WHAT WOULD JESUS DO?

WHAT WOULD JESUS DO?

Wherein a new generation undertakes to
walk in His steps

by

Glenn Clark

MACALESTER PARK PUBLISHING
COMPANY

St. Paul, Minnesota

WHAT WOULD JESUS DO?

Copyright, 1950

by

MACALESTER PARK PUBLISHING COMPANY

Published in the United States of America by
Macalester Park Publishing Company
1571 Grand Avenue, St. Paul 5, Minnesota

PREFACE

Ever since *In His Steps* appeared at the close of the last century, I have dreamed of writing a sequel to it. Now on the fiftieth anniversary of its first appearance in book form, that dream has been fulfilled. Just a few months before the death of Charles M. Sheldon I had the good fortune to meet him in his home and receive there both his permission and his blessing for this undertaking.

The chief characters in this book are the grandchildren of the chief characters in Dr. Sheldon's book. They find themselves confronted with the problems of this age just as their grandparents had been confronted with the problems of their age. The solution to these problems in both cases is found in the answer to the simple question, "What Would Jesus Do?"

My soul's sincere desire—and I am sure it is shared by Dr. Sheldon in heaven—is that fifty years from now the third book in this series will appear, written by someone under the guidance of the Holy Spirit, in which the Kingdom of Heaven will be even more apparent than it can be made to appear in the age in which I am writing now. If my book is a mere stepping stone connecting the shores of these two centuries I shall be satisfied.

May the reader of it derive a blessing measured only by his need, and limited only by his capacity to receive, is the soul's sincere desire of the author.

Glenn Clark
Saint Paul, Minnesota
May 7, 1950

5

CHAPTER I

"Know ye not that I must be about my Father's business?"

THE REVEREND CHARLES S. MAXWELL eased his lanky frame into his pulpit chair and mopped his ruddy forehead while the choir led the congregation in the closing hymn. Despite his athletic physique, the hectic week he had just been through, climaxed by the sermon he had delivered on this sunny August morning in 1945, had left him exhausted. Sermon-making ordinarily was a difficult task for him, and this time it had been unusually so. Besides, this was only his third Sunday in a new pastorate, and a man was human enough to want to put his best foot forward. The sermon he had prepared to give had to be entirely reconstructed on Friday after Japan offered to accept the surrender terms. Now that he had finished, with the approving eye of his congregation upon him, he had a nagging feeling of incompleteness, as if he had forgotten to say something—something extremely important, vital to the times and to the day.

The church was well filled this morning, even the galleries which ran around the church clear to the pulpit.

Raising his head, and smoothing back his dark brown hair, damp with perspiration, he surveyed the men and women who had listened so attentively to his words, seeming by their nods and smiles and grave attention to approve of what he had said. It had been a militant, a victorious sermon. "God disciplines us, His beloved children, with sorrow and suffering and even sometimes death when we depart from His way. You, in turn, as loving parents, must sometimes resort to harsh punishment in the disciplining of your children. And we, as a nation, found ourselves assigned the sad but necessary task of disciplining another nation in a seemingly harsh and terrible way when it defied God's laws. The United States, more than any other nation in history, was founded and has flourished upon Christian principles. In the twentieth century, America has become God's chosen land, even as in the days of Moses, God chose a people to carry high His Word. Even as Joshua fought the battle of Jericho, and with the help of God caused the walls of that great city to fall upon its evil inhabitants, even so have we, as a nation fought a glorious battle, and with God's help have caused the very atoms of the air to come to our aid to destroy the enemies of God-given rights."

Charles Maxwell sighed, and clasped his hands together over his black robe as the congregation and choir sailed on into the fourth stanza of "Onward, Christian Soldiers." The physical warmth which had accompanied the fervor of his sermon had left him, and with a shock he realized now that his hands were cold, almost icy. Sweet and clear above the other singers he could hear the beautiful voice of the first soprano in the choir behind him. Trying to throw off the feeling of depression that had suddenly come upon him, he turned his head slightly so he could see her face. His glance took in the well-cut features and the nose that reminded him of Hoffman's "Boy Christ." He shook himself and slowly rose and was in his place behind the pulpit as the last notes died away.

He stood a moment in silence under the restive gaze of a congregation whose thoughts by now were occupied by the roast in the oven at home, or plans for the remainder of the day. "Next Sunday, be back and bring your friends. We have defeated the enemy, but we have not yet won the war. And we are very far from winning the peace. This will be the biggest job our nation has ever faced. Next Sunday I shall tell you what we must do to win the peace."

The words he spoke were exactly the words he had planned to say, but suddenly Charles Maxwell was struck with the audacity

8

of his statement—"I shall tell you what we must do to win the peace!" Certainly nothing very humble about that statement! Without time to analyze the feeling of shame and embarrassment that swept over him, he lifted his long right arm in the familiar gesture of blessing, bowed his flushed face and stumbled into the beautiful words of the benediction: "And now, may the grace of the Lord Jesus Christ, and the love of God, the Father, and the fellowship of the Holy Spirit, be with you all, Amen."

As the organ boomed into the postlude, Charles hurried down from the pulpit and strode out to the south vestibule. By the time the first of his people reached him, he had regained his poise.

"Mighty good sermon, Parson," came from the first to greet him, a gnarled old gentleman with a long, bony nose. "A good, hard-hitting man's sermon—just what I've been trying to tell these softies who thought it was just real mean of us to use that bomb on the dirty Japs! We've heard you only three times, but each time's better than the last, young man. You may catch up with your old Grand-dad yet."

Charles Maxwell smiled. He knew he had a high mark at which to aim. Coming fresh from the seminary to undertake a parish made famous by his grandfather, the great Henry Maxwell, was not an easy thing to do. For a moment a question clouded his mind, chilly as an autumn breeze—what would Henry Maxwell have thought of his grandson's sermon this morning? But the concern was quickly brushed away by the admiring voice of a large lady who pressed in upon him.

"We certainly will be back next Sunday!" she exclaimed, an assertion eagerly seconded by a half-dozen others crowding around. "We can't wait to hear what you have to say about winning the peace."

Over and over again similar remarks were repeated as the congregation trooped past. Suddenly Charles felt something go flat in the pit of his stomach, and the chilly breeze swept over him again as he realized with full force that he had no idea what he would say next Sunday.

9

As he stood in the sunny doorway just in sight of the stained glass window which was the pride of the church, shaking hands and smiling—so that by now his face and his hand were both getting a little stiff—and making appropriate responses to the remarks of his admiring congregation with the outer part of his mind—down in the inner part, out of some recess of memory, he heard the voice of one of the most popular teachers in the seminary: "Build up their enthusiasm, get the congregation on tiptoe by the topic you announce . . . then break your neck to satisfy them. Be sure you don't let them down."

Charles realized he had stepped out in the reckless method of the gambler. Could he fulfill the expectations of these people? Could he meet his promise? Just how were we going to win the peace, anyway?

The press of people had passed now, and he looked back into the cool interior of the church, where he could see just a few lagging behind. He started back down the aisle, moving wearily and almost oblivious of the quiet voices of those left in the sanctuary. Then he became aware of a group coming up the aisle towards him, so engrossed in their conversation that they had not seen him approach.

"I don't care, Arnold," said one of the young women, whom Charles recognized as the soprano whose voice had so enthralled him for a moment at the close of his sermon, "it's just not right, and I'll never believe it was—no matter what you say, or what Mr. Maxwell says. It was wrong and it can't be justified!"

The handsome young man she spoke to so defiantly Charles saw was Arnold Eton, a member of the Board of Deacons and president of the garment factory in lower town. He moved with a soft, feline grace, his eyes fixed on the girl in amused cynicism. "Come now, Frances," he purred, "you're being unrealistic. I grant you I never expected such a militant sermon from our boy wonder. But I was with him this morning, all the way. You're a babe in the woods, Frances, you don't know what it's all about."

"Oh, Arnold, Frances, don't quarrel!" spoke up the other

young woman with them, a look of genuine distress on her pretty face. "I think you're both taking him too seriously. He looks so sincere, so—so—good. I can't believe— Anyway, it's too pretty a morning—" she broke off as she looked up and saw Charles approaching. "Oh, here's Reverend Maxwell now!"

Eton reached out to shake hands with Charles, putting his other arm possessively about the beautiful girl he had called Frances. "Ah, Mr. Maxwell, we were just discussing the fine sermon you gave us this morning. I don't believe you've met Frances Page, our soprano." He met Charles' look with a wink over Frances' head. "Miss Page didn't quite agree with all you had to say."

"Arnold, please," murmured Miss Page, but Eton went on.

"And this pert little redhead on my right is Florence Bowen, first contralto in the choir. I don't think she's decided yet just what she does think."

Something in Eton's felicitous tone bordered on the sarcastic, and Charles Maxwell suddenly felt, however unreasonably, that he must defend the lovely Miss Page, even if she didn't like his sermon. "I'm not so sure myself that what I said was right," he said, looking directly into the cool blue eyes of the girl. She met his gaze with something almost like contempt—or was it only disappointment?—then looked away. "When I planned the sermon, I felt that it was right," Charles went on, "but I know I have a lot to learn. At any rate, I'm sorry if I have disturbed you, Miss Page."

Her eyes moved up and searched his face. "This is the first time I have heard you preach, Mr. Maxwell," she said slowly. "When I heard that you were coming to this pastorate, I was glad. I hoped—after all my grandmother had told me about your grandfather—"

Charles exclaimed, "Of course! I should have known who you were at once! You are the granddaughter of Rollin and Rachel Page—that Rachel that my grandfather used to tell me so much about! Where have you been these three weeks since I arrived?"

"She has just returned from a year of studying music in New York," blandly interposed Eton, the smile suddenly gone from his face.

"Headed for the Metropolitan," added the red-haired Florence proudly.

"I was quite aware of your voice this morning, Miss Page," said Charles. "I'm sure your friends' faith in your career is justified."

"Come along, Frances, we'll be late for dinner," broke in Eton almost imperiously. Then to Charles, the sardonic smile returning to his face, "I hope you can make good on your promise for next Sunday. 'How to win the peace' is rather a broad subject."

As Charles Maxwell's gaze followed them out of the church doors and down the broad steps, he noted what a contrast the two girls made. The even features and chestnut hair of Frances complemented the snub nose and freckles that went so well with Florence's red hair. He watched them thoughtfully for a moment longer, then went back into the church and joined the old sexton in gathering the bulletins from the pews.

"Oh, dinna ye bother about thae bulletins," exclaimed the latter, turning his ruddy face under a thatch of white hair so that he could look straight into the face of Maxwell. "I'll do a' the cleanin' up before evenin' service. Dinna ye worrit."

"I'm not worrying, Mr. MacIntosh," said young Maxwell with a smile. "I'm just tired of thinking—need a little body work to get me back to normal." His tall figure moved rapidly down the rows slipping the used bulletins into his large hands.

"It maun be a strain tae gie them sermons tae a kirk fu' o' people," said the sexton, sympathetically. "I dinna see how ye parsons do it." After a pause, he continued. "By the way, that wes a gude sermon. Better than laist time."

Maxwell looked up quizzically. "What do you mean, Sandy? What was the trouble with the sermon last time?"

"Laist week yer sermon came frae the buikcase an' it hit the buikcase. Gude—but it hit the buikcase. This sermon came frae

12

the heart an' hit the heart. I wouldna know if ye were right or not—but it came frae the heart."

"I see," said Maxwell slowly. "A thing only reaches the place it started from."

"That's how I see it, Parson," replied Sandy with his crinkly smile.

"Old MacIntosh," thought Maxwell as he turned to leave, "is a candid fellow. If I hold my ear close to him, he may help to keep me straight."

As he arrived next door at the big old parsonage he now called home, the mood that had been upon him after his sermon returned to him. He let himself into the little garden through the weatherbeaten iron gate that led from the church-yard. A sense of dissatisfaction and unrest seemed almost to suffocate him, and his nerves tightened with what, if there had been good reason, Charles might almost have named as a sense of impending danger. But what danger could there possibly be in the sunlit, smiling world that met his eyes here? In the little parsonage garden, roses nodded in the welcome breeze that had suddenly sprung up—roses that had been planted by Charles' grandfather, that saintly man who had given his life to the search for Jesus' footsteps. The grass that Sandy so conscientiously kept within its bounds was brilliant in its August lushness; and an ancient willow shaded a white wrought-iron bench that had once been given to Henry Maxwell by a loving congregation. On this bench, Charles mused, his grandfather must have sat for many long hours, counselling some troubled soul, or meditating upon the God he seemed to know so well. Surely his presence was in this lovely spot, where the work of his hands was still evident and alive. And in such a hallowed spot, no danger could lurk, no fear could live . . . unless . . .

In such a mood as he had never known, Charles sank upon the bench and put his head into his hands. "Something is working in me," he thought. "God is trying to tell me something, and I have been so far from Him, although I call myself His messenger, that I cannot hear what He says." He sat motionless, and the little Sunday afternoon sounds went on around him unnoticed—two children ran shouting past on the other side of the tall hedge that hid the garden from the street; a boy whizzed by, whistling, on his bike; somewhere a group of girls was laughing. But Charles did not hear. And it was only when his housekeeper came looking for him to say dinner was ready, that he roused himself and went in to eat in unaccustomed silence under the concerned eye of Mrs. Bailey.

CHAPTER 2

"Behold, your house is left unto you desolate."

E
ARLY THAT AFTERNOON Charles Maxwell went back to
the church study to prepare for the young people's meeting he was to lead that night. The unquiet, unsatisfied
feeling that had dogged his footsteps home after his sermon that
morning accompanied him now on his return to the church.
Entering by way of the sanctuary he sank into a rear pew and
let his eye roam over the empty room so full of past memories.
It was an old church. The pulpit was not imposing, nor the three
pulpit chairs. Behind was the choir loft and behind that the old-
fashioned organ, its gilded pipes exposed to view. He raised his
eyes to the gallery which encircled three sides of the sanctuary,
almost to the pulpit itself. How he had loved to run around this
as a boy when the church was not in session, imagining he was a
horse on a race track! In the twinkling of an eye he was plunged
into a flood of nostalgic memories.

He remembered as a little child sitting here beside his little
sister, Dottie, his towering, silent parents on either side. Beyond
the high pew ahead, he had not been able to see his grandfather
in the pulpit and he didn't care, being occupied with a box of
colored crayons and a book of huge, outlined Biblical characters,
whose flowing garments craved to be colored.

He remembered a walk in the woods one day with his grandfather, his own chubby hand fiercely gripping the immense cal-
loused hand of the old man. One memory stood out on that walk
—it was when his grandfather had seated himself on a fallen log
and called him. "Kneel down, my lad, and let me put my hand

15

on your head and invoke a special blessing on you before we go home." Special blessing! Was there something invisible handed down that day from grandsire to grandson?

That was the last memory he had of the old gentleman. Shortly after that his parents had moved away, and had never returned to that city again. Their business had not prospered. Something had gone wrong. For twenty years his father had been paying off old debts. When the last one was paid, his father left the field of business and had gone into consular government service. Being a natural linguist, he was very happy in his new work. He was now in the Foreign Embassy office in Sweden. His sister, Dottie, had married a medical missionary, associated now with a great hospital in India.

"We are an international family, it seems," his vivacious mother had written in her last letter. "I feel that God intended it to be so. Your father and I are very happy in this field of service. You will have to look after America while we are gone. We are very proud to hear that you have been called to your grandfather's church. Our prayers are with you."

Their prayers? Yes! He certainly needed them now.

After his graduation at Northwestern, where he had won a letter in football and been active in debate, he had taken his theological training at Andover Newton and had immediately after been sent as a chaplain to the armed forces in Europe. Right after Germany's surrender he was called to First Church. With practically no church experience at all! Churches ordinarily didn't do things that way.

The reason for his call, he had been informed, went way back to his Andover Newton days. He had a little church in a New England village which was his charge during the entire three years he was a student there. Things had happened in that church. Permanent results had followed that ministry, and when three members of that village church had moved to Raymond and joined First Church, their enthusiastic story had led that church to "grab" the young man before some other church had discovered him.

"I may have had something in those early days," mused Charles. "A freshness, an original spontaneity and faith that three years of theological studies and three years of war has tarnished I'm afraid." Then turning his eyes upward toward the vaulted ceiling, he said, "Grandfather, why did you let them call me to this big church? Dear old saint in heaven, if I ever needed your blessing it is now!" Then he arose and went to his study.

As he entered, he had a strange feeling that he was not alone. He suddenly felt as a man who is being secretly watched or hunted. Not a thing in the study was in motion. Everything was in its place—and then he saw it—a face! The face was attached to the thin body of one sitting perfectly motionless in the pastor's big chair behind the desk. A gaunt, tragic face, with eyes somewhat aslant—a Japanese!

"I beg your pardon, Meester Maxwell. I am Kamada—Meester Kamada." Now the face was moving, a face of drawn agony that did not awaken pity so much as horror, because of the tragedy in it. "I beg your pardon a thousand times, but I am in trouble—here." He put his small hand upon his chest. Speechless with surprise, Charles stood watching him as though frozen to the spot. "The trouble is in my soul." He was now out of the chair and bowing low. His smooth voice, the English faultless, with only a trace of Oriental cadence in its intonations, went on. "I beg your pardon. Sit down. But will you pray to God to forgive me? I may do something the good Jesus would not approve. There is one man—only one—whom I must kill."

With the last words, his voice had risen, and, so quickly that Maxwell could not follow the motion, the Japanese drew a revolver from his pocket. Involuntarily, Maxwell reached backward to the door. But the smooth voice, low again, resumed its sing-song way. "Oh, no, I would not kill you, not any good American. Do not fear for yourself. It is a Japanese who has outlived his time. He is empty. He is a coward and he should better die."

Finding his voice, Charles spoke almost harshly, "Please, give me the gun. You must forgive the man." Regaining control, he moved forward to the little man. "Sit down and talk this over with me."

"Talk?" The sad face was lighted for a moment with what was almost a smile. "Talk? You are so kind to give me of your time." What might have been a smile had disappeared as he continued, "Talk will do no good. There has been too much of talk already. I promise that I will kill nobody. NOBODY!" Suddenly he laughed, a harsh sound without mirth. Placing the gun in his pocket he strode past Maxwell, who stood now in complete bewilderment, as he reached the door.

Pausing abruptly he turned back to the young minister and spoke rapidly. "Very well, I will talk. You talked this morning, and I was here because I was lost and alone—I think that I am lost and I try to find myself. The good Jesus, they told me, taught love, and because I am unloved in all this land, I think perhaps I can find some love in His church, among His people. And so I came this morning, and I listened to you talk." He paused, his brilliant eyes fixed upon Charles with such a penetrating look that Charles felt suddenly weak and reached out for the desk to steady himself. Feeling for his chair, he sank into it.

The Japanese went on, slowly, enunciating deliberately, as each word sank into Charles' soul. "You said in your sermon this morning that killing 100,000 human beings in Hiroshima was right because it saved a million American boys and ended the war sooner. We were bad children, we must be punished. But I ask you, would God not have punished us in His own way for misusing his energies? Does an older brother place a revolver to his little brother's breast and destroy him for disobeying their father? Surely this is not right?"

Kamada sighed deeply, as if weary to the depths of his soul. He passed a brown hand over his forehead, then looked again at Charles, who watched him, hypnotized. "Maybe you are right. Ministers of the Gospel are always right. Otherwise, they wouldn't be ministers of the Gospel." His eyebrows lifted.

"Would they?" He straightened, and with renewed energy went on, "But why—why could you not have dropped the bomb on a desert island? My countrymen would have surrendered just one week later. Just one week. Already Japan was ready to surrender, but America was sleeping. Sleeping, and dreaming the dream of God's chosen people. Could it be that Jesus was sleeping, too?"

With another mirthless laugh, he turned and was silently gone. Maxwell sat rigid in his chair, feeling helpless to move, even to call the man, to deflect him from his crazy errand of murder, wherever it was.

The paralyzing thought that something he had said had brought another human being to this hysterical state of mind was so overwhelming that for long minutes he remained motionless. At last his lips moved stiffly in an attempt at prayer. "God help him. God forgive me, God forgive me, God forgive me." He moved a little, resting his elbows on his knees, his head in his hands, trying to see the picture whole. The little Japanese had come to his church that morning, searching for love and guidance, rejected by the other human beings who sneered and pointed at him on the street—"another dirty Jap"—"oughta kill 'em all off"—"I wouldn't ride in an elevator with one"— "run 'em out of the country"—. How often had Charles heard these words, snatches of conversation on the streets, in the stores, in civilized parlors. He had never said such things himself, to be sure, he had no particular animosity for the Japanese, nor for any other race. All during the war he had been vaguely aware that the Japanese, too, were children of God, with hearts that beat, and blood in their veins, and minds quickened by the intelligence that could only come from God. But he had never really thought out the implications of his vague awareness. Obviously, Japan, as a nation, could be misled, and justify her actions with her own brand of logic. Somehow it was easy to work up a logical defense for wholesale murder; he had done it himself only this morning.

And the little Kamada, knowing himself innocent, knowing

his own heart free of guilt, had sat this morning and heard his countrymen whom he loved even as Charles loved his own countrymen, branded as guilty of defying God's laws, and deserving the harsh punishment they had received. The knowledge came sharp as lightning into Charles' mind that Americans had, by assuming the burden of this punishment, defied God's laws as criminally as any Japanese or German had ever done—and the punishment, when it came, would be swift and inexorable. Unless—was there no way out? Ignorance of the law is no excuse, whether of man's laws or God's. But surely, somehow, penance might be done. What was the answer?

Stiffly, he stood and walked to the window. Sandy MacIntosh sat on the smooth lawn behind the church, reading to his little granddaughter. The child looked up and saw him standing there, laughed, and waved. Charles made a little gesture with his hand, and turned back to sit at the desk.

Let's think this thing through, now. The Japanese, Kamada, had come to the church as to a sanctuary, seeking love. He had met with rebuff, with condemnation, subtle and broad though it may have been. "And what man, if his child ask him for bread will give him a stone?" The man was hungry, and Charles had given him a stone. He was thirsty, and he had refused him of the cool water of love. "And inasmuch as ye have done it unto the least of these, ye have done it unto me." Did I turn Jesus from my church this morning? thought Maxwell, in an agony of despair. Whomever Kamada kills, his blood is on my hands.

As clearly as if she were in the room with him, there rose up before Charles the image of Frances Page, as she had met his eyes this morning. What had it been in her look—contempt, pity, disappointment? "It wasn't right," she had said to Arnold Eton, in that silvery voice, "I don't care how you and Mr. Maxwell try to justify it, it just wasn't right."

"God, help me!" he breathed, pressing his hands hard against his temples, blotting out the vision of Frances' appraising eyes. That atom-breaking thing in Hiroshima had not stopped. It was still breaking atoms in men's nerves, in men's minds and souls.

Would its chain-reaction never stop? Perhaps this was the explanation of the feeling of danger that had reached him this noon even in his peaceful garden—danger and death were loose in the atmosphere of the whole earth—set free by arrogant Americans when they had split an atom and used it to destroy.

The proud ivory tower of logic which Charles Maxwell had so laboriously built through the last week when he was writing his "Victory" sermon, which had inexplicably begun to crumble after the service this morning, whose columns had trembled under the onslaught of the honest eyes of Frances Page, had now been completely undermined by the visit of the Japanese, and with the walls that had seemed so proud and strong crumbling to bits about him, Charles found himself floundering in the quicksand upon which it had been built.

He rose and walked slowly into the sanctuary. It was an auditorium that would hold twelve hundred persons. That morning it had been filled. How many of them had gone away secretly hurt, unsatisfied, knowing instinctively that might does not make right—and yet helpless to defy the logic of it?

He wanted to be alone; he wanted to pray. He wished he knew how to pray as the men of God in the olden times had prayed. He wanted to pray with power, as he had never prayed before in all his life.

His steps turned to the little chapel that had been added since his grandfather's day. He paused in the doorway and drank in its exquisite pale-green freshness. On the left wall hung the picture of a Christopher Wren spire. On the opposite wall, in a built-in shelf stood the ancient silver communion set, the pitcher and the four cups.

As usual, his spirit quickened as his gaze momentarily took in the entire front of the chapel. He did so enjoy the warmth that fairly radiated from the expansive wine-red dossel curtain behind the altar and approved of the soft interplay of light and shadow in its velvety folds. Then his attention centered on the white altar and the white pulpit. Both shone in their pure whiteness against the background of rich red. Carved on the front of the pulpit was the Celtic cross, symbolizing God in Christ reconciling the world to Himself. The altar was covered with a white embroidered cloth. He noted the three carved panels of the altar: the left one with the two interlocking triangles symbolizing the Star of David, the central one a circle with radiations like tongues of flames symbolizing the Sun of Righteousness and the right panel, with three interlocking triangles creating a nine-pointed star, symbolizing the nine fruits of the Spirit.

On the altar, in its center, stood a beautiful golden cross bearing the letters I-H-S, representing three Latin names for Jesus. He liked to think they also stood for "In His Steps." It was flanked by two candles, and they, in turn, by two Japanese inlaid vases containing maiden-hair ferns. Suddenly he noticed that both the candles were lighted. This startled him. It was not the custom to light these except upon important occasions. Someone must have been here. As he started toward the front between the rows of seats the thought came to him, "One of the candles is burning for me and *my* needs; the other for the Japanese boy who came to me with *his* need."

He hurried up the narrow aisle and started to kneel at the low platform before the pulpit when he saw a man already kneeling there. The body was slumped awkwardly over the platform. One hand, fingers curled backward, rested limply on the floor. Beside the hand lay the revolver he had seen that afternoon.

"Mr. Kamada!" he gasped. "My friend, are you all right?"

No, he was not all right. His "friend" was dead. A widening pool of blood on the floor carpet where it dripped from the wound in his breast told the story.

So this was the "Nobody" that Kamada had said he must kill!

Shaking violently, Charles Maxwell ran to find Sandy MacIntosh, and nearly collided with him coming toward the prayer room.

"I heard a strange sound comin' frae that room a bit ago— like a muffled shot." The tousled white hair added to Sandy's startled look. "I wes just outside on the grass. What happened?"

"Something terrible, Sandy, something terrible. A man has

killed himself. Go in and see." Charles' voice rose and nearly broke. "I'm going to call the police. Don't do anything until they come!"

He had just got to his study and placed the call when a heavy rap came on the door. He gave a start. "Come in."

As Sandy entered, he was too shaken to speak but he handed Charles a blank sheet torn from the back of a hymn book. Then he found his voice. "I foun' that on the low platform beside him. Will the police be here soon?"

"As quickly as they can pick up the coroner," Charles replied, his eyes already searching the scribbled paper. As Sandy left, Charles sat and held the note in his cold hands and read the scrawled words over and over again.

"I am studying at the college here to go back and preach Christ to my people. All my family and relatives and, above all, my little sweetheart, lived in Hiroshima. Now they are all dust. In the time required to take one breath my world was destroyed. Will my people receive a Christ that would let a Christian nation do that, in His name? I am confused. I leave my confusion."

Overcome, Charles Maxwell buried his head in his arms. He had tried several times this terrible afternoon to pray. Always something had stopped him. His heart felt a great need to touch God in prayer. Even now he found it impossible to get started. He said a few words, but they went no higher than the ceiling. It seemed the very air was filled with breaking atoms. If the chain-reaction would only cease long enough for him to find God! "If the flying atoms would only stop jamming my wireless long enough for me to get a message through!" He opened his eyes and found them on a level with the telephone right before him on the table.

"If God could be reached as easily as a friend by the telephone!" he sighed. "Oh, Father, why are You so far away today?"

His hand reached out. A terrible craving gnawed at him to call someone who could connect him with God—to call him right away. He could not stand this sense of separation—not in this

23

dark hour. Frances Page! Strange the way that name, that face, that voice intruded itself upon him at this moment. A strange yearning came over him to seize the phone and call upon her for help. Could *she* connect him with God?

He knew now why some people who have great need and weak faith often stand deeply in need of a priest. That is what he, a priest himself, stood in need of right now. Suddenly the loneliness of his calling welled up within him—the loneliness and the terrible responsibility of it. What if again he should fail a weak one when he came for strength and succor? That was what his Japanese friend was seeking—that was what he came for—and had he failed him?

When the sexton came he found him kneeling with his head still bowed upon his arms.

"Pardon, sir. The police hae com'."

"Thank you, Sandy," he sighed. "Tell them I'll be there at once."

He opened the Scriptures at random, a desperate longing in his heart. "I can't make my words reach you today, O Father. Speak to me through your Holy Word."

He opened the Bible and his finger rested upon Isaiah 32:2: "And a man shall be as a hiding-place from the wind, and a covert from the tempest, as streams of water in a dry place, as the shade of a great rock in a weary land."

"Oh, God!" he murmured to himself as he moved towards the door. "Make me that man. Let me be that for my people. For your people, O Lord. I am not asking to give great and famous sermons, or draw great multitudes. But I must never again fail my people when they come to me in need. Teach me to pray, that I may become henceforth the type of man that is in this verse!"

CHAPTER 3

"Launch out into the deep, and let down your nets for a draught."

AFTER ALL the painful detail of the inquest of Kamada's death, and the preparations for shipping his body back to a distant relative on the West Coast, had at last been attended to, Charles Maxwell sat late one night at his grandfather's massive old desk in the study at the manse. Weary as he was, he could not face the prospect of going to bed, there only to struggle with the demons—or had they been angels?—with which he had been wrestling since that awful afternoon last Sunday when Kamada had thrown his words back in his face, and he knew that he had failed as God's messenger.

He had put off even thinking about the next Sunday's sermon. He had known that he must come to some peace with himself, and with God, before he would ever be worthy to enter the pulpit again. He knew that he had acted and spoken according to the best of his beliefs at the time, and enough people had applauded his sentiments so that he could have maintained the rightness of the doctrine he had expounded on that basis if nothing else. But he could not take this easy way; he knew that he had reached a turning point, a crisis in his own growth, and there was nothing for it but to work it out within himself and get his thinking straight.

He had turned to the Bible, but somehow, in his state of mind, the words were a taunt to him. "We are the words that you have used to justify sin," they seemed to say. "You do not understand us at all." Should he go back and retrace his steps to find where he had taken the wrong turn—or should he forge ahead, and make a new path to the highroad?

And so it was, at 9:00 on this sultry Wednesday evening he had gone to his study in the manse to try to write a sermon, knowing it was time he began to make some preparation for next Sunday, whether he felt like it or not. After sitting for some time motionless in front of a pile of blank white paper on his desk, he dropped to his knees beside the old-fashioned swivel chair in the dim room. From the church across the way came the intermittent snatches of song that told him choir practice was still in session. "Oh, God," he whispered, "show me the way, show me the way. 'One step enough for me . . .' I will struggle no longer within my own little intellect for the answers to my questions. I know that the answer is here, somewhere, and I know you will reveal it to me." The words had come to him involuntarily, without plan, but suddenly he began to feel at peace. He knelt, without knowing for how long, his head against the smooth wood of the desk, as a little child at his father's knee, tired out from a long day full of childish woes.

It seemed a long while that he knelt there, not thinking, but feeling himself more and more relaxed, more at peace, when suddenly he heard sounds in the entry. The breathless voice of a young woman was saying, "I know it's late, Mrs. Bailey, but I wanted to talk to Mr. Maxwell for just a bit. It's quite important, really." With a start, Charles realized that this soft voice could belong to no one but Frances Page. He glanced at the watch on his wrist, and saw that it was only 9:30. What could bring her here at this hour? Rising abruptly, he went to the door and opened it to see Frances talking to his housekeeper.

"Why, Miss Page," he greeted her warmly, "how nice to see you again! I didn't have time to drop in at choir practice tonight." And to Mrs. Bailey, who had apparently been stoutly defending her minister's right to privacy while he wrote his sermon, he said, "It's all right, Mrs. Bailey. I couldn't seem to get started writing tonight, anyway. Won't you come in, Miss Page?"

When Frances had seated herself across from him at the desk, Charles spoke again. "This is a real surprise. If it were anyone but you I'd ask if I could help you, but somehow I feel it's the other way around, and I should ask, 'Can you help me?' "

Frances lifted her eyes in surprise, "Oh, I don't know how I could help you! I know it's very forward of me to call on you this way, but I've had you on my mind very much the past few days. And then, today, I saw you coming out of the coroner's office, and you looked so tired and worried, I—well, somehow, tonight, when I left the church after choir practice, and saw your light on, I had such a strong feeling that I should stop in and see you —I don't know, really, why I came!" She laughed, a musical sound in the quiet room, and went on, "I guess I sound awfully confused—I know men make fun of woman's 'intuition'—but that's really what brought me here." She paused, regarded Charles thoughtfully for a moment, then said, "Maybe I *can* help you. You tell me why I'm here."

Charles picked up one of the freshly-sharpened pencils that he had laid out when he sat down to write, examined it intently, then handed it to Frances. "Here, Miss Page," he said gravely. "Perhaps you would like to write my sermon for me."

She flushed deeply, and said in a reproachful tone, "You're not serious—you're making fun of me." She rose, saying, "I'd better go. Maybe my woman's intuition was wrong, after all."

He sprang from his chair—put a detaining hand on her arm. "No, no, don't misunderstand me! I *am* serious—here, please sit down again." He continued earnestly, "I mean it—you've got something, some understanding that goes deeper than anything I've got. I do need help! I've been on my knees here, tonight, ever since I left the prayer meeting, seeking guidance. Your coming here as you did must mean that you are the answer, or have the answer, to that prayer. Please, don't be hurt—sit down!"

This last was spoken almost like a command, and Frances sank slowly back into her chair, her eyes fixed on Charles' face.

"Very well," she said at last. "Talk to me."

Charles walked slowly to the open window which looked toward the church and leaned against the window casing. He could see Sandy MacIntosh moving slowly through the church, putting out the lights one after another. He stood in silence for a moment, then turned to Frances again. With a little wave of his arm toward the darkened building, he said, "Look there—that's my church. It will be full of people next Sunday, coming to hear me tell them how to win the peace." With a short laugh, he shoved his hands in his pockets and walked back the length of the room. "How To Win The Peace! Who do I think I am, anyway!"

He turned abruptly back to Frances. "I stood up there last Sunday and said a lot of high-sounding words about how gloriously we won the war, how we were God's chosen people, how we had used the weapon God had given us to destroy those who defied his laws. If the world followed through on that theory, why, when Ben Franklin discovered electricity, why didn't we use it the first chance we got to electrocute the next nation we had a fight with?"

Frances continued to watch him in silence, and Charles went on. "Almost as soon as the words were out of my mouth, something deep within me revolted against them. It was all I could do to stand up there after the service and accept the compliments of that majority of my congregation who agreed with what I had said. Instinctively I knew that I was wrong, and yet my intellect would not give up and admit that its dictates were false, that the logic was—" he shrugged, "—all haywire."

He sat again in the big swivel chair and spread out his fingers upon the white paper which still lay on the desk. "The blood of the man Kamada is on my hands, and yet I presume to stand up again in front of that congregation and tell them what we must do to win the peace."

His eyes raised and met those of Frances, who leaned forward to exclaim, "No, no, don't say that!"

"But it's true! That poor wretch had come to church that morning seeking peace and love. And what did he get? A slap in the face! I am overwhelmed with my own stupidity, my own unworthiness to represent myself as a minister of God! Probably most of those who read about his death have thought, 'Well, there's one Jap who knew what he was good for—nothing!' I've heard people say that on the street—nobody cares—'Just another dirty Jap,' they say. But he wasn't—he was a child of God, and I destroyed him, when I could have saved him!"

He ran his fingers through his hair in a desperate gesture, then looked up again at Frances who was watching him wide-eyed. "I don't know why I should unburden all this to you—you knew it was wrong—I heard you telling Eton so, just before you saw me last Sunday. Well, now you can say, 'I told you so.' " Frances started to protest, but he interrupted with a gesture. "Oh, I know you wouldn't actually say that. I'm sorry. But I can see things now so much more clearly than I did, even a few days ago. It seems incredible even to me, that I could have taken such a stand. The point is now, what comes next? What is the answer? *How can I tell my people how we are to win the peace, when I cannot find any peace even within myself?*"

They sat in silence for a moment. A cool breeze had begun to come in through the open windows, fluttering the curtains. Charles sighed, then straightened in his chair. "Just before you came in, I had begun to find a little peace. Maybe it was because at last I realized I could do nothing, even understand nothing, of myself. I was beginning to give up, to let go,—let God come in and tell me what to do. Maybe I hadn't been giving Him a chance. And so He sent you. Now—" Charles smiled wryly at the silent girl, "now you talk to me."

Frances Page sat quietly for a moment, seemingly absorbed with the design of the grain of wood in the old oak chair. The thought crossed Charles Maxwell's mind that here before him was one of those rare women who could be completely still, making those with them relaxed and still as well.

"I think you are taking too much personal responsibility for what happened," she said at last. "I haven't heard many others who seem to care, they thought it was good riddance. I haven't heard anyone in all the persons I have talked to condemn you in the least. I suppose, if the truth were known, that a great many fine Japanese people have died of broken hearts at the hands of us Americans who call ourselves Christians."

"And there will be more to come," broke in Charles.

"The students at the college," Frances continued, "wouldn't sit beside him in a class, people on the street sneered when they passed him, the little boys called names that they had learned from their parents when he walked by—they are responsible for his death as much, or more, than you. It was a tragedy, to be sure—but somehow it seems we silly little humans have to burn our hands before we learn to shun the fire. That's how a child learns, and we are still children in our understanding."

Slowly, as if searching for each word, she went on, her face very grave in the lamplight, and Charles did not speak. "So it has happened, and you have learned something by it. You had already begun to learn, even before Kamada's death. God was trying to tell you something, and your intellect, as you say, was too proud and jealous to let you open up to the new knowledge that was trying to come through. And so at last, when you had reached the point of desperation, you realized you could do nothing of yourself, and you gave up. You became really as a little child, humble and receptive. I can tell you nothing now that you do not already know, because you have opened up your heart to God. Instead of searching frantically for the key, you have begun to realize that the door wasn't locked, after all." Frances smiled then, and picked up the pencil from the table where she had put it so abruptly a few minutes before. She reached across the desk and handed it to Charles, all in one graceful motion. "Here," she said. "You don't need me. You can write your own sermon."

Charles reached forward to take the pencil and said, with a little smile, "Give me a text."

Very thoughtfully, Frances said, "I hope you won't think I'm irreverent, but I never could believe that God stopped speaking to us through men when John finished Revelations. I think He still speaks to us through our poets, our writers, our scientists—through men in every walk of life. Perhaps a hundred years from now, someone will have compiled a Bible from the teachings of men in the Twentieth Century. I've been thinking, ever since you began to talk, of a line from Sidney Lanier's 'Marshes of Glyn'—' . . . as the man who hath mightily won God out of knowledge and good out of infinite pain, and sight out of blindness, and purity out of a stain.—' If we, as individuals, could learn from our mistakes,—could not nations, too? If enough in this marvelous country of ours could say, 'God, forgive us, for we knew not what we were doing,' perhaps then we could win purity and peace out of the stain of war."

She glanced briefly at Charles, and when he made no move to speak, continued, musingly, "God has no chosen people, not in the sense of races or creeds. I believe God's chosen people are the humble, those who have gotten a clear picture of their place in the scheme of things, those who love mercy, and do justly, and walk humbly in the sight of the Lord. When men become arrogant and proud, they run too far away from the flock, and get lost."

Charles still sat in silence, there seemed to be nothing more that needed saying. He had never known such peace, and he was reluctant to move or speak to break the spell.

"You know," Frances said suddenly, "I think your grandfather had the answer. Grandmother Rachel has told me about his wonderful experiment in living which began when he challenged his congregation with the question, 'What Would Jesus Do?' and actually tried following in his footsteps, every day, every hour! It was so thrilling to hear her tell it! But there's the answer to everything, really. If only we would question ourselves, 'What would Jesus do?' and then try to follow through with the answer, we wouldn't get into nearly so much trouble in our lives. If, as a nation, we had acted on those principles, in all the common, every-day things, why, we'd never gotten ourselves into the position of thinking war was necessary, much less killing off thousands of people with an atom bomb!"

31

"You're right," mused Charles. Suddenly he jumped up, banged his fist on the desk, and almost shouted, "That's it! That's it!"

"That's what?"

"My sermon! What we must do to win the peace! Just do whatever Jesus would do, that's all! It's so simple—and so complicated. Because of course not everyone will agree on what He'd do—but it's got to start somewhere! We'll start it here, in this little town, in our little church—maybe we can get others to help—it could grow and grow—if we had the faith!"

"Oh, yes!" Frances' eyes were glowing, as she began to understand Charles' outburst. "It would be marvelous, if we could get even a small group working together, trying to live in that way— it would change everything, I know it would—the whole world, maybe!" She laughed aloud. "Oh, if anyone saw us, he'd think we were crazy, wouldn't he?"

As if coming back to earth, Charles suddenly looked at his watch, and exclaimed, "What has happened to the time! It's nearly 11:00, and I've kept you too long! Let me see you home?"

Frances began to pull on her sheer white gloves, saying, "No, thank you, I have my car." Her eyes twinkled as she said, "Do you suppose my parents will believe me if I tell them I've been helping you write your sermon?"

CHAPTER 4

"If any man will come after me, let him deny him-self and take up his cross and follow me."

THE FOLLOWING SUNDAY found the church filled with eager, expectant people. News of the "hari-kari," as the newspapers insisted on calling it, of Kamada in the chapel of the First Church, had spread all over the nation. The Associated Press had picked it up and sent it around the world. The announcement that Charles Maxwell had made the preceding Sunday had drawn back his entire congregation and many strangers. As he sat in his simple straight-backed chair behind the ancient pulpit, Maxwell looked out at the throng before him, then lifted his eyes to the great stained glass window above the gallery, of Jesus the good Shepherd standing among His sheep. He closed his eyes and prayed, "Father, I feel like the little sheep Jesus carries in His arms. I am in your arms this morning, dear Father. Hold fast to me now in this hour. I thank Thee in all humility for Thy revelations to me in these past days, and for showing me the error of my thinking. Speak through me now to these Thy people, Father, speak through your servant today. Bless the sheep of this pasture."

He prayed all through the opening hymn. As the congregation sat down, amid the flurry of hymn-books being slipped back into their racks, the arranging of dresses and the clearing of throats, he lifted his gaze again to the great stained glass window. He rose and waited for the restlessness to quiet before he read from the scriptures in a voice strangely tense.

"For behold, it shall come to pass in the latter days, saith the

Lord, that I will pour out my Spirit upon all flesh: And you sons and daughters shall prophesy, your old men shall dream dreams, your young men shall see visions: And also upon the servants and upon the handmaids in those days will I pour out my Spirit, and ye shall know that I, the Lord, am in the midst of you."

As he sat now, hands outspread along the arms of the pulpit chair, a soprano voice filled the sanctuary like a voice from heaven itself. Someone he knew was thinking about him, praying for him. A deep quietness filled Charles Maxwell, something like lethargy and yet atingle with something lethargy does not have —a great, vibrant peace.

When the solo drew to a close, he found himself rising to stand before the hungry eyes of that packed assembly. "Help me, Lord," he prayed inwardly, "and help me, you little one of the singing voice." For in that moment it came to him with divine certainty that the child of song sitting behind him was incandescent enough for the power of God to come through. He felt the Holy Spirit taking hold of him. Quietly he pushed aside his notes and stepped out beside the pulpit, up to the very edge of the platform. He opened his lips and the words began to come:

"I stood in this pulpit last Sunday, posing as a man of God, and justified mass murder because I was exhalting patriotism above God. And a man who had come here seeking peace and the love of his brothers went away and took his own life because I had destroyed the last hope of his bewildered soul. But in a sense, he gave his life that I might live; for the little man named Kamada pulled me out of that trap of wilful self-deception." In a voice low but so vibrant that it penetrated every corner of the quiet church, Charles Maxwell murmured, "God rest his soul."

With the eye of every member of his congregation fixed upon him the tall young minister moved slowly around to the other side of the pulpit, and began again in purposeful, clear tones. "A few years hence atomic energy will be harnessed by scientists and engineers to serve us in a thousand different ways. It will take the place of oil and coal; a thousand things we now depend

34

upon will be rendered obsolete. The world is coming into a period of material plenty. Will there be spiritual plenty to control it?"

Charles paused, and felt instinctively a restlessness growing in the air. He was not saying the things he had been expected to say, and he knew he was going to disappoint a great many "practical" minds who had hoped he would go on being as "sensible" as he was last Sunday. He plowed ahead: "Our nation, and other nations, will also busily develop their knowledge of atomic power for destructive use—for war, altho the sign on the road may read, 'Preparedness.' There is no known defense against atomic bombs. I believe in preparedness—but the only kind that really counts is good will."

Although a sweeping search showed Charles a great many skeptical faces among the approving ones, he went on. "There is only One who knows the secret of bringing good will to men and peace on earth, and that One is God. The only preparedness is preparedness of the soul.

"Fifty years ago in this church, my grandfather conceived a dream. From this pulpit he threw out a challenge. This week I found in a cubby hole in my grandfather's old desk a copy of that sermon, and I shall at this time read to you a portion of it."

Some of the older members of the audience sat alert at this mention of Maxwell's revered predecessor.

" 'What I am going to propose now,' runs my grandfather's words, 'is something which ought not to appear unusual or at all impossible of execution. Yet I am aware that it will be so regarded by a large number, perhaps, of the members of this church. But in order that we may have a thorough understanding of what we are considering, I will put my proposition very plainly, perhaps bluntly. I want volunteers from the First Church who will pledge themselves, earnestly and honestly for an entire year, not to do anything without first asking the question, What Would Jesus Do? And after asking that question, each one will follow Jesus as exactly as he knows how, no matter what the result may be. I will, of course, include myself in this company of volunteers, and shall take it for granted that my church here will not be surprised at my future conduct, as based upon this standard of action, and will not oppose whatever is done if they think Christ would do it. Have I made my meaning clear? Our motto will be, What Would Jesus Do? Our aim will be to act just as He would if He were in our places, regardless of immediate results. In other words, we propose to follow Jesus' steps as closely and as literally as we believe He taught His disciples to do. And those who volunteer to do this will pledge themselves for an entire year, beginning with today, so to act.' "

Charles Maxwell placed the paper on the pulpit and looked genially over the audience. "I saw smiles of recognition on some of your faces as I read those words. Yes, it was an interesting experiment. For several years it did great things for our town. You probably all know some of your older friends and relatives who accepted the pledge. But this is a challenge that cannot be offered lightly and cannot be taken up without great sincerity, tremendous zeal, and a considerable amount of courage. What Would Jesus Do? has been the subject of many sermons since my grandfather's day, in this pulpit and all over the country. It has rarely been taken to heart. My new friends," he said, gently and firmly, "I think you have the courage and this is the crisis."

The skeptical faces scattered throughout the congregation had assumed blank looks, having been faced with a proposition which they could not, in all decency, dispute—not publicly, at least. And as the sense of peace and power continued within him, Charles saw that most of his people sat alert and interested. In a friendly, welcoming voice, he continued, "I am going to ask all those who want to take this pledge to meet with me at a special service tonight in the little chapel. There we can talk this thing over in detail, and map out this adventurous journey into real living. We shall try to follow Jesus as completely and literally as possible, regardless of the immediate results."

He left the pulpit and came out to the very edge of the platform. "Jesus was the only perfectly natural person who ever walked this earth. He followed laws of love as faithfully as the sea follows the laws of the tides. We as individuals and as nations have been living unnaturally. We have been breaking laws. This terrible war from which we are just emerging was the inevitable consequence of impractical, unnatural ways of living. If we persist in remaining out on the lunatic fringe of this revolving world we shall sooner or later all fall into the ditch."

Eyes alight and in a ringing voice, Charles went on, "We speak of 'winning the peace,' as if it were another battle in which we might gain victory by force. But peace is a quiet thing, coming from within. It is something we must earn, not win. There is no 'Chosen Race.' God's chosen people are the humble, whatever their language or color or birthplace. Remembering this, and as diligently as our scientists worked in their laboratories to find the secret of atomic power, let us labor as scientists of the spirit, and in life's laboratory see what far-reaching changes might be wrought in our lives and in the world if we consistently apply the chemistry of love to every experience that comes. If we step out on faith, in His steps, who knows but what the route to the pot of gold at the end of the rainbow will be but a straight and narrow path, easily trod, with sunshine all the way? Those who will join with me in this adventure, come out tonight!"

As Charles returned to his pulpit chair, the choir softly moved into the familiar strains of "Lead, Kindly Light," and he sent up a fervent prayer of thanks, his mind seconding the words, "One step enough for me . . ." "Thou hast shown me this step, oh, God; I know that the next will be made plain to me as well."

After the benediction, a great silence fell upon the worshippers. Instead of rising as usual and breaking into animated conversation, they remained seated. Gradually a gentle hum of conversation broke out, more a composite of whispers and sighs than anything articulate and vocal. Slowly they began to move out, saying little to Maxwell as he stood at the door, but with an

37

extra pressure of the hand, a wordless look, or a murmured "Thank you," telling him that his words had reached their mark. Charles Maxwell glanced down the steps, and saw the people gather in clusters outside, joining in conversations that gradually grew more animated.

There was a faint sound and Charles turned back suddenly to see Frances Page behind him. Gravely she gave him her small gloved hand and spoke. "Today I felt that I was listening to a prophet." Without giving him time to speak, she was gone, and Charles watched her join Arnold Eton where he stood apart from the others on the sidewalk with an impatient stance. He had not seen Eton leave, and thought wryly that the man probably had not found much to commend in today's sermon, remembering his face among the skeptical, disappointed ones in the congregation.

Charles smiled, and with a light heart turned back into the church, feeling younger and freer than since he was a little boy, and was doing something that pleased his Father very well.

CHAPTER 5

"What is that to thee? Follow thou on."

THAT EVENING, ten minutes before it was time for the specially called meeting to begin, the little chapel was full to overflowing and people were blocking the halls that led to it. Whether it was curiosity or earnest, sincere zeal that brought them, Charles did not know.

When there still remained five minutes before starting time, Charles joined them.

"In a way, I am sorry," he announced, standing by the altar, "that we must leave this little room, as this was the place where I thought it was natural to start a movement as sacred as this. But I am glad there are so many of you who were interested enough to overflow this room. Let us move to the church parlors."

Ten minutes later when the confusion of changing from one room to another was over and all were comfortably seated, Charles said, "Let us drop the curtains of our eyelids and step into the secret place of the Most High for a few moments of silent prayer."

The instant all heads were bowed the silence grew like something tangible that could be felt and heard. The very presence of the Christ seemed to be in their midst. As the moments went by the Holy Spirit Himself seemed to descend upon them and fill the room. Charles closed the period with a simple prayer.

Then clearing his throat he began:

"Coming home to Raymond has always been a dream of mine. I call it home though my folks moved away while I was a small

39

child. Now that this war is over I realize that I have come home to Raymond for a reason."

Feeling all eyes fixed attentively upon him, Charles continued. "A man died in this church, in the little chapel we have just vacated. He died not by his own hand, but by my hand. No, don't shudder. It was by your hand, too. We are so interwoven one with another that no one can escape his share in this total war guilt. I talked with many boys in the Army, and most of those who were in combat have a sense of remorse. It was kill or be killed, they told me. When I saw what we did to that forlorn, frustrated lad whose entire family had been blasted into dust one day in Hiroshima, I decided then and there that this world is not a fit place to live in as it is. It is not a fit place unless we can make it a little more like heaven. Don't think that is impossible. It has been the chief burden of the Lord's Prayer for two thousand years—Thy Kingdom come on earth as it is in heaven. The time has come when that prayer should begin to have some effect. The time has come when we should cease saying it merely in words, and begin saying it in action. And what better action for bringing in the Kingdom than trying to follow in the steps of Jesus in every way we possibly know how?"

After a pause, Charles concluded with a smile, "I have said all I intend to say tonight. Now it is your turn. What are you going to do about it?"

Immediately there arose on the front row a man of around sixty, tall and straight, slightly bald, but with sharp, piercing eyes.

"I am Richard Norman, owner of the *Raymond News*. My father, fifty years ago, participated eagerly in your grandfather's pledge and ran into many difficulties. When he died, twenty years ago, I reversed his policy because it seemed to be out of step with the times. Maybe it was I who was out of step. My conscience has been hurting me ever since. While the pastor was speaking right now, a whole vision leaped into my mind of what we could do with that paper. Would it be the proper place to tell of it now?"

40

The eager exclamations from all over the room actually startled both the pastor and the speaker. Before Charles Maxwell could respond beyond nodding his head, the general excitement seemed to invite Mr. Norman to go on.

"As I sat here it came to me. Would Jesus be whooping it up for liquor and tobacco? Would He delight in spreading crime and scandal for all to see? That set me to thinking. And that led me to some resolving. Here are some resolves. There are some things about the paper I can change right now." He paused as if to get his thoughts in order, then continued decisively. "I am going to take no advertisements of liquor or tobacco, beginning the first of next month. I am going to put the big news in the big places and have all crime news put through a condensing and dehydrating system and placed in small type on an inside page. I have one man on my staff who would make a marvellous condenser and dehydrator."

Everyone laughed. When they had subsided he went on.

"On the middle of the front page in a box, I am going to have a meditation for the day." He stopped, as if letting the idea grow in his mind. "I shall start writing to leading ministers and spiritual leaders tomorrow, asking each to furnish the prayer thought for one day, three hundred and sixty-five great spiritual leaders to contribute one each for the year. Maybe we can start a new syndicate and other papers will follow suit."

Hardly had he finished when another voice exclaimed, "I, too, intend to put this pledge to work in my business and I want your prayers."

"Stand up, Mr. Wright," said Charles, recognizing in him another member of his Board of Deacons, the vigorous young owner of the Wright Department Store.

Jonathan Wright rose slowly to his full six feet. "I have failed to meet this test in my department store. I am going home tonight and put in a good long time in prayer for guidance, and I mean it when I say I want the prayers of all of you."

His long figure was hardly deposited in his chair when three more were on their feet, eagerly waiting their turn.

"One at a time!" laughed Charles. "This is getting exciting. Let us hear from this lady here on the front row." As he looked at the sweet-faced, elderly lady, as sweet and beautiful in her white hair as most young women are in their golden, his glance was drawn to Frances Page seated beside her, her eyes aglow. Why had he not been wise enough to infer that this older woman was none other than Rachel Winslow Page, the great friend of his grandfather?

"I just want to say that nothing has moved me in fifty years as much as the service this morning and the vision that is taking form tonight." Her sweet contralto voice was in refreshing contrast to the masculine voices that had just spoken. "When my dear husband passed away two years ago, his last words were, 'Rachel, I will be with you in heaven, opening a little wider if possible the gates to let the King of Glory come in and fill your life as never before.' I have truly felt his presence, and never so much as tonight. I feel as if all the heavenly host were near to us, joining in a divine partnership to bring heaven down to earth. I am too moved to talk further. But it warms my heart to see the response to this heaven-inspired leadership of our pastor in putting the dream of a new world into action."

She paused, then sank back in her seat. Frances grasped her hand and put her other arm around her shoulder. Charles Maxwell's eyes had been fixed, fascinated, upon the beautiful face of the grandmother. They now passed to the equally beautiful face of the granddaughter in her young loveliness, and for a moment, he felt himself almost trembling with the shock of finding her eyes, exceedingly bright and glistening with tears, fixed full upon his.

Before Charles had time to call on another, a veritable stream of words came pouring through the walrus mustaches of a lean, elderly man on the front seat.

"See here, young man," he said, not rising. He tossed his shaggy locks of grey hair and clenched his two bony hands around the top of the cane they held. "While you're talking about what Jesus would do, don't forget how he overturned the tables of the money changers. We've got to put teeth in this if we get anywhere. The demon that is destroying America is greed, old demon greed." His deep bass voice paused a moment, then the flow continued. "When Jesus went from Nazareth to Jerusalem the scenery wasn't defiled by whiskey advertisements every mile and cigarette signs at every cross road. They had money changers then, sure, but their profits were picayune and microscopic compared to the profits of our munitions manufacturers and addiction trusts today. We'll never stop drunkenness, crime and war till we take the profits out of everything that fosters these things."

"Take the profits out!" ejaculated a bald headed man sitting beside him, "Take out the profits! What do you mean, Mr. Babcock?"

The mustaches were now working overtime. "You heard what I said!" the voice boomed. "And don't pull any raised eyebrows stuff about Babcock, the millionaire, turning communistic. The grass roots in our economic system are good, but most of the clover and alfalfa is being crowded out by burdock and mustard. And by the great horn spoon, the weeds that threaten to stifle our way of life aren't so much communism, but greed, greed, greed. That is the fifth column, right in our midst which has caused all of our wars, has caused three-fourths of our crime and if we don't stop it in time it will create nine-tenths of the chain reaction that will destroy our world."

"And what is that chain reaction?" asked the bald headed man.

"Communism is nothing more nor less than the chain reaction to greed run rampant. Mark my words, if we don't get Jesus into our economic system mighty quick, we won't have any economic system left in which to practice what Jesus told us to practice." His voice fairly shook the room. Then in a quieter tone he added, "If Editor Norman thinks we have enough free enterprise left in America for him to conduct his newspaper as he thinks Jesus would do it, just let him push over one or two tables of the money changers and see what happens to him. I give him three

43

years before he is walking the streets, looking for a job. What he is planning is right, but he can't do it piece-meal. Until we get at the roots of the entire system, the evil will go on and on till our civilization destroys itself."

Charles could not take his eyes from the speaker. Could this violent outburst be coming from the retired millionaire, Babcock? Could this be old C. J.?

And now the booming voice went on, "Does Editor Norman really want to do what Jesus would do? Does he really have the intestinal fortitude to knock over the money changers' tables? Then the first thing he will do will be to remove the iron curtain that is hanging over our own news channels almost as tightly as it is hanging over Russia. He will have to lay bare the way our oil interests and other greedy monopolies are reaching out over the whole world in ways that may involve us in a new war almost before this one is ended."

"This is absurd!" exclaimed the bald headed man sitting beside the speaker. "Now you are going too far, Babcock."

"Too far nothing," the deep bass boomed, and with one hand on his cane and the other on the chair, Babcock slowly rose to his feet and faced the audience.

"I am a pacifist, and I'll tell you why. Fifty years ago I took the pledge under my friend Henry Maxwell to walk in Jesus' steps. Twenty years later I voted for a second term for Woodrow Wilson because he ran under the slogan, 'He kept us out of war.' A year after he was elected, Ambassador Page wrote Secretary of State Lansing that the only way to prevent a collapse in the stock market was for the United States to come into the war. So we contrived to get in. 'A war to end war,' they told us. Bah! It was a war to prevent economic collapse. It was the war that *started* wars. We thought we were making this world safe for democracy, but it was a war that destroyed democracies. Churchill himself said that if the United States had not gone into the war it would have ended in a stalemate; there would have been a negotiated peace instead of a Punic peace, com-

44

munism would never have been born and a million English, French and German boys would not have died.

"Twenty years later I voted for Franklin Roosevelt who assured all mothers that their sons would never be sent into another foreign war."

"Hold on," cried a young man in military uniform on the back seat, "you don't mean to imply that we shouldn't have gotten into this war."

"I certainly do!" came the booming answer. "What about these four freedoms we fought for? Freedom from want. Bah! Never was the whole world so dying of starvation and want as it is this very hour. Freedom from fear! Fiddlesticks! Never was an entire nation—yes, a whole world—so filled with fear as it is today. Had Christ been in control of the White House and of American business He could have prevented this war before it even began.

"Ladies and gentlemen," now his voice lowered. "I just told you how fifty years ago I pledged Dr. Maxwell, my dear friend, Henry, that I would try to walk in the Master's steps. In 1918 I lost my only child in a commercial war on Flanders' field. His wife, my sweet daughter-in-law, died of the shock. My wife and I took their little baby into our home and raised him to manhood. In 1941 he was conscripted for World War II. A week before Japan surrendered we got word that this young lad was killed, the last of my line, in an air raid over Tokyo. Yes, I am a millionaire. But what does that mean to me? I accumulated millions under America's highly vaunted system of free enterprise. But what does it profit a man if he gains the whole world only to lose his sons? And mark my words, if some one doesn't break our own iron curtain and reveal how we are being used as pawns for selfish interests we are in for another cycle of wars that may bring the whole world to destruction. So I will back Mr. Norman in all he undertakes to save the peace. But if he goes all the way, God save the pieces."

45

CHAPTER 6

*"Render to Caesar the things that are Caesar's and
unto God the things that are God's."*

THE FOLLOWING MONDAY morning, young Jonathan
Wright called a meeting of managers of all the divisions
of his company. The eight managers were already seated
in comfortable green leather chairs in Wright's office, and as
Wright entered, a soft buzz of conversation which had been
audible as he approached the room ceased abruptly. Each of the
managers greeted him as he made his way to the head of the
conference table and seated himself. Jonathan sat silent for a
moment, half turned from the men before him, looking thoughtfully out through the large window which gave one a view of
half the town of Raymond.

The group matched his silence, and Jonathan could feel their
questioning minds pulling at him, their curiosity about this
unscheduled meeting filling the atmosphere of the room. Then
for a moment the importance of what he was about to say filled
his mind, obliterating even the sense of the presence of others.
His whole being went out in one heartfelt prayer that he might
have guidance as he went into the meeting, that the right words
would be spoken through his lips and find receptive minds among
the men who would have the responsibility of carrying out his
plan.

Slowly, with eight pairs of eyes watching him intently, he
turned back to face the men at the table. "Let me tell you why
I asked you in on a busy Monday morning," he began. "This
meeting is going to make history for the Wright Department

Store. What I have to say will come as a surprise to you. Perhaps you won't like it." No sooner had the words left his lips than he detected a restive stir among the men before him, a lifted eyebrow here and there, a quizzical smile. "No," said a voice within him. "That won't do. Don't take the defensive. Assume that they'll like it, because it is right and good and honorable, and they will have no other course than to accept."

Jonathan looked at each one around the table. Here were men whom he had known most of his life, men he had worked with every day for three years, men who called him "Jonathan," and in whose homes he had visited. But how well did he know them, really? Men in business, he suddenly realized, were like actors on a stage, speaking the accepted lines, waiting for cues, presenting a front to the world which did not necessarily express their true selves at all.

How well did they know him? countered the voice within. They knew him, he supposed, as an earnest and aggressive young man who had so far followed previously established policies of the store—policies which had lately evolved, not so much from the idealistic leadership of his father and grandfather, but from the materialistic "hard-headed" practices of his advisers. They knew him as a moral and conscientious young man, a churchgoer who had not heretofore shown evidences of trying to practice in any outlandish way the things he heard the preacher say on Sunday. Well, it would be a shock to some of them when he came out with this new policy.

Especially to men like Bill Peters, vice president and Jim Long of the Hardware Division, these inseparables who sat together now at the end of the long table and exchanged a half-amused, half-puzzled look. Peters, especially, Jonathan felt, had long considered himself the real head of the store, and had only tolerated Jonathan's nominal leadership. Bill Peters' eyes seemed to be saying to Jonathan, as he turned from Long and looked up at the head of the table, "Well, all right, Boy Wonder! Come on, out with it! If it suits me, O. K. If not—well, it won't get far, anyway, so why worry?"

The rest of the men, Jonathan thought, could be counted on for a reasonable amount of support. His eyes travelled along the table and tried to weigh them all, one by one, as if he could look into each soul and see there whether the tendency to follow like sheep in the path of the strongest leader—himself or Peters—would overbalance the amount of real conviction and innate goodness in each of them.

Suddenly he realized that the silence was stretching into minutes, and the managers were beginning to become restless and looking even more puzzled.

Smiling, Jonathan relaxed his scrutiny of the men and leaned back into his chair. "Forgive me for seeming so mysterious, gentlemen," he said. "This thing I am going to propose is terribly important to me, and I would be very disappointed if you didn't agree. But I won't be mysterious any longer."

Leaning forward again, Jonathan gripped his hands together, and said, "I have to warn you, it'll boost us or bust us, but that is not the most important thing. The most important thing is that, as Christian business men, we have a moral obligation to bring Christian principles out of the churches which we enjoy on Sunday, and put them into the world of business which occupies us on all the other days. In other words, I want this store to be run as if Jesus Himself were going to come around and inspect it once in a while, just as the auditor comes around to inspect the books."

With a half smile, Jonathan looked around the circle of faces, all of which were watching him intently. "I know I'm not being very fashionable, gentlemen, when I bring the words Christian and Jesus and even God into a business meeting of department store managers." His glance, travelling around the table, came to rest upon the steely eyes of Bill Peters, and he continued, "It is a 'sin and a shame,' as my grandfather used to say, that the civilization we know has gotten so far away from God that a person risks being laughed at if he mentions His name in polite society. Well, we don't have to mention His name if you'd rather not. We might only antagonize people if we did, and that wouldn't help our cause any. But we can slip over some things on people, without their knowing it—things like going out of our way to be generous and helpful to our employees—and encouraging them to be increasingly kind and courteous to our customers. Any student of Dale Carnegie will recognize the value of such practices in winning customers and influencing employees," he smiled. "But, seriously, even aside from their value in creating good will, such practices will increase our income for the store."

There were murmurs of approval from the little group, and the hard look on Bill Peters' face softened a bit.

Unable to sit still any longer, Jonathan got up and began to walk back and forth from the window to his chair. "Fifty years ago my grandfather got religion, as the old-timers would say. He gathered his managers together and laid down some rules, like the Golden Rule, that he wanted the business to be run by. In spite of opposition from certain factions among his men, to the surprise of everyone, the business prospered. From being one of the smaller department stores in the state, it became one of the largest. Our record to this day shows we are doing a bigger business than any store in a city of our size in this section of the country."

The faces about the table seemed to be watching Jonathan with approval, and he continued, still pacing back and forth, "One of the rules Grandfather laid down was that we were not to advertise in the Sunday papers. Every manager said that would sink us. To the contrary, it seemed to be the spark plug that got us going. Grandfather persisted in this policy till the day of his death. Father carried the same policy, in this and other things, farther, with even greater success. Every step that he took to be more unselfish, the faster the business came along."

Abruptly, Jonathan turned from the window and leaned his hands on the massive conference table, his face darkening. "But the heart went out of it, men! Somewhere along the line, we stopped doing good for its own sake, and began simply keeping up the appearance of doing good, purely for the money to be made by maintaining a reputation as a benevolent and charitable business institution. The heart went out of it, I say, and we became corrupt, because our motives became corrupt. We got into the habit of being good just because it paid. The directors grew more and more materialistic, donating money to some good cause with one hand—and incidentally getting their pictures and much praise in the newspaper—and laughing up their sleeve on the other hand. How did this happen?"

Jonathan sat down tiredly in his chair, beginning to be spent with the force of his feeling. For now he had come to that part of the store's history which he had never understood, the baffling phase of his father's life and that of the store which he hoped someday to unravel. Slowly he continued feeling the intent gaze upon him of all the men in the room who had so far listened in silence.

"How did this happen? I hope some day to know what brought about the change in my father's life that took the sincerity out of doing good, and consequently the satisfaction out of it. Whatever it was, Father seemed to relax his control of the store, and it passed into the hands of more supposedly business-like men. They kept up the outward appearances, yes, but here and there changes were made that began to destroy the foundation upon which this great institution was built. When Father died suddenly three years ago, as all of you know, I found myself the head of the most hard-boiled firm in town."

Again Jonathan paused, collecting his thoughts. Was it only his over-wrought imagination, or had he really glimpsed a sardonic, knowing smile on the lips of Peters at the mention of his father's loss of control of the business? He knew, of course, that his reference to business-like men could have been interpreted as a blow at Peters and his cohorts. He had not meant to be critical; he honestly believed that the materialistic conduct of the business which had characterized it in recent years had been damaging. But how to persuade these material-minds that a different course, a course they might call impractical and too idealistic, would help? Well, all he could do now was to go ahead on faith, speak his piece and let them have their say, hoping they would give his plan a chance. He plunged ahead:

"I want us to try this year to renew that old spirit that started us on our road to success fifty years ago. I want, with your cooperation, to reinstate some of the working principles on which my grandfather established this business: things like granting pensions to deserving employees, vacations with pay, installing a comfortable lounge with a nurse in attendance for tired or ill customers—we might even throw a bang-up party for our workers on Christmas Eve! And let's train our clerks that courtesy is the better part of efficiency, that it is profitable to take a little extra time with a customer, taking a personal interest in his purchase, rather than getting rid of him as soon as possible to wait on someone else." He smiled, and with a twinkle in his eye, addressed Bill Peters. "Perhaps our worthy personnel manager will say if clerks take extra time with every customer, that we'll have to hire more clerks. Well, all right, let's hire more clerks. If a few extra salaries to pay each week is going to break us, we're pretty bad off, anyway, and had better be looking around for a few changes to improve matters. The good-will created by friendly clerks might possibly bring in enough more customers to pay the salaries of those extra clerks. What do you men think of this? Is this too big a step to take all at once?"

"It won't be a big step for me," spoke up Sam Crocker, the jovial head of the women's ready-to-wear division. His gruff good nature characterized everything he did. "I just fired a clerk yesterday because he wore such a long face he drove customers away. His wages were being garnisheed because he got too expensive a wedding ring like all the rest of them do."

Smiling broadly, Crocker looked around the table. "He was only married two months and thinks he's got trouble. Can you beat that? Wait till he finds out, eh, boys?" Laughter went around the circle, melting for a moment some of the hardness between the men.

Leaning forward, Jonathan was poised, a determined smile on his lips.

"Just a minute, Sam. I think you have the problem for us right there. I was in the treasurer's office when this young chap —Pete Phillips—from your department was there, Sam. I found that the orders were that he be fired. I don't blame you, Sam. Before last week I would have written the fire order myself. But let's look at this boy. He had bought an expensive engagement ring, I found. Much too expensive. But a high pressure sales artist told him how easy it was to pay for it on time. Then, getting married, it has been one bill after another. So he went to a loan company that looked o.k. because they advertised the most in town. The interest was lots higher than he realized and when he couldn't pay it the company went to court and are legally taking his pay from us, garnisheeing it. That's what got you, Crocker, and I don't blame you. It is the custom to drop a man like that for it reflects on his usefulness to a store. That's what I thought, anyhow, until I talked it all over with young Phillips and got a lot of his background. That's what we should do more—get the background of our people. Do you know he has been taking night school courses in merchandising, Sam?"

"He has?" exclaimed Sam.

"He's been taking them for two years plus working. He is back at work today, Sam, and I think he will make out all right. I got our store lawyer to help him figure it out and I think he'll get in the clear in another six months or so. I think he'll also be a real asset for us someday too. And after hearing his appreciation for my helping him, I know he's grateful.

"It got me to thinking, though. And I had some talks with some local people. Why can't we help these employees be free from such money troubles? An organizer from the credit union outfit is coming in this week and maybe we can get one of these set up here. All kinds of companies have them and it will help get small loans at low interest rates. We are going to give it a try.

"This is just what I have in mind. The kind of way we should be moving. I kind of had the idea that we were just in it for money. But we are really in it for other reasons too. If you don't remember anything I say today, remember this: We're going to get a different kind of spirit in this store from now on. And I want your help for I've made my errors too." He turned to Ed Olsen, the natty store treasurer. "I want you to forgive me for grilling you each meeting on the income and outgo of the store. I know you, as treasurer, can't help a great deal of it. Thank heavens, this has brought me up to my senses. I guess I was giving you ulcers and me too." Ed looked startled then returned Jonathan's good natured grin.

Jonathan rose again, and leaned his clenched fists on the table, but turned a smiling face around the attentive group. "I know you will all have things to say, but give me just another minute, and I'll be through, and wanting to hear what you think. I've been up all night—with my Bible on my knees. I got especially interested in Paul. He was a great organizer, and what he did was permanent. He built on three great principles—Faith, Hope and Love. Let's begin with Love. It sounds preachy to talk of love in business, I know, but you know what I mean—harmony and teamwork.

"Last week I came back from New York on an airliner of the company that has never had an accident. An inspector was on board and do you know what he told me? His chief job is to make sure there is no tension or discord among the members of the crew. If there is, he smoothes it out if he can, but if he can't he transfers the offending members to other flights where harmony can prevail.

"If any of you have any jealousy, bitterness or grudge against anyone else on the staff, come and talk it over with me and we will see if we can't get it solved. Or better still, see the man you have the grudge against. Try to fill the clerks working under you with the same spirit. Don't drive your clerks from now on—encourage them! In other words, let's turn our store into something more than a treadmill. Let's start to make it one big happy family."

Something on the face of Bill Peters caught his eye.

"What's on your mind, Bill?"

"It's just this," began Peters, and for the first time Wright noticed the way the iron-grey of Peters' hair seemed reflected in his eye. "Our business isn't any too good of late. It's been running on a danger line for two years. We do need something changed—perhaps firing some weak sisters—cleaning out some dead wood and adding more efficiency. That's why it's bad business to encourage slackness when we need tightening up."

Bill Peters was fifty, and Jonathan Wright was thirty. Bill was first vice president, and head of operations. For years he had been the indispensable man, the one the business could not go on without. Keen, shrewd, experienced in nearly every phase of the business, Jonathan's father, before he died, had depended upon Bill to break in many of his new men.

"Mr. Wright," continued Bill, frankly, "I don't want to be critical, but I don't believe what you are talking about will work. I believe you are beginning at the wrong end. We should put a little more drive into our working force before we get too sweety-sweety. We should produce more profits before we think of distributing charity. Our first duty is to our stockholders. After that comes the customers. You can't mix sentiment and business."

Jonathan got up and went to the wall and turned on the electric light.

"This is not sentiment I am talking about, Bill, but something as hard as nails. When I pressed that switch the one wire in there which was unconnected got connected up. Before I did that there was a break in the circuit and the light was off. But when the circuit was made complete the lights went on. I am not being sentimental when I say that to complete the current of harmony and good-will in a group of strong men will increase the unseen power of that organization.

"I played tackle on the Yale football team, and I have seen games lost because the circuit was turned off, and I have seen games won when the circuit was turned on. I have seen where one man out of accord with the spirit of the team could shut off the whole circuit. Men, we are going to have a business which, some way or other, keeps the circuit of harmony and good will turned on. For the last five years we have been trying the 'drive' way. Now that I have taken over the management, I am going to ask you to try the other way, and see how it works. That's all now. I'd appreciate it if each one of you would keep this new idea in your hearts. Thanks for coming. Uncle Henry, will you come to my office?"

When the meeting ended, Bill Peters and Jim Long slipped out of the room first of all. The others lingered a few moments in the hall looking from face to face.

"That young boss of ours means business," said Hal Simpson, the efficient head of the men's clothing division. "This is the first time in twenty years I ever saw anyone go against Bill Peters. Jonathan's father was under Bill's thumb as long as he lived."

"Funny," said Harvey Smith, of the credit department, "that little flash of fire in his eye did more to make me believe he knows what he is talking about than all the love he had been preaching to us before. I believe it will take a little fight to get more love into our crowd. We've all been pretty edgy the past year."

"I don't know," questioned one, "I am afraid he antagonized Bill."

"Well," continued Harvey, "I liked it. Maybe that's what it needs. I guess it takes a little vinegar to make my soda water fizz."

The entire group burst into laughter at this. Jonathan, on his way to his private office, heard the laughter and it made him wince a little. Were they laughing at him? But at that moment Sam Crocker was saying,

"Fellows, did you see that light go on? Remember this, what young Jonathan was giving us is straight common sense, as sure as the law of gravity. We must all pull together. Keep the current turned on."

"You're right," said Harvey Smith, "Let's give it a try."

In his private office, Jonathan faced Uncle Henry.

"What do you think, Uncle Henry?" he asked quietly. "Did I say the right things?"

Uncle Henry, fat and baldish, manager of the house furnishing division, was the oldest member of the staff, a conscientious member of his church, and for seventeen years superintendent of its Sunday School.

"Jonathan," Uncle Henry replied, "your Father would have been proud had he heard you this morning. It's about time someone said what you said."

"There's one more thing I wanted to talk about, but I didn't think it would be best to bring it up before them all. What would you think about having a prayer room somewhere in the store, maybe on the top floor, away from the noise and confusion?"

"A prayer room?" mused Uncle Henry, wrinkling his forehead in thought. "Well, I don't know. It would certainly be unusual! Do you mean for the employees?"

"I had in mind one for the employees, and another for the customers," said Jonathan.

"Do you think it would be used very much?" asked Uncle Henry.

"No, not in the beginning, but after it had proved helpful to some, the idea would spread. Besides, I want to prove the practicality of Christianity to people who don't already know it! I sincerely believe that if you give just a ten minute thought to God some time during the day, your whole day works out better. At least that's what I'd like to prove to people! Isn't it worth a try?"

Uncle Henry's eyes were alert with interest. "Jonathan," he said with a wide smile, "it certainly would be fun to try. I'd just suggest one thing. What about calling it a quiet room instead of a prayer room? Not because it's better but just to creep up on the idea for those who would immediately fight the kind of impression they have of a prayer room."

Jonathan laughed. "That's a good point," he said. "You don't know how much I appreciate your wisdom and your help, Uncle Henry," he said, rising and extending his hand. "Thank you!"

CHAPTER 7

"I am the true vine and ye are the branches."

O N A MONDAY MORNING following a Sunday where the attendance had been most gratifying, Charles noticed a letter in his morning mail from the office of the president of Lincoln College. He pulled it forth from the rest, and found it contained an invitation from Dr. and Mrs. Egbert Page for his presence at dinner Thursday evening in their home. In the corner was the word, "Formal."

Charles held the invitation in his hand and turned it over as he tried to visualize who would be there. He had not yet met President Page, but he was eager to meet him. The latter had been in such demand as a speaker out of town that he had not spent one Sunday in Raymond that fall.

"He is a real prince o' a man," said MacIntosh when Charles asked his opinion of him. "A' he needs is tae be chucked onto a white horse and hae a white beard hung on his chin and he wad be an exact replica of Robert E. Lee."

"What kind of wife does he have?" asked Charles. "I have met her at the church door several times, and she impresses me more as a socialite than a college president's wife."

"I' her youth she wes the belle o' the ballroom," said Mac-Intosh, "the only bairn o' one o' the auldest and best known families o' Raymond."

"I will be very glad to meet them," said Charles as he hurried into his study. But above all, Charles looked forward to meeting again that wonderful grandmother, Mrs. Rollin Page, whose sweetness had seemed to fill the whole room at the specially called meeting. And Frances! Would she be there? He had not seen her, except fleetingly, since the night she had come so impulsively to his study, and helped him clarify his thinking after Kamada's suicide. By now it seemed almost like a dream that she had been there at all.

When the evening came he donned his "boiled" shirt, black bow tie and tuxedo, and rang the door of the stately mansion a few minutes before six-thirty. It was a warm September evening, and the smell of new-cut, well-watered grass filled the air as he stood on the wide veranda and saw the vast sweep of lawn all around him.

A Negro woman with a white tea apron came to the door, took his hat and ushered him into the parlor, its high walls decorated with rivers, bridges and castles reappearing at regular intervals. There he found nine persons assembled, nine who were destined to change and mould the entire course of his life.

Dr. Egbert Page was a tall man of about forty-nine years, erect and yet relaxed. He greeted Charles with a very genuine, sincere courtesy that combined dignity with graciousness. Pomp and ceremony had probably been a common thing in his life, but Charles felt instinctively that they bored him. Not so his wife. He knew she loved it all—that it was she, not he, who had wanted this little party to be formal. Wherever a social affair took place, Charles guessed, she would be right in her element.

The sexton had told Charles that she came of a home of wealth and had not been entirely in sympathy with the way her father and mother-in-law, the Rollin Pages, had given most of their money away to help worthy causes. Her portion, Sandy had said, she had carefully nurtured, and it was obvious that she was taking a great deal of satisfaction in planning for her daughter what she had failed to achieve herself—the uniting of two considerable fortunes in one. The Frances Page–Arnold Eton match had been something of a triumph for Carolyn Page, whose art in bringing people together in the right way and at the right time was largely responsible for it, if all were told.

This evening she was bringing another choice group together —another work of art.

When they were gathered around the table, its white cloth laden with gleaming silver, Charles sat as guest of honor at Carolyn Page's right, and at his right sat Mrs. Rollin Page. Next to the latter sat Mr. Andrew Marsh, attorney for the railroad, and next to him, Mrs. Belle Wainright. At the end sat Dr. Egbert Page, listening at the moment to the lively chatter of Mrs. Marsh at his right. Next to her sat the huge figure of Arthur Wainright, coach of the college's football team, then Frances and beside her and right opposite Charles sat Arnold Eton.

As they unfolded their napkins, Carolyn Page turned to Charles and whispered, "Did you know that there is an art about selecting guests for a dinner party just as there is an art in arranging flowers?"

"No. That is a new one to me."

"Yes, I have two hobbies—flower arrangement and guest arrangement." (Charles for the first time now noticed the beautiful flowers on the table.) "I have been threatening Egbert for some time that I was going to start both of these courses in Lincoln College if I could induce the trustees to furnish an appropriation large enough." Charles glanced around to see if the rest were listening, but at the moment all were paired off in little dialogues.

"Behold the little twosomes," continued Mrs. Page, with an air of proprietorship. Her alert eye had noticed Charles' survey of the guests. "Want the recipe for arranging a dinner party? Well, put this down in your notebook. First, everyone should be seated beside someone he would like to talk with. Second, there should be an alternation at rhythmic intervals of private little tete-a-tetes, with larger, more general conversations where all talk to all. Third, the party should not be too large. The ideal number is ten or twelve. And finally, if possible there should be an equal number of men and women."

"Really!" laughed Charles. "You do have this down to a fine art! It sounds very simple."

"But those are only the first steps," smiled Mrs. Page. "That's

59

only the multiplication table of it. Wait till we get into higher algebra and solid geometry."

"I hope we don't get into cube root!" laughed Charles. "There is where I would flunk out."

"It's almost as involved as that!" she laughed. "Let's start with the first rule of higher algebra, that there should always be certain special types of people present, and that everyone should be different from everyone else."

"But I thought a common interest was essential to good fellowship."

"A common interest, yes, just as a common denominator is essential when working on a problem. But the *numbers* must be different. What fun would there be adding 444 to 444?"

"You are right," said Charles. "Go on, please. You certainly know your mathematics!"

"Well, in the cast of characters, one type that is absolutely essential is the clever man. He should be a charming, debonair, cavalier type, such as Andrew Marsh, for instance."

"And he just asked us," broke in Mrs. Rollin Page, who was listening at this moment, "why all the bond issues in the Second World War were lettered E, F, and G."

"Yes, why was that?" asked Arnold. "Give us the answer, Marsh."

"Because," replied Mr. Marsh, "only Eleanor, Franklin and God knew where the money was coming from."

After the laughter had subsided the conversation again broke up into twosomes. Carolyn Page turned to Charles and lowered her voice:

"Take a good look at Arthur Wainright across yonder. Big nose, big features, a prince of a man! He has everything but doesn't know it. Out on the athletic field he is always barking at his men to work harder, try harder, play harder. He's at home on the athletic field, but put him in a tuxedo and a white shirt and his lips close up like a clam. He is shy, self-conscious. He doesn't respond to conversation, he doesn't laugh at a joke, he just sits there like a bump on a log."

"I imagine he is not popular at dinner parties," ventured Charles.

"On the contrary, he is!" Carolyn broke in almost before the last word left his lips. ("She's faster than a machine gun," chuckled Charles.) "He *is* popular!" and she raised her eyebrows and waved her spoon under Charles' face. "I'll tell you why. Once in a while he *does* smile at a joke, and that smile is ample reward for a whole evening spent in efforts to bring it out. Once in a while he *does* open his mouth and speak, and when he does it often is so appropos that it stuns us all into silence. Once in a while he cracks a joke and because it is so unexpected and so perfectly fits the situation, it breaks the whole gathering up in hysterics of laughter."

"I wish you could explode a little nitroglycerin under his lips tonight. I should like to see the Hercules perform."

She laughed merrily. "No, I am afraid he won't open up tonight. He has a tremendous respect for Egbert that amounts almost to awe and he looks upon Frances as an angel not of this world. He blushes and gets paralyzed every time she speaks to him."

"I am afraid you didn't do such a good job in your flower arrangement when it came to placing him, Mrs. Page. You should have seated him next to you, perhaps."

"Oh, no! I did much better than that!" she laughed. "I placed him by Mercedes Marsh," and now she lowered her voice and spoke in his ear. "Mercedes, sitting at his left, is absolutely the most fascinating woman in Raymond. She could have been a Cleopatra had she lived in Egypt, or a Marie Antoinette if she had been born in France, or a Mary Magdalene if she had been born in Palestine. I just wager that Mercedes' and Andrew's courtship must have been like Anthony's and Cleopatra's— good enough for a book, and a very modern book at that. If anyone can thaw Wainright out, she can do it."

They were interrupted by a scream of laughter arising from the other end of the table. Charles turned in time to see Mercedes Marsh, her face screwed up in an agony of mirth, turning to the big man beside her. "If you ever spring anything like that again you'll slay me!" and she was off again, laughing with the abandon of a teen age girl. Egbert Page was laughing heartily also.

"See here, see here," exclaimed Andrew Marsh, "what's doing? Let the rest of the gang in on this."

"Not on your life!" cried his wife, still shaking with laughter. "Mr. Wainright insulted me and I will sue him for libel if he ever repeats it."

"Well, then, I guess we'll have to give it up," said Carolyn Page, and then turning to Charles: "Tomorrow I'll make Egbert tell me what it was all about. I can't bear to miss any of Wainright's humor."

"It may not sound so good when repeated," offered Charles.

"True," she agreed. "But to go on with my flower arrangements. Note that I placed Mrs. Wainright, the plump, comfortable, pin-cushion sort, between Egbert and Andrew Marsh. I set this typical house-wife down among the shining lights just as a shock absorber is placed on a lively car."

At this point Carolyn signalled Lulu, the Negro maid, to bring in the next course.

"Now give me the rest of the cast of characters," said Charles, "You are getting me terribly curious. Who are the other essential ones?"

"Well—one is the ingenue—you know, not the leading lady type, but the coquettish girl who serves as a foil for the leading lady."

"I see, you mean someone to flirt with the debonair man."

"Exactly."

"And who fills that bill here?"

"My modesty forbids me from saying outright," two dimples accentuated her sudden smile. "You see, I am keeping my talents under a bushel."

"Do you imply that I am that bushel?" his laugh was spontaneous. "I am afraid that Mr. Marsh should have had this chair of honor."

"No, no!" she laughed. "If his tongue and my tongue get started wagging together, no one else would have a chance.

"But," she added quickly, "remember that the Mrs. Ingenue is *not* the leading lady, and Mr. Debonair is *not* the leading man."

"And who are they? You have me excited, now."

"We have two leading ladies—each in her generation. Mother Page there to your right, and Frances opposite you; for you see, if anything happened we always have to have an understudy to take over."

Charles glanced across at Frances and met her smile. He noticed that she and Arnold had ceased their private tete-a-tete and had suddenly become interested in what her mother was saying.

"And who are the leading men, Mother?" Frances asked eagerly.

"Well—" Mrs. Page hesitated, "we happen to have two leading men here tonight."

"And which ones are they?" Frances' eyes sparkled with expectation.

"Arnold Eton on your side of the table, and Charles Maxwell on this side."

"I see you put the table between them," exclaimed Mr. Marsh, a sally that was greeted with a burst of laughter from the rest who were now all following the dialogue, "so they won't fight it out at a dinner party."

"Thank you for giving me so high a role," said Charles. "And which of us, I might ask, is the understudy?"

"Neither. You are two contrasted types. It would be impossible for either to understudy the other. Arnold represents the 'stand-pat' stalwart. You represent the adventuresome pioneer. That's what makes life interesting. It is contrast that creates drama. So it's time for the ingenue to drop backstage. I have been basking in the footlights long enough. Now the rest of you talk awhile."

63

"In other words," said Eton, who was now giving absorbed attention to all these closing remarks, "you are putting us in a bullpen to fight it out between ourselves—the old and established against the new and untried."

Charles thought he detected a touch of scorn in his voice that went deeper than jovial banter. While others were laughing, he caught a cold glint in the other's eye that pierced him like a rapier.

Mrs. Rachel Page suddenly turned to Charles and said, "Egbert and Andrew and I up at our end of the table, while you have been engaged in *frivolous* conversation at your end, have been discussing the feasibility of trying to walk in Jesus' steps in college life. Egbert thinks it would work. Andrew thinks it would tear the whole college to pieces."

"Yes," said Mr. Marsh, "when a young man stands for Christ's way in a modern college he is surely sticking his neck out."

"I think," said President Page, "that you have a martyr complex, Andrew."

Mr. Marsh exclaimed, "Great scott, no! If a young man takes a stand on the race question at a southern college he would be ostracized; if he turns down his wine glass at a drinking party at a big university he would be called a sissy; and if he bowed in prayer before he started his meal at another college he would be called a crackpot."

"Not at Lincoln!" exclaimed Frances, "and if his life and character were expressed in courtesy and kindness, he might win others to his way of thinking and acting."

"But even at lily-white little Lincoln College," taunted Mr. Marsh, "you will have to admit that there are things that take courage to do and whenever one acts with courage—bang! down comes the social order!"

"How does that apply to our 'lily-white college'?" smiled Dr. Page.

"Well, supposing a teacher of history insisted a certain war

vas necessary. Would a student who disagreed have the courage
to rise up and walk out of the classroom?"

Mrs. Rachel Page turned to him quickly. "If a student really
asked, 'What would Jesus do?' I don't think he would get up
and walk out in the midst of a lecture. The courteous way would
be to sit patiently till it ended, and then tell the teacher privately
and in a loving way the point where he differed."

"Some diplomat, some diplomat!" grinned Mr. Marsh, "So
you believe that following Jesus completely would actually make
a student popular!"

"What I am trying to tell you," replied Mrs. Rachel Page, "is
that there is one thing you must put above courage and that is
love. Jesus took the courageous way, it is true, but He always
took the love way *first*. And in a Christian college, like Lincoln,
there may be a *few* times when the Christ way would bring
ostracism, as you say, but in ninety-nine times out of a hundred
a courageous act, if done lovingly in the Christ way, would win
the love and respect of others rather than their condemnation."

"Aha," said Mr. Marsh. "Win friends and influence people!
To me that would cheapen religion. It would spoil the whole
thing."

"Don't you yourself agree," asked President Page, "that on
the whole, the more one loves others unselfishly, the more he is
loved in return? What harm is there in that?"

Rachel Page broke in: "We are referring to a Christian college,
you must remember, Mr. Marsh, and a Christian church. Of
course, in cocktail groups that don't profess any religion, a tee-
totaler might be very unpopular. And in a big business company
a director who proposed reducing dividends to pay a minimum
annual wage might be unpopular with the other stockholders.
In those cases Mr. Marsh is right. Courage often *is* demanded,
and the one who stands on his convictions in such instances will
surely make enemies."

Arnold Eton cleared his throat at this point, and Charles saw
that he was eager to break into the conversation.

"I noticed you mentioned directors in business, Mrs. Page
I don't think that Jesus would interfere in the business world a
all, ever. Don't you remember how He said, 'Render unto Caesa
the things that are Caesar's and unto God the things that ar
God's?' There are God's laws and there are business laws.
don't think it is the part of religion to try to interfere with th
natural laws of supply and demand."

"Don't you think," expostulated Marsh, "that if Jesus wer
here today He would make some efforts to prevent periods o
unemployment and cure these cycles of recurring hard times
I, for one, have sometimes wondered if Jesus might not favo
some Socialistic patterns if He came here today."

Eton's eyes flashed. "No!" he thundered. "To me even t
think that is sacrilegious! The periods of depression are acts o
God, just like the tides of the sea, and they can't be tampere
with. Left alone, the law of supply and demand will regulate a
our economy. If the ministers of America started going out o
their way to try to tell business men how to regulate their busi
ness, the whole church would go toppling down to its very base.

"But Jesus did something about poverty in His day," sai
President Page. "For instance, the feeding of the five thousand.

"Oh, that!" exclaimed Arnold. "I think that was a purel
religious act of Jesus, neither miraculous nor sociological.
think Jesus took the two fish and the five loaves that the littl
boy gave him and said to the multitude, 'See the generosity o
this little boy. He is going to divide his little with everyone els
How many would like to do the same?' Immediately scores o
others who had brought big hampers full of food for their ow
private use would catch the contagion and divide theirs as wel
There never yet has been a pot-luck supper where there wasn
twice as much food as any of us could eat."

"I am not sure I accept your explanation of the miracle o
feeding the five thousand," said Rachel Page, "although I d
admit that the love that would unlock the hampers of those wh
had to share with those who did not have is as beautiful and a
Christlike a deed as any so-called miracle that Jesus coul

perform. But in this modern age of split atoms, I don't believe that any miracle of Jesus was impossible. Once you explain one away there is a temptation to explain all away. Would you explain *all* the miracles away, Arnold?"

"Oh, by no means, Mrs. Page. I accept, for instance, all of Jesus' miracles of healing."

"Then," said Charles Maxwell, "you wouldn't say that a minister is going out of his proper field when he prays for the sick?"

"Not when he prays for the sick in the proper way a minister should. Prayer is a part of a minister's work. But he is going out of his bailiwick if he tries to make people expect that cures will come from his praying."

"But," said Charles, "I thought you said that you believed in miracles of healing."

"Yes," said Arnold, "In *Jesus'* miracles of healing. But ministers are not Jesus by a long shot. What is possible for Him is not possible for them. And, what's more, doctors and hospitals take care of all that today. So why should preachers trespass into fields where they have no business to go?"

"Then you don't believe one should follow in Jesus' steps?" continued Charles.

"Decidedly not! I did not from the first, and I do not now. People should worship Jesus and attend church faithfully, and ministers should stick close to the gospel. But it is dangerous, yes, even sacrilegious when one gets the notion he should *imitate* Jesus. Only an egotist would boast of accomplishing what Jesus did, and only a crackpot would expect to work miracles through prayer."

"Oh dear, oh dear!" exclaimed their hostess. "We are getting farther apart now. Let's all retire to the parlor for our coffee where the chairs are more comfortable."

As they rose and pushed back their chairs, Frances remarked, "I am sorry, but Arnold and I can't be with you all evening. We have tickets to the symphony, and I know you wouldn't want us to miss it."

"Run along," said Mrs. Marsh, in a maternal way, "and leave us older and wiser heads to settle the problems of the universe."

"Older and wiser heads!" Charles smiled. "But Arnold," and he turned to the departing pair, "I hope you won't brand me as an egotist because I differ from you on the matter of answered prayer."

"No, but I do warn you, don't be a crackpot." And again Charles caught the cold, cruel gleam in his eye. "Stick to your last, young parson, stick to your last." And taking Frances by the arm he stalked to the door.

"I guess your leading men," said Mr. Wainright to Mrs. Egbert Page, "are going to fight it out on this line if it takes all winter."

"But I must say one thing more," said Arnold, turning in the doorway to face the entire group. "If one comes right down to brass tacks, it is easy to show how absurd it is to try to imitate Jesus. To be consistent, one should grow a beard, wear a flowing garment, and adopt the trade of a carpenter."

"You are right, Arnold," Charles responded amiably. "Imitate is not the word—but not because it is going too far, as you say, but because it is not going far enough."

"Not far enough!" gasped Arnold amazedly.

"No, not as far as Jesus Himself asked us to go. He asked us to abide in Him as He abides in the Father, to be a branch of Him, blood of His blood, flesh of His flesh, soul of His soul, spirit of His spirit. To get in absolute union with Christ is the very highest form of walking in His steps. When you do this, you will find yourself truly walking in the steps of the inner, living Savior, and not trying to walk literally in the footsteps of a distant, externalized, historical figure whom you have never seen. No one living today can tell us exactly what Jesus looked like, but there are thousands of consecrated souls who have actually met Him in the interior cloisters of their hearts."

"Come on," said Arnold, turning impatiently away from Charles with the manner of a man dismissing the utterly impractical, "Frannie, we'll be late to the symphony. Let the Reverend dream his dreams."

Frances had moved close to Charles and was giving him rapt attention.

"Please go on, Mr. Maxwell!" she said quietly, her eyes appealing.

"Wait till Sunday!" exclaimed Arnold with a hard laugh. "This is the night for the symphony. Come along, little dream girl. Come down to earth."

Slowly Frances withdrew her gaze from Charles and looked up reprovingly at her escort.

"I do think you should be more considerate of our guest of honor, Arnold." She slowly slipped into the long, dark cloak Arnold held for her.

"Remember, girl," he said, "the first number is Tschaikovsky's Fifth."

"You broke a Tschaikovsky's movement of the soul just now," she murmured, as she fastened the cloak about her throat. "Goodbye, all."

As they passed out the door she turned and smiled back at Charles.

"Save some for next Sunday," she called.

As they moved toward the parlor, Rachel Page slipped her hand in the arm of Charles and drawing him very close whispered:

"I wish you *would* develop that thought farther in your sermon soon, Mr. Maxwell. Frances and I would both love it. And I do want to have a long talk with you some day about all of these deeper things. And about Frances, too! May I?"

"The joy will be all mine," he replied. "There is nothing I should like better than to make such a conversation a weekly thing."

"That would be like heaven to me," she said simply. "It makes me think of the days when your grandfather used to visit with Rollin and me. God bless you!"

Chapter 8

*"I thank thee, O Father, Lord of Heaven and earth,
because thou hast hid these things from the wise and
prudent, and hast revealed them unto babes."*

O<small>N A SUNNY</small> Monday afternoon about ten days later, Charles Maxwell looked out his study window and saw Mrs. Wainright hurrying toward the Gothic entrance of the church. The plump, commonplace Mrs. Wainright, the "pin-cushion" easy-going wife of the athletic director, was coming to see him. He wondered why. When he opened the door in response to her knock, instead of the calm, complacent face he anticipated seeing, he beheld a face tied up in a grimace of woe and a lower jaw trembling so violently that she could not speak. So amazed was Charles to see this transformation of a calm woman into a hysterical one that for a moment he, too, was speechless.

"My little Meredith, my only child, is dying," she gasped, between her convulsive sobbing. "Save her, Pastor!" She leaned against the wall for support, and buried her face in her hands.

"What is the trouble with your Meredith?" he asked gently as he helped her to a chair. Her sobs choked her so she couldn't speak.

"Try to tell me what the trouble is, Mrs. Wainright," his voice was soothing.

"Double pneumonia," she gasped between her sobs. "The virus kind that penicillin can't help. The doctor says it has gone beyond the aid of medicine."

"Are they giving her oxygen?"

"She's under an oxygen tent right now. But it's no use—it's no use." Sobs shook her again as she buried her face in her hands.

"Have you had a specialist?"

Regaining her self-control, she mopped her eyes.

"Yes, six doctors sat in consultation at the hospital this morning. They said—they said—she can't live." She shook with sobs. "So I have come to ask you to pray to God to save her."

"Oh," thought Charles, this was the one thing he hoped would never enter his door—an out-and-out call for healing, and his thoughts became audible on his lips, "Oh, that Jesus were here in this hour of need!"

"But He is here! He *is* here!" cried the woman, desperately. "You said so in your sermon yesterday. You said He was here as truly as He was in Galilee. That He is a living Christ, not a dead Christ."

"I meant spiritually He is present . . ."

"And if He *were* present," she interrupted, "He would touch my little daughter and make her well. Ask Him, Pastor, to do that now! Now! Now before it is too late!"

"I will gladly pray. But Mrs. Wainright," he went on, searching carefully for each word, "I want you to know that my prayer for healing is only the human prayer of a very weak but earnest pray-er. And before I pray it will help if we can get the atmosphere all clear. In the first place, we must be prepared to accept the will of God."

"But it is *not* the will of God," her face was tense, her eyes fixed pleadingly upon him, "it can't be, to take my only child. A loving Father wouldn't do that to me!"

"Are you sure you don't over-adore her—idolize her—let your affection for her crowd out your love for God or for others?" asked Charles, hesitantly.

"Oh, Pastor, of course I don't!" she denied passionately. "My love for Meredith has made me love all children more, and love God more; it has bound my husband and me together. And Arthur simply lives in little Meredith. This will devastate him. It will kill him!"

Tears came to Maxwell's eyes. As she gave way again to her sobbing he bent over her and laid his hand softly on her shoulder. All his heart went out to her in this hour of supreme need.

"Oh, God," he murmured, "help me, if it be Thy will."

He knew, then, that he was being watched. In the partly open door stood little brown-eyed Agnes, the ten-year-old granddaughter of the sexton. School was out, and she was evidently looking for her grandfather. She pushed the door wider and came right in, her brown pigtails bobbing against her blue dress.

"Please, Pastor," she said, "I heard you talking. Let's pray to Jesus to make Meredith well. She's in my room at school. She's awfully nice."

"All right, my dear," he exclaimed, strengthened beyond words by this simple reinforcement of a little child. "Sit down with us, Agnes, and let us pray."

She went at once to the window seat, the afternoon sun gleaming on her shining braids. "You sit here, lady," she said, "and I will sit on one side of you and hold your hand and Pastor will hold your other hand and he will ask the good Jesus to heal Meredith."

"Good, good!" exclaimed Charles Maxwell, eagerly. "That will be perfect!" He sat as directed by the child. A new calmness and confidence was in his voice. "Let us all be still for awhile after I finish my prayer," he said.

It was a rather stumbling prayer, but Charles was not thinking so much of the words as he was of the tremendous faith of the little girl sitting at the side of this woman in need. With such simple faith present he felt that words were almost unnecessary.

In the silence that followed, a great peace began to fill his heart. The woman's sobs ceased. Suddenly Agnes hopped lightly down from the window seat.

"There!" she exclaimed, clapping her small hands together. "Meredith is well. The good Jesus is so wonderful!"

"Let us trust that it is so," said Maxwell, quietly, looking up at the confident child.

72

"I know it is so, because He told me." She returned his gaze, with her calm brown eyes.

"How did He tell you?" asked Charles, putting his large hands on her little shoulders.

"See that plant over there?" And the child pointed to a potted fern in the study window-box.

"Yes, why?"

"Well, when we were quiet I looked at it, and I thought, 'If God can send life up through that little plant, He surely can send life up through little Meredith.'"

"If God so loves the grass of the field which today is and tomorrow is cast into the oven—" slowly repeated Charles, "how much more shall He clothe you—with health—O ye of little faith!"

"Oh, God, so be it!" exclaimed the woman, in a voice trembling with emotion. "Thank you, Pastor. Thank you, dear little girl. Thank you, thank you!" and she rose as if to go.

"Do you have transportation?" Charles asked, rising.

"Yes, my sister brought me in her car." She hugged Agnes tightly for a moment, then straightened and was gone.

A little ache was in his heart as Charles watched her hurry down the walk.

"Too bad if—" he choked and added, "No, I mustn't think that. Oh God, help Thou my unbelief!"

As he was preparing to leave his study a few minutes later, the phone rang. It was a man's voice.

"Is this the Parson?"

"Yes."

"This is Arthur Wainright. Is my wife there?"

"No, she has just left. Is it something important?"

"Something terribly important." His voice almost rose to a shout. "Little Meredith has just passed—" the voice broke, so charged it was with emotion, and Charles' hand holding the receiver shook. But the voice continued—"passed the crisis and the fever is abating. The doctors can't believe it. It's almost too good—" his voice choked again and broke and there was a brief

73

pause—"too good to be true! I hardly know how we deserve it."

"Thank the Lord, thank the Lord!" exclaimed Charles.

"Say, Parson, you were praying, weren't you, with my wife just now?" The voice at the other end ceased with something like a sob.

"Yes."

"I haven't been inside a church for a year, Parson." The voice halted, then went on. "I let my wife carry on my church work by proxy. But, Parson, from now on I'm coming to church with her! God bless you! Thanks a million." And he rang off.

Charles looked out of the window. A large limousine was passing by. On the front seat, alone, his hand on the wheel, sat Arnold Eton, eyes straight ahead.

"That little mustache makes him look like Hitler," he thought. "I hope he doesn't hear of this healing. He may start a little purging."

CHAPTER 9

"Judge not, that ye be not judged. For with what judgment ye judge, ye shall be judged. And with what measure ye mete, it shall be measured to you again."

ONE MORNING Charles had just completed a purchase at Jonathan Wright's store and was strolling around leisurely, for some reason loathe to leave the store. It seemed to have a restful atmosphere he had not felt there before. Perhaps it was because it was in the morning hours before the rush of customers turned it into its customary bedlam. A peace and serenity lay upon it, like the deep woods in summer.

As he was passing the hosiery counter a voice called to him: "Oh, Mr. Maxwell!"

Maxwell turned to see a pretty, dark-haired clerk who was a member of the First Church choir.

"Have you heard the latest?" she asked eagerly. "Mr. Wright is building a prayer room on the top floor where customers can rest and pray whenever they wish."

"What!" exclaimed Charles. "Is it open for use now?"

"Not quite completed, but finished enough to show what it really will be when it is all done. Why don't you go up and look at it? You are the one who inspired it."

"Things are happening fast here!" smiled Charles. "A prayer room in a department store, think of that!"

"Two prayer rooms, to be exact," she explained, "one for customers and one for the firm. Mr. Wright asked for volunteers and over half of us volunteered to take a fifteen-minute prayer vigil once a week. Isn't that wonderful?" The girl's eyes sparkled.

"It certainly is," asserted Charles heartily.

"And what is more," she went on gaily, "Mr. Wright gave a party to all of us last week in which he announced a new profit-sharing plan, which thrills everybody except a few big stockholder higher-ups in the firm," she finished, making a wry little face.

Charles stepped into the elevator and said, "As high as you can go."

The top floor was exclusively used for displaying rugs. It seemed immense, and at this hour was very quiet. There were no customers, and only two clerks chatted at the far end.

"Anything I can do for you, sir?" called one as Charles made his way between great piles of thick rugs.

"No thanks. I just came to take a look at the prayer room."

"You'll find it at the far end way over yonder."

Charles always loved the odor of new lumber and he took a deep breath of satisfaction as he entered the little chamber.

"Plain, unstained walnut boards, and fresh sawdust on the floor. It has an atmosphere already! I almost wish they would leave it bare like this always, as simple as a hermit's cell. But—of all things!" he exclaimed, as a movable kneeling bench caught his attention. He knelt upon it, to find his knees nestling down in the soft carpet cushion which covered it. He rested his elbows on the altar rail, and all of the tension went out of his shoulders.

"God bless you, Jonathan Wright," he said softly, "and all who enter here."

"How marvelous to find a sanctuary like this in the very vortex of a city's commercial center!" he thought, gratefully. "And how wise to locate it on the very top floor where the great rugs softened and filtered out all obtrusive sounds." He glanced back at the entrance. The door, not yet placed on its hinges, was resting against the wall. When completed, he saw at once, it would be a room absolutely sound-proof, completely isolated from the outer world.

"I wonder how it would feel," he thought, "to kneel in a quiet

76

place like this for fifteen minutes. I will just pretend I am one of the clerks in Wright's store!" As he lowered his head he wondered, "Will fifteen minutes be long enough to remember everyone who pledged to walk in His steps?"

Ten minutes or more had passed when he heard footsteps approaching. He slid over on the kneeling bench to make room for others who might wish to join him. But the footsteps went by. He heard them entering the door leading to the company prayer room.

"Heavenly Father," he resumed his silent prayer, "please send down deep blessings on Mr. Wright for this lovely gift to us of Raymond. May Thy presence always go with him and protect him in his great vision and guide him as he tries to lead his employees to walk in Thy steps. Amen."

Suddenly he heard voices in the adjoining prayer room. The unplastered unfinished walls were like a sieve for voices to come through. Two men had entered, concealed from sight of all outsiders, evidently unaware that every word they spoke was distinctly heard in the adjoining sanctuary.

"See here, Jim Long," began one in a heavy, rasping voice, "we've got to spike these fool notions of that young Jonathan and the time to do it is right at the beginning. The moment he starts this profit-sharing idea with the entire force the smaller the melon will be for us at the top. And if he gets a few more crackpot ideas like spending the company's surplus on prayer rooms and social centers, the less the stockholders can divide."

"Well, how can we stop it?" Jim Long drawled.

"Either of two ways," snapped the other. "Buy out a majority of shares and take over control—"

"That would break us," interrupted Long.

"Or use the little lever we used to pull on the old man—"

"You mean blackmail?"

"Call it what you will, but it worked with him."

"Listen," said Jim Long slowly, "all that old Milton did was what you and I know was entirely an innocent attempt to help someone in trouble. But on account of his Sir Galahad complex

77

and his inexperience in things of this world it could easily be made to look like an indiscretion."

"Exactly, and like a fly in a web the more effort he would make to fight, the worse it would be for him. Knowing that, the old man made no effort—that was where we won over him."

"Ha!" Jim's laugh was short and unmirthful. "And it took a wily Machiavelli like you, Bill Peters, to give it just the little push it needed to put the old man, hook, line and sinker, right in our hands!" As the suave voice of Long ceased the sound of low chuckles followed.

"Well, there it is in a nutshell," said Bill Peters' rasping voice. "It was sufficient to shut off the reforms the old boy was about to start. What more need we ask?"

"But how can it hold this young upstart?"

"Don't you see? The son worships the very ground the old man walked on, and never so much as now that he is dead. He will go one-hundred percent farther to protect the old man's memory than the old man would go to protect himself."

"Ah, you old horsethief! You deserve to be hung!" And the two laughed uproariously.

"All that remains now is to tighten the screws. Come on, Bill, let's go."

Their footsteps and their laughter both died away. Taking a deep breath, Charles peered out the entrance and saw the elevator door open and receive them. He went straight to where the rug clerks were still chatting as they unrolled a great rug together.

"I beg your pardon, but can you tell me who those two men were who just went down?"

"Certainly. They are the two vice-presidents of the company, William Peters and James Long."

A few minutes later Charles called at the office of Jonathan Wright. Jonathan received him cordially.

"I came to congratulate you on your new prayer room," and Charles seated himself in the handsome mahogany chair Wright had indicated.

"Oh, did you see it?" Jonathan Wright's face lighted up boyishly. "What did you think of it?"

"I consider it an inspired idea." He paused and looked Wright straight in the face. "And now, my beloved friend, I want to report to you the very first service it has rendered you. It may carry a shock, but it also carries a salvation."

"What do you mean?" asked Jonathan, his eyes intent on Maxwell's grave face.

"I mean I have found the go-ahead light for all your plans."

"You did? Tell me about it," said Wright.

"Close the door, and I will."

The very next morning Jonathan Wright found a note in his box asking for a conference with Bill Peters and Jim Long. "Set your own time," it ended. "We have something important to take up with you." He asked his secretary to call them right away. Within ten minutes the two men were standing in his office.

"As vice-presidents we thought it was fitting that we sat in on an executive council with you," said Bill Peters, clearing his throat importantly.

"Yes, we thought it was about time," drawled Jim Long.

Jonathan sat down calmly and waited till they were settled before he spoke.

"All right, men. What's on your minds?"

"Because of our long experience in the store," said Bill Peters smoothly, "we thought we would give you a full outline of the way *we* would run the store if we were you. Last night we worked out a complete program of procedure in the form of a written outline. I had my secretary type it this morning with several copies. Here they are." He fumbled in his brief case and brought out several sheets of neatly typed paper. "Jim and I feel firmly convinced that we have a right to be consulted hereafter on all future moves before you announce them to the staff. You own the great majority of the stock, that is true, but just because a man owns the automobile is no reason he has a right to drive all his passengers into the ditch. You will find that we have amended many of the moves that you were proposing."

Jonathan took the paper and looked it over a long time in silence. When he finally looked up both men were eyeing him closely.

"My father it was, I believe," mused Jonathan, "who appointed both of you vice-presidents. Let's see—how long ago was that?"

"A long time ago. Very shortly after we entered the firm," said Peters shortly. "But what has that to do with it?"

Jonathan, his hands clasped over his vest, looked straight into the eyes of the two men, ignoring Peters' question. "Yes, I think I remember. I was a boy then. There were others in the firm, as I recall, who thought that they deserved the promotion as much as you did. It caused a little split in the ranks. And, by the way, it was shortly after that when most of the new reforms my father had initiated came to an abrupt end." He took up his silver letter-knife and toyed with it lazily. "Did you happen to have anything to do with that?"

"Well," said Bill Peters heartily, with a wave of his large hand, "there is the up-in-the-clouds way of doing business and there is the practical way of doing business. It happens that we two belong to the practical way of doing business, and I think we were a great help to your father."

Jonathan could see that inwardly both men were tense and excited and yet exceedingly confident. It was clear that they were aware that they had a tough man to deal with, and that they were prepared to be tough themselves. Jim Long's eyes flashed and he started to speak, but Bill waved him back. He seemed to be waiting until Jonathan, by some chance remark, might give the opening that he was waiting for before stepping in to make the "kill."

Jonathan straightened in his chair and spoke firmly.

"My answer to you is that I don't like your program as outlined here. I intend to go on with my own." He paused, then

80

added abruptly, "I have said all I have to say. Now will you please lay *all* your cards on the table?"

"That's what we came to do—" said Peters with an air of triumph, an ugly smile on his face, "lay our cards on the table. We won't beat about the bush, Mr. Wright. It is perfectly true that we kept your father under our thumb, and if you try any hare-brained schemes of playing free and loose with this store, where we have invested so much of our money, we are going to put on pressure that you won't like." This last was uttered with deliberate emphasis.

"You can stop right there," said Jonathan quietly, rising and folding his arms. "I want you to know, once and for all—that nothing you can do will ever force me to budge one inch. I know exactly what you are driving at. You think you have 'something on' my father." He smiled and slowly shook his head. "Well, that blackmail won't work any longer. I am on to your cold-blooded game. Pick up your cards and go home."

Astounded, Peters and Long sat speechless. There was a quiet but tremendous firmness in Jonathan's voice and manner, but no trace of irritation or personal spite. He was speaking as impersonally as the oracle of Delphi.

"If my father ever made a misstep," he continued gravely, "it was the only one he ever made and all the good he has done has so completely erased the memory of it that the good Lord has long ago forgiven him. His life was filled to the brim with good works. The only thing that worried me about him was that he didn't go further in the reforms that his father, and my grand-father, began in this business. I see, now, that in the gentleness of his character, he soft-pedalled those reforms under the brutal force of blackmail you applied upon him. He figured that the hurt that you could bring to his children would more than offset the good he could do by continuing those reforms." Jonathan walked around his desk and half-leaned against the front of it, his square hands spread on its shining surface. "Well, I am here to tell you that you can go ahead and do anything you want.

You are and have been playing fast and loose with the reputation of a good man. Every word you speak against him and every act you take will swing like a boomerang back upon yourselves, and those nearest and dearest to you." He straightened to his full height and the eyes of both men followed him as he finished forcefully, "My compassion goes out to you, if you, in your ignorance of the laws of destiny and in the face of the grace of God, persist in your dirty work!"

The men sat as if stunned. Neither made a move to reply.

"Unless you change your attitude," Jonathan Wright continued, strolling back behind the desk, "I am going to ask you to find yourselves other positions in other stores at the end of the month. Your salaries will continue till the end of the year. We can't do business on the plane that I intend to do it, with such pockets of poison and infection in our midst. Broadcast anything you wish. From this moment your evil hold on this store is broken, and I am free to go on with the reforms my father and grandfather had so carefully planned."

Jonathan seated himself in his swivel chair and looked steadily at the two men a moment. "That's all," he said then with finality. "Take it or leave it," and he swung around to his desk and started looking over the business program of the day. Neither man spoke. Finally Jim Long looked furtively at Bill Peters. Peters, without raising his eyes, moved slowly toward the door. Jim hesitantly followed, and they went out, leaving the door wide open. Jonathan arose and went to close the door. He paused a moment as he saw them continue in single file down the corridor of counters, heads down, neither speaking. Then he walked briskly to the elevator and said, "Top floor."

The prayer room was still in its unfinished state. Amid the fragrance of freshly sawed wood, Jonathan Wright knelt at the little shrine and said softly, "Thanks, dear Partner, for showing me the way. You gave me the courage, now give me the wisdom. But above all, let your love heal these two pitiful, darkened lives. Bless this little sanctuary. Let it continue to bless all who enter here. Bless this evidence of your handwork. Amen."

CHAPTER 10

*"Behold the fowls of the air, for they sow not, neither
do they reap, nor gather into barns; yet your heavenly
Father feedeth them. Are ye not much better than they?"*

As CHARLES MAXWELL stepped out of the manse into the
bright sunlight the next morning, he was greeted by a
bass voice.

"Get in, Parson, and I'll drive you downtown if that's where
you're going." Arthur Wainright's big hand was beckoning from
the open door of his car.

"Okay, coach!" was the cheery response. "I wanted to drop in
at the bank, but isn't it out of your way?"

"Nothing is out of my way for you, Parson," he said, sincerely.
"I guess you know why."

"How is Meredith?"

"Just perfect. She will be home tomorrow. The doctors can't
understand it." He grinned wistfully. "I don't know if I do,
either."

"Nothing is impossible with God," said Charles Maxwell
cheerfully, as he climbed into the car.

Wainright had a little trouble with the starter. "An old
model," he apologized. "There she goes. Say, Parson, I'm an old
model myself when it comes to religion. I wanted to ask you at
the party the other night what you think Jesus would do if He
was a football coach? Would it be sacrilegious to ask that?"

"Oh, by no means. That is exactly what He was—I mean a
coach of a great team. If you ask me, Wainright, I would say,
give your squad the same advice Jesus gave His team."

"That doesn't make sense to me," said Wainright with a puzzled frown, as he swung out to pass a car. "You don't mean the Sermon on the Mount, do you?"

"I mean the sort of pep talk Jesus gave His entire squad of seventy athletes of the spirit before He sent them out to win souls for the Kingdom. He said first, 'Travel light.' Only one coat, only one pair of shoes. By this I think He meant for them to carry no surplus baggage of jealousy, fear or resentment to pull them down. Second, He told them to be in perfect harmony with the rest of the team and be loyal to the purposes that held them together. And third and most important of all, He told them with special emphasis not to press down too hard for results."

"Well, what do you know!" exclaimed Wainright, turning a moment to look wonderingly at Maxwell. "That's the only thing we did last year whenever we prayed—pressed down for results. But didn't Jesus press down for results?"

"Listen to what He said," and Charles quoted, smiling: " 'Rejoice not that the demons are subject unto you; rejoice rather that your names are written in heaven.' The only results Jesus pressed down on was for His men to keep in tune with the power of heaven and let the Lord do the worrying about results in this world."

"Let the Lord do the worrying?" pondered Wainright as he brought the car to a stop in front of a traffic light. "Well, that is a new one to me. Do you know, Parson, I almost worried myself into arthritis, anemia and a nervous breakdown last year the way our team lost games! You know my job depends on winning at least some of the games!"

"Life is too short!" said Charles. "Forget the inconsequential things like making this opposing team or that opposing team subject unto you. Concentrate on the real goal: to get your boys to do justly, love mercy and walk humbly with their God. Justice, mercy and humility constitute the indelible ink that writes names in heaven. Translated into football jargon that would be, drive hard, play clean and keep in step with the will of God."

Wainright gave Charles Maxwell a quizzical look. His tanned hands gripped the steering wheel tightly as his grey eyes looked off down the street, then his grip relaxed. He said slowly, "Maybe I begin to see a little light. The only times we prayed last year were right before the games. Then we prayed awfully hard, and always for results. Sometimes till my head ached."

"And you lost all your games?"

"Practically all. Now it so happens that most of our boys have come back, but they have a defeatist attitude. How can I change that?" The big hands shifted the gears and the car leaped ahead. Green lights showed for three blocks ahead.

"Don't let defeat worry you," said the young minister. "It was an old saying in my college day, 'Beware of a team of defeated veterans!' "

The coach gave a sigh of relief. "When the season gets going," he said, "we may shake off that fear and even have a chance at the championship. But the hitch comes that the very first game we play just two weeks away-is against the very best team in the entire League—last year's champions. The boys are afraid they have a jinx and are sure to lose." He brought the car to a stop in front of the bank, where Charles had told him he was going.

"Then I'll tell you the best way to shake them out of that feeling," said Charles, as he opened the car door. "Teach the boys to pray to be better channels of God and when game time comes, tell them to let go, forget victory, and play with all the pep they've got for the sake of the team, for the glory of the college, and for the joy of the game itself." He turned and looked squarely at Wainright. "And by the way," he added, "don't look so downhearted yourself; remember you are in it for the joy of the game, too." He stepped out the door.

"Wait a minute, Parson," the long arm and big hand of the coach prevented the door from closing. His large face with all its large features was peering out at Charles. "Parson, I am famous for making my boys work hard at everything they do. But you think we should do a little more loafing when it comes to God?"

"Yes, a little redemptive loafing would be a good thing," smiled Charles. "Let go and let God. Concentrate more on the letting go."

A quizzical expression passed over the face staring out of the car.

"Your advice, Parson, reminds me of Pat, who wrote back to his brother in Ireland, 'Come over to this country, Mike. I got a mighty good job. All I have to do is carry a hod full of bricks up ten flights of stairs. There is another man up there who does all the work.' "

Charles chuckled as he recalled the words of Carolyn Page, "When he does spring a joke it is very apt."

"Yes, coach, remember there is a Man up there who does all the work."

"Well, keep us in your thoughts, Parson," and Wainright slowly drew shut the door of his car. "Thanks a lot. I think I've got the idea. Here's trying!" And the soft wheels of the car went purring down the street.

The way Arthur Wainright applied this advice would have done Charles Maxwell's heart good. The next day he reminded the boys to keep a prayer in their hearts for the college and then startled them by adding, "And give a thought to the poor kids who not only can't go to college, but who don't get enough to eat. Especially remember all the suffering children of Europe."

As the week went by the boys began to wonder what had come over their coach. The climax came when the day of the game arrived. They had all gathered in the dressing room ready for the coach's final instructions. As Arthur Wainright looked around he thought he had never seen a more sober, heavy-hearted, gloomy-faced group of boys. Despair in some faces, a make-believe daring in others. He didn't tarry long. Glancing around the room for an inspiration, his eyes lit on the dingy back wall.

"Fellows," he began, "we have been praying for the college and the unfortunate young people of Europe all week. They are what count. We are not so all-important. This game isn't going to settle the destiny of the world. Some of you have been getting pretty low about it. This game is just a game—that's all. It's a place to develop manhood and courage and good fellowship. Above all, it's a place to have a good time and help your friends and folks have a good time—the folks who will be out there rooting for you. Now go out on the field today and have a lot of fun. Don't be concerned about the outcome. Today have the time of your young lives."

He turned and pointed to the picture over the lockers. "If you can see through the dust on that old picture of Ben Hur racing in the Coliseum," he said, smiling broadly, "you'll see how I'm thinking of you. Like those horses—all working together for the thrill of the game! Tell you what—I'll be Julius Caesar and you be my gladiators! Go out there and give the crowd a Roman holiday! That's all. Now get a move on you."

He walked quickly to the door and was out of the room. The boys looked wide-eyed from one to another.

"What does the Old Man mean?" asked one.

"Is he a little off his nut?" asked another.

"I never heard anything like that before!" exclaimed curly-headed Harlan Douglas, laughing. "A Roman holiday!"

Then Tuffy Sullivan, the tall captain, got up from the bench and turned to the men as they stood and sat around the room, almost dazed and certainly surprised by the coach's words and quick exit.

"See here, fellows;" the captain shrugged his shoulders, "the only thing I can make of this is that the old boy doesn't expect us to have a ghost of a chance, and he isn't going to wear us out emotionally trying to build us up to do something that no one thinks we are capable of doing. So he is telling us indirectly that he doesn't want us to take the situation too seriously, but to go out like a bunch of kids and have a good time."

"So nothing is expected of us!" said the big center. "Well, that's a relief! We might as well have some fun while we're at it."

"Nothing to lose and everything to gain! Hip, Hip, Hurray!" shouted Harlan Douglas.

The boys ran out upon the field, the captain leading, a long, thin line. A small round of cheers from the home bleachers greeted them.

"They look pathetically small," thought Charles Maxwell, sitting with President Page on one of the top seats. "Wonder how Wainright put it to them."

The boys were deployed now, tossing the ball back and forth. Presently there were three balls in the air, boys alternately passing and catching, usually on the run.

"They look more like a bunch of kids at recess time, shouting and laughing at each other," mused Charles Maxwell, "than a college team out to fight or die for their alma mater."

The grey autumn sky broke slowly and one small ray of sunlight hit the grandstand as the rugged Overland boys trotted on the field while great cheers now roared from the opposite stands. The Overland substitutes scattered on the field to pass and kick the ball, but the first team squatted in a line and began running signals with magnificent proficiency and precision.

The captains flipped a coin for choice of goals and the Lincoln boys went scampering out over the field to receive the kick-off.

"Just like a bunch of kids at recess time," Maxwell was still thinking. "They didn't even line up for practice signals. I declare!"

The Lincoln boys rallied around the lad who received the kick-off and threw themselves in the way of opposing tacklers with remarkable abandon. It was a good return, but immediately when they tried running the ball from scrimmage they were stopped on the line every time. The punt was good and the Overland man was downed in his tracks.

Playing on defense, the Lincoln boys let go with all the abandon they had shown at the beginning of the game. They "swarmed" through their opponents' lines, stopping every play before it got well started. And so the game see-sawed back and forth through the first half, neither side being able to make first down once. The Lincoln stands were amazed by the remarkable defense of their outweighed team against this powerful foe.

The first half had been a kicking game with the advantage in favor of Lincoln. At the start of the third quarter, Overland made three first downs in a row. Reaching the middle of the field they were held for downs and forced to punt. Lincoln's back and captain, Tuffy Sullivan, was hurt on the play, and Harlan Douglas replaced him. Running on the field, the diminutive quarterback looked like a cocker spaniel among bloodhounds. He barked out the signals with a boyish relish, in a high, almost singing voice, easily heard in all the stands. They gained fourteen yards on the next three downs.

"First down!" shouted the referee. The home stand was yelling now. Their team was moving at last. The team was so close to the sidelines that the boys, panting and standing in a circle, could hardly hear Harlan's signals above the yelling.

"Boys," he exclaimed as they got in the huddle, "remember we are Julius Caesar's gladiators and our only job is to give the Romans a holiday. Let's get going!"

As the team leaped into formation, Harlan rose from his squatting position behind the center and addressed the startled spectators in the stands:

"Ladies and gentlemen: the next play will see Mr. Sparks of Lincoln, fast and free, run like forty around Mr. Neilson of Overland," and before either players or spectators were prepared for it, the ball was snapped and Tubby Sparks was running for a ten-yard gain around the opponents' left end.

"And now," sang the pigskin troubadour, "you will be enlightened and entertained by the choppy, plunging fullback, Mr. Bright, trying to find a hole between Mr. Purvis and Mr. Brockman." Mr. Bright didn't see the promised hole between the rugged guard and tackle because it wasn't there, but a big hole loomed just outside of Mr. Brockman, which he took for a seven-yard gain.

"And now if the back pews are all wakened up, the rest of the game will be resumed in silence. The beautiful, silvery voice of Harlan Douglas will not be heard in the land for on the next play he will try some fancy steps himself, but where he goes nobody knows—not even himself. After that, for reasons of major strategy known only to Napoleon, Grant and Eisenhower, all plays will be announced in a whisper."

The stands were roaring with laughter, even the stands holding the Overland rooters.

Zigzagging down the field, eluding some tacklers and swinging loose from others, Harlan picked up thirty-five yards. He carried the ball on three more successive plays, and then handed it to Tubby Sparks to carry it over for a touchdown. The game finally ended 6 to 0 for Lincoln.

When the team reached the dressing room, they found the coach sitting there fanning his large lean face with his hat.

"Gosh!" he kept saying over and over again, "who in the world would have thought it!"

"And whatever got into you, Doug, to turn into a barker at the Fair?" asked Tubby Sparks. "Want to make a side-show of us?"

"And what a side-show!" came the muffled voice of the big center as he pulled off his sweater. "Wow!"

"Hip hurray!" echoed a dozen voices.

"Just giving the Romans a holiday!" grinned Douglas.

Yes, it *was* a holiday that the fans of Lincoln College would never forget!

Chapter 11

"Thy sins are forgiven—arise, and take up thy bed, and go unto thy house."

CHARLES HAD not anticipated that any publicity would come from the healing of little Meredith, but he was counting without Meredith herself. Three days after her return from the hospital, the news had spread all over the school yards. It began with the children in her room and by the time it had reached the upper grades, it had grown in the telling. From the school it passed out into the city, and from the city back into First Church. An ax falling on a stick of cordwood couldn't have cut more cleanly. The church was split neatly in half. Fortunately, save for Arnold Eton and sour Mrs. Gentry, the spirit of condemnation did not last long.

"He is young and we must expect some mistakes," was the general comment of those who recoiled at the first shock. "But why didn't he leave this sort of thing to the doctor?"

Mrs. Gentry, however, was more emphatic.

"He is turning our church into a cult!" she exclaimed, and her tongue once started did not cease wagging.

And Eton, usually so calm and self-possessed, did not try to conceal his irritation.

"It is nonsense to claim that prayer healed that girl. The doctor, the nurses and the hospital did it. This man will have us the laughing stock of the city if he makes such claims."

"He doesn't claim anything," matter-of-factly replied Andrew Marsh, "excepting that God helped the doctors. It's the Wainrights who claim this healing came through Maxwell."

Opposition upset Arnold Eton. In his business he had always had his own way. His prejudice was deeply rooted and this opposition was all that was needed to set him off.

The vehemence of his explosion astounded Mr. Marsh.

"It's ridiculous!" he shouted. "This man thinks he is a healer!"

"Young man," Marsh said calmly, "this isn't as terrible as you make it out to be. Jesus healed people."

"Yes, but does this man think he's Jesus Christ?" The way he spoke the words sounded like profanity. "We shall see," Eton concluded, with a menacing tone, "how long this thing keeps on."

"How long it keeps on," was the crux of the matter as Charles sensed it when Mr. Marsh reported this conversation to him. "I shall *not* keep on," he resolved inwardly. But the very combination of circumstances surrounding the event made it almost impossible for him not to keep on. The problem was intensified by the calls for healing prayers that came pouring in upon him from every side.

"I never dreamed we lived in such a sick world," Charles remarked wonderingly to Sandy one day. Meanwhile Mr. Eton's face grew colder and colder, and Mrs. Gentry's tongue wagged sharper and sharper.

There was only one way out of this dilemma, as Charles could see it, one sure, sound way to handle these calls for healing— and that was to train his people to do their own praying. As a matter of fact, at this stage Charles had very little faith in his own power in prayer. Faith had healed Meredith—this he knew, but it was little Agnes' faith and not his that had opened the flood-gates of heaven.

The next day found him in the city library asking for all the books available on prayer, especially on prayers for healing. He was disappointed that there were so few. He went to bookstores and finding their stock of religious books very slim, he finally wrote direct to the religious book publishers, Abingdon-Cokesbury, Harpers, Macalester Park, Augsburg, Fleming Revell, and some Grand Rapids companies, for their catalogues. As a result of this quest he finally acquired a large shelf of books on prayer which he could use as a sort of lending library adapted to meet every need. When people came to him for help, he would shove a book into their hands and tell them to read it and then try talking to God as best they could, and see if the problem would not solve itself. But what he anticipated would be an easy solution turned out to be a big job: finding the right books, reading and classifying them and directing them to the special needs of special people. He wished the seminaries had offered a special course in guiding their students to the right literature for meeting specific needs, especially for deepening the spiritual life of the people.

"The trouble is," he thought to himself, "that we church members too often merely scratch the surface of this profoundly deeper life of the spirit. If I hadn't been led into this adventure of trying to walk in His steps I would never have discovered how poorly equipped we religious leaders are in the deeper phases of Christian life."

The very next day an emergency call came from the hospital that could not be declined. It was Jonathan Wright on the telephone, his usually calm voice tense and excited.

"Jim Long's little grandson is here at the hospital with a critical case of mastoid, and his suffering is beyond words. One would think the little boy's head would crack. Besides, he has an awfully high fever. Jim's wife is here, too, and is begging me to use my influence to induce you to come. She is a good friend of Mrs. Wainright and she believes your prayers for Meredith were what turned the tide. Will you come as quickly as you can? If prayer ever accomplished anything, I can't think of a greater opportunity than this. And, by the way," finished Jonathan wryly, "there is one sadly cracked soul here that needs it as badly as this little cracked head."

"I'll be right over," said Charles. So this was the little grandson of the Jim Long whose drawling voice Charles had overheard that day in the prayer room!

Jonathan Wright met Charles at the entrance of the hospital. They passed silently through the cool, clean halls to the door of a room from whence childish moans were coming. The strong odor of drugs smote Charles' nostrils as they paused at the threshold.

"You go in alone," Jonathan whispered.

Beside the bed the nurse was bending over a little boy. At the foot stood the parents and grandparents. Down the hard lines on Jim Long's face were trickling little shiny tears. His face, to Charles' amazement, was the only one where the agony had broken through.

Suddenly his wife, a plump, matronly woman with kindly eyes, turned and saw Charles by the door.

"Oh, Mr. Maxwell!" she exclaimed, rushing to meet him. "Mr. Wright said he would phone you. We all heard what you did for Meredith Wainright. Pray for our little Jackie as you did for her!"

Charles Maxwell walked slowly to the bed and paused a moment. All eyes were on him. He spoke quietly, as a strange feeling, half peace, half excitement grew in his mind. "Dear friends, would you all be willing to kneel down while I pray?"

The young mother of the boy, a sweet, brown-eyed girl with raven-black hair, asked softly, "Here by the bed?"

"Wherever you wish."

The nurse interrupted in a cool, efficient voice. "I just gave him another shot that will dull the pain for a few minutes. When it wears off I will be in again," and she went out and closed the door softly behind her. They all knelt down, the mother and grandmother on one side of the bed, Charles and the father on the other, and Jim Long, the grandfather, his face still all cracked up in sobs, knelt clumsily at the foot.

"Dear Lord," began Charles in a gentle voice so as not to waken the restless child, and letting his words come as they would, "please look down upon this family gathered here, with love in their hearts for one another and faith in their hearts for Thee. If there is any blockage, any hurt between any of them,

94

please wash it away. We thank Thee for the loyalty and love that binds them all together. Use that love and loyalty as the wave-length through which Thy healing love may reach this child with power."

Charles was silent for a moment, reaching out inwardly for the unquestioning peace that did not come. Realizing that this must be a specially difficult case, he resumed his prayer.

"Father, if there be any deep resentment in any hearts here for anyone else, please, please wash it away in Thy redemptive love. And if there be any sins, forgive them, O Lord."

"Amen!" came an agonized voice from the foot of the bed. "Amen, Amen, O Lord!"

"And now, Father," continued Charles, "we come to Thee with pure hearts and trusting souls, ready to avail ourselves of Jesus' promise that where two or three agree asking anything —yes, anything—in His name, it will be done. Father, we agree in asking for the healing of little Jackie, and we ask that anything necessary for that healing in our hearts be here accomplished. We lift him into Thy healing love and leave him in Thy care, with confidence that whatever is best for him will be done. In the name of Jesus Christ, Amen."

For long moments no one stirred. The little child moved uneasily and writhed and his moans grew louder. Charles opening his eyes saw the little lids on the pillow open and brown eyes stark with pain stare into his. Suddenly all the compassion of heaven itself was pounding at Charles' heart. Gazing at the boy he was conscious of the floodgates within him opening and all this compassion flowing over the lad. A tremendous urge, an uncontrollable urge to lay his hands over the little boy flowed over him, the simple, instinctive urge anyone feels toward taking up a hurt puppy or gathering in a crying baby, but multiplied, as Charles afterwards described it, by infinity itself.

He placed his hands upon the boy's hot, burning cheeks and then let them slide up and cover the ears. The boy did not take his eyes off of him. He continued to groan, but he did not stir. Charles felt heat pass through his hands and flow as it were up his arms. He had never had an experience like that before. Gradually the little face grew cooler and cooler. In ten minutes, which seemed like ten hours, all the fever was gone, and the little lad was breathing easily in a restful sleep.

As Charles rose stiffly he noticed that one by one the others had already risen and were gathered around him, staring unbelievingly at the boy. The father was standing by Charles' shoulder, his eyes fixed in amazement on the face of his sleeping son. Jim Long alone remained kneeling by the bed's foot, his iron-grey, thatched head still buried in his hands.

"Father, look what's happened!" exclaimed the son, in a broken voice.

Jim raised his head and his blood-shot eyes blinked fitfully, Then he looked up at Charles, who was already picking up his hat to go.

"Pray for me, too, Parson!" and there was a look in Jim's eyes like the eyes of a wounded hound. "Pray as hard as you prayed for him," and his long finger pointed at the sleeping child. "We can never thank you enough. We'll make this right for all your trouble." And he buried his head again in his hands.

"Never mention it," Charles said simply.

As Charles went out he met the nurse with a hypo coming in.

"You won't need that!" he said, smiling, and immediately found the arms of Jonathan Wright enfolding him.

"How was it?" His face was filled with anxiety.

"God has taken over so you can drop your concern."

"Oh, thank the Lord!" And Jonathan almost crushed him in his embrace.

The moment Charles reached the church his head began to ache with the most wracking headache, something he had never known before in all his life.

"The excitement," he thought. "Perhaps something I ate for lunch." But as he sat down in his study and found it impossible to concentrate a thought suddenly struck him.

"Of course it wasn't the excitement! Of course it isn't anything I ate for lunch! It was the healing! I must have pressed down too hard. I was so eager for the little lad's sufferings to abate. Perhaps I let a little, just a little, of my own personality get into it—all unconsciously. And because I breathed a little of my personality into the boy, a little of his pain was breathed into me. Strange, but I didn't get this when I prayed for little Meredith!"

And thus was revealed a new truth to Charles Maxwell, one of many he was destined to learn in the school of prayer, that the closer one gets to a case, and the more one puts oneself into it, the more need there is of putting oneself through a cleansing, purging process before and after.

"With Jim Long there and the tremendous things at stake," he thought, "I did a little of what I warned Wainright *not* to do —I pressed down a little too hard for results."

"Come with me, MacIntosh," he said to the sexton as he hurried to the little prayer chapel. "Stand here beside me as a dear old Father Confessor, and listen well as I confess my sins and shortcomings before the Lord." He knelt and prayed simply, "Father, I here and now resign as General Manager of the universe. Thank you for accepting my resignation." And when he rose from that prayer, his headache was gone.

CHAPTER 12

*"He that receiveth a prophet in the name of a prophet
shall receive a prophet's reward."*

Word of this second remarkable healing travelled far
and wide. While the interruptions to his work had
been frequent enough before, Charles Maxwell now
found his days so filled with people coming to see him and with
letters craving answers that his time for sermon preparation had
practically come to an end. This caused him such deep concern
that he let it overflow one day in the presence of the old sexton.

MacIntosh was at his work bench in the basement when
Charles found him. A bright green child's chair from the nursery
classroom was on the bench, freshly painted. MacIntosh lay
down his brush and wiped his wrinkled hands with a grey rag
stained with green.

"Dinna let it bother ye, my lad," the old man reassured him.
"The same thin' happenit to yer grandfaither. An' ane day he
said tae me, 'Sandy,' he said, 'Sandy, I hae mak a diskivery.
Time is elastic i' heaven, an' ten hours sometimes gae past as
easily as if they were ane!' But I always noticed, Mr. Maxwell,
that when people's troubles were the greatest an the preacher's
time for writin' sermons shortest, thae Sundays he preachit his
greatest sermons. Yes, believe me or na, thae Sundays Gude put
the sermons richt intae his mouth."

"But you must remember that you knew my grandfather in
his later years," objected Charles. "By that time he had stored
up reservoirs of reading and study and personal experience that
I haven't as yet achieved."

"Never mind, me laddie," Sandy assured him. "Ye are pickin'

up a lot of personal experience fast. An' if the Laird taks awa yer time, He will gie something worthwhile in return. Time is elastic i' heaven. Trust yer Laird, Lad."

What MacIntosh said, Charles found was very true. Never were his sermons more powerful than the Sundays after a week filled with interviews with people who laid the anguish of the world upon his heart. However, there was one limitation to this type of speaking spontaneously from his heart and extemporaneously from his head. On such days he often had to draw upon his own personal experiences, and strangers in the audience hearing him for the first time—and there were more of these now than ever before—might easily get the impression that Charles Sheldon Maxwell, who at heart wanted to be the humblest of men, was trying to draw attention to himself and his experiences, and not to God and God's experiences through him. It is so easy for those who want to see black to see it even in the whitest sky. At such times he found great solace as well as great inspiration in this prayer that he had put together slowly through many months of praying: "Father, I belong entirely to You. Everything I have is Yours—my mind, will, body and soul. All my reputation is Yours. I give it utterly to You. Henceforth my reputation is Your reputation and Your reputation is my reputation, for I have nothing of my own apart from You." After that he felt less concern over what people might think of him.

As he was sitting at his desk one morning in his daily meditation he began to feel the tensions clear and suddenly the solution formed itself as he spoke aloud his thoughts:

"Most of these questions people bring to me individually could be discussed and answered in a general meeting—leaving only the private, personal problems to be brought to me individually. Why not set aside one morning and one evening to be devoted exclusively to answering these longer questions and solving these major problems by corporate prayer?"

That led to the following announcement the next Sunday morning:

"Friends, your response to the challenge given from this pulpit two months ago that you square all your actions by the test question, 'What would Jesus do?' has been so far-reaching, not only from church members but from many strangers besides, that I am, frankly, overwhelmed by the needs and the questions people are pouring in upon me. I now see that the evangelism of this new age is going to revolve around the question, How? *How* shall we pray? *How* shall we find God? *How* shall we attain union with Him after we find Him? To answer these questions that center around the *How*, I propose to set aside two periods each week. On Friday mornings from ten to eleven-thirty we shall study the technique of prayer. Wednesday evenings will be set aside for a new, twentieth-century, stream-lined prayer meeting, where we shall discuss, witness and pray, and, if God so wills, expect answers to our prayers."

Not only did it mean that time was saved, but it meant a far greater generating of power for First Church, for very soon Charles Maxwell discovered that he now had available two great reservoirs of spiritual energy that he could draw upon for any need that might arise.

The Wednesday night group was almost equally made up of men and women—anywhere from forty to seventy-five persons in all. The Friday morning group was made up almost exclusively of women, over half of whom came from other churches in the city. This, to his surprise, proved to be the real power group. He was soon made aware that the cream of all the praying women of Raymond were gathered before him. Those from other churches told him the meetings enabled them to be of more help to their own pastors and their own church programs than they had ever been before.

In his morning gathering he found a sprinkling of New Thought students, some earnest Moral Rearmament people, and many who had found a new hunger and thirst for deepening their spiritual lives at camps and Ashrams. He was delighted to find several Catholics. And there were two orthodox Jewish women, one with a beautiful, Madonna-like face who was exceedingly anxious to add the wisdom of Jesus to her own synagogue teachings. Three lovely Negro women came and their faith, Charles felt, brought a special blessing. And yet so rarely did a man come to this group that whenever one did come he felt self-conscious and out of place and rarely came again. One day Charles was surprised to see an elderly, stately man enter with his "vest on backward" as Charles loved to term it. His amazement grew when he recognized in this new face the Right Reverend John Aldrich, rector of the leading Episcopal church of the city.

When the meeting was over, Reverend Aldrich came forward and said to Maxwell, "You have a great message, my young friend. It's a pity you must speak only to women, for it's the men who really need this—men who are plunged into the practical work of the world, and it is the men the world needs to solve world problems in a Christian way." He had a deep, resonant voice with a slight English accent, a voice of culture.

"It is true that men are the Senators and Governors and heads of our big business enterprises," replied Charles, "but women have the mystic touch. Like water they can flow around and into the heart of what men are doing. In my opinion, *praying* and *doing* are the same things. A president of a business firm, in sending out telephone calls and telegrams, is building a great empire of business. His wife and daughter in this Prayer Laboratory you have just visited are sending out prayers that can be building something greater than an empire of business—their prayers can be establishing the Kingdom of heaven on earth."

"Do you mean that you actually think these prayers we prayed this morning in this church parlor will ultimately make things *happen* in the world of business, or politics, or statemanship, as actually as the practical *work* of statesmen and business men make things happen?" queried Aldrich skeptically.

Charles liked the directness of the man. "Yes," he replied firmly, "I certainly do. 'Go into the inner room,' said Jesus, 'and when you have shut the door pray to your Father who is in heaven, and your Father who heareth in secret shall reward you openly.' And," he continued, "whether men or women go into that inner room, it makes no difference. A woman is just as powerful in prayer as a man, for in the sight of God there is no Greek nor barbarian, Jew nor Gentile, bond nor free, male nor female. If the men won't come, let us train the women."

"But think what the men are missing!" said the rector regretfully. "I certainly wish the impact of your faith could reach the men of this city. They don't take to prayer as quickly as the women, but their need for it is just as great, if not greater."

As Charles nodded assent, Aldrich continued. "What I should like to do is this. I am a man's man myself, and in my parish out there in the Country Club district there happen to be more of the influential business men of Raymond than in any other church in the city. To be very frank, I cultivate them. Not because I kow-tow to wealth, but because I believe in men. And I believe in the influence that successful, efficient men can be to others. I belong to their golf club and join them in their bridge club and in their chess club and knock around with them a lot. But in bringing the gospel to them, I admit I have watered it down considerably. Your challenge has gotten hold of me this morning and I am resolved to put more iron into my sermons hereafter. I believe my men will respond to it. I want to bring them into the contagion of what I caught this morning. I believe they are ready to move from the What to the How, as you call it. And now I have a proposition I would like to unfold to you. Would you like to hear it?"

"You are getting me excited!" eagerly responded Charles, who had been listening intently. "Just wait a minute and I will see that lady over there waiting to ask me a question before she goes, and then we will go into my study where we shall be uninterrupted."

Once seated comfortably in the study the rector began:

"I have been in this parish for twenty years now, and have perhaps specialized on men more than any minister in the city. You are new here, but a number of the older men remember your grandfather very vividly. While some thought his ideas were a little wild, and many thought he was a little old-fashioned,

I find that at the bottom they all held a very high respect for him. Now this is not a large metropolis like Chicago and everyone knows what everyone else is doing. Men have been talking about you over their cigars and coffee. Some scoff, but many of the business men are with you—men not in your church. Many would like to meet with you. But men can't come out Friday mornings and men don't like to go to Wednesday evening prayer meetings, especially in other men's churches. But they all like to meet at luncheons in the middle of the day. Therefore I should like to suggest, Mr. Maxwell, that you take lunch with me and a little group of business leaders next Tuesday noon, and talk over a plan of getting a group of men to lunch together one day every week, say on Tuesdays, and talk over ways and means of running their business as they think Jesus would do."

"God bless you!" exclaimed Charles Maxwell. "If you really believe that the men you have in mind sincerely want this, nothing would give me greater happiness than meeting with them. But I think you should be the leader, not I."

"I will be the convenor, but you are to be the catalyst or spark-plug of the gathering. I have been looking for someone like you ever since I graduated from seminary. I have always been so sorry that your grandfather left before I came here. We ministers need to be filled up just as much as laymen."

And so the Tuesday Luncheon Club was born, an event that marked a turning point in the history of Raymond.

CHAPTER 13

"Yet lackest thou one thing: sell all that thou hast, and distribute unto the poor, and thou shalt have treasure in heaven: and come, follow me."

THE FIRST Tuesday Luncheon was well attended. Reverend Aldrich had done his work well. He had personally invited by letter or by phone a hundred "representative men" of Raymond whom he thought might be interested in "a new kind" of luncheon meeting to be held just for men, but with a purpose all could tie on to. Over fifty came. They met in the Gold Room of the Raymond Hotel.

"They told us we could have this room every time if the number runs over thirty-five," said Reverend Aldrich in his speech of greeting. "If you men turn out this well every time we won't be pinched into a smaller room!"

Charles looked with keen interest around the table, at the men engaged in hearty conversation. At his right was Jonathan Wright, then Richard Norman. Next was Andrew Marsh, counsel for the railroad; then came shy, quiet David Paul, principal of the local high school; fat, bustling Albert Abernathy, grocer; pompous A. G. Cummings, insurance man; serene, complacent J. C. Smith, jeweler; and at the far end of the table, old Mr. Babcock, the retired capitalist. Most of the others were men in the business activities of the city, strangers to Charles Maxwell.

As it was just the beginning of the football season, talk was all about Lincoln College's prospects for the coming season.

"Last season was disastrous," said Andrew Marsh, shaking his head sadly, "but since they got safely past the powerful Overland team, they have a good chance to win the championship, I hear."

"I was told," ventured Mr. Paul, with a shy smile at Charles, "that Reverend Maxwell had something to do with that victory."

"Sure!" barked Mr. Babcock. "Psychology did it."

The talk drifted on to the big teams of the nation, Army, Navy, Notre Dame, University of California, Texas, Minnesota, Michigan, Alabama and Oregon State. But when the luncheon was over, the conversation turned to the deeper purpose for which they had come together. Reverend Aldrich rose and told them quite simply of his visit to Charles Maxwell's Friday morning group. He gave an impressive picture of the power he felt there, and ended by confessing how jealous he felt over the women's having a monopoly of what he knew the men needed too.

"Now as this began in Mr. Maxwell's church, I have asked him to repeat the challenge that he made that night."

Charles found a responsive group before him. When he concluded he said, "I think these noon meetings should not be lecture periods but experience periods, and I know that we shall all be interested in hearing how the editor of our city paper, Mr. Richard Norman, finds it working out in his experience since taking the pledge."

Norman rose, his face aglow, a smile on his lips, but he spoke seriously. "Perhaps you don't know that I'm the most practical of men. I am a downright hard-headed man if there ever was one. I don't see how such an idealistic father as mine ever had so realistic a son. I am determined to prove to the world that the good way is also the strong way, the successful way. It is nature's way and nature is no failure. When the bees go forth carrying pollen they come back carrying honey."

Shifting to a firmer stance, he hooked his thumbs in his vest pockets and said: "Well, when I began making plans for carrying pollen to my readers, I began collecting mason jars to hold the honey. Don't get me wrong. When I say honey I don't mean money. Honey comes in lots of ways other than dollars. First of all, in the form of a happy home. Next in the form of an army of silent helpers—Fanner Bees, my wife calls them, referring to the bees whose busy wings keep the hive sweet and clean.

"I thought how wonderful it would be if I had a whole army of men skilled in prayer praying for me and my newspaper. The audacity of the thing took my breath away. But, men, that seemingly impossible dream has come true. With the help of the parson and my wife—and she has read more on prayer than anybody I ever heard of—I picked out the three hundred and sixty-five most spiritual men in America as far as we could determine them, and asked each to write a meditation and prayer for one day for my paper. I began with Fosdick and Rufus Jones and didn't stop till I had included a number of Jewish rabbis and a number of Catholic priests—and yes, several very sincere, Christ-like leaders in what my wife calls the 'Impatient Creeds.' "

"The what?" queried Jonathan Wright, in a puzzled tone, from across the table.

"Oh, those groups that got impatient with the evangelical churches' attitudes towards prayer and ran off and started big and little cults of their own.

"Well," continued Norman enthusiastically, "this correspondence has opened doors to friendships with some of the finest men in the land. Their little messages are wonderful. I am hoping the idea may take root and spread to other papers. My secretary is preparing a multigraphed letter right now to go out to editors all over the land to see if it is worth syndicating.

"Men, I have made a great discovery. For every bad thing done which the papers flaunt before the public, there are a hundred kind deeds done which the papers never mention. I have several reporters making it their special job to ferret out deeds of sacrifice, heroism and love, and dress them up as dramatically and fascinatingly as the most thrilling stories from Scotland Yard could possibly be. We are also running a series of stories on answered prayer. As for crime, it is easily condensed

and dehydrated and we have one inside page that the staff calls the 'garbage can' to hold all that. This crime news is completely surrounded with advertisements, usually of the very dullest kind."

The laughter that greeted this was so loud and prolonged that Norman himself rapped for order.

"But in conclusion, let me say this: I expect to be taking an editorial stand on some issues that may not be popular with my advertisers. The financial sledding in the future may not be easy."

Following Norman's talk, Reverend Aldrich asked Jonathan Wright to tell how his experiments of walking in the steps of the Master were working out.

As Wright rose to face his friends his long frame gradually unfolded until he towered above them. He spoke with deep modesty.

"I have simply been living in heaven ever since I resolved to test every act I undertook by the yardstick, 'What Would Jesus Do?' At home everything has been marvelous. At my store we are having one long, happy story. Take that Prayer Room, for instance. Now that it is finished I wish everyone in the world could see it! There are two sections—one for employees and one for the customers. The employees' room is very small as usually there is only one in there at a time, but she usually remains on her knees for fifteen minutes. When I suggested we start a continuous stream of prayer every day within working hours I was amazed that almost half the employees volunteered. The result is no one need keep a period more than once a week. Each volunteer has a fifteen-minute vigil in the prayer room and already many are telling me that this little prayer time is already blessing their entire week. They can hardly wait until their turn comes around."

"Do they do this on company time?" asked Mr. Marsh.

"Of course they do this on company time, but it is already inspiring many of them to keep a similar vigil *daily* at home, either morning or evening, on their own time. In fact, they have all taken home books on prayer from our book department and some of them 'train' all week in order to make that fifteen-minute period in the prayer room more effective."

He turned to Norman and laid his hand on his shoulder.

"By the way, Richard," he smiled, "you would be interested the way they all go for those stories of heroism and answered prayer in the *Raymond News*."

"But don't you have Jewish clerks?" interrupted David Paul, the principal of Crocker School. "Do they participate also?"

"Yes, we have a score or more of Jewish people, and they are just as eager as the rest to participate. I give them exclusive use of Saturday morning vigils, which is their Sabbath, you know.

"Another feature is the profit-sharing plan that holds such possibilities that I should like to describe it to you some day.

"And another interesting aspect is the fifteen percent of the total earnings each year going to the Lord. This fifteen percent, you know, from the net corporation earnings, is deductible for income tax purposes. Our stockholders came together and agreed on this and had a regular love-feast planning how we could use it to establish some very badly needed playgrounds for children in the congested parts of the city. Only two strenuously objected, and one is now completely won over, thanks to an experience shared in by Reverend Maxwell. From the other we are trying to buy his shares, but the stubborn mule doesn't want to sell. He, by the way, is our only problem—and a pretty tough one at that, and about him I covet your prayers. Right now he is no longer on the grounds. He is getting a new job.

"But, men," continued Jonathan Wright, his enthusiasm growing as he proceeded, "the most unique thing of all is the hearty esprit de corps and the loyal teamwork that has spread through every department of the organization."

Reverend Aldrich exclaimed, "Gentlemen, everything he says about his store is true! One feels the atmosphere of good will the moment he enters the swinging doors."

"What I am interested in," said Mr. Paul, "is the public

prayer room. Do the customers make any use of their section of it?"

"Not as much as I wish," replied Wright. "People evidently do their ordinary praying at home and, I am sorry to say, most of them probably don't even do that. Out of thousands of daily customers, perhaps less than twenty-five use it each day. Their motives may be partly novelty, partly a real need, and in some cases their needs are met. One woman came in great distress. Her need was so great that she simply had to find a sanctuary to get close to God, she said. She had gone to a modernist church late that afternoon, but the doors were locked; then she went to a very fundamentalist church, hoping it would be open, but it, too, was closed for the weekday. Then she thought of this prayer room and came at once. A great peace came to her when she entered the room and she stopped in the office to thank me before she went out.

"Another thing has interested me greatly. Friends tell me that when they have appointments to meet someone downtown, they tell them they will find them in the rug department. That always means that they will find them in the prayer room—the best possible place! Often they chide their friends for coming too soon!"

So the first meeting of the Luncheon Club ended with a real sense of mission in trying to do what Jesus would do. Here was laid the foundation for men of all callings to meet together and share what they could do to "walk in His steps."

As Arthur Wainright was driving Charles back to the church he said:

"I have an important question to ask you, Parson. My wife and I have given a lot of thought to the part that little Agnes had in the healing of Meredith. As Belle related it to me, Agnes was absolutely sure that our girl was cured when she looked at the potted plant on the window sill. Is that right?"

"Yes," replied Charles. "She was using a method spontaneously which Jesus used deliberately."

"What do you mean?"

"Do you recall," asked Charles, "how the woman with an issue of blood *knew* the tear in her body could be hemmed up when she saw how beautifully Jesus' garment was hemmed up— that beautiful garment, 'all of one piece and woven from above'? And do you recall how the Roman Centurion *knew* that his beloved bond-servant, trained from childhood to obey every command given by one in authority, would have to obey a command to be healed when given by one who 'spoke differently from the scribes and pharisees in that he spake as one having authority'?"

"I see," said Arthur Wainright. "Cures come when one goes beyond mere believing to absolute knowing. Is that right?"

"Yes. And that absolute knowing is stimulated by a parallel experience in his own life, in a field where he is particularly familiar."

"Is that why Jesus spoke so often in parables?" asked Wainright.

"Undoubtedly," said Charles.

"I'm glad to hear you say that!" exclaimed Wainright, as he drew his car to a halt in front of the church. "Belle and I have done a lot of experimenting with prayer since Meredith's recovery, and as both of us are very practical-minded, we have been using incidents of our daily life in just that way—as sort of parables. And, believe you me, we have been getting answers to our prayers, too. It's been remaking our lives. We prayed just yesterday for a special problem of Belle's and we *know* it is going to be answered."

"Why do you know?" asked Charles.

"Because of the great peace that came to both of us."

"There you said it," exclaimed Charles, "I have been discovering that when a prayer falls into the arms of peace, it has fallen into the arms of God and all will be well. And when the peace manifests in a still deeper way—as a profound sense of joy, then I know that God's way and my way will be the same."

"Our cargoes," mused Wainright, "come to us only over calm seas. I discovered that this football season."

Charles started to open the door to the car.

"Wait a minute." Arthur's long arm detained him. "There is one thing Belle and I want your advice about. Now that Meredith's life has been saved, we want it to be saved for some good purpose. She is a very spontaneous, original little girl—does wonderful things at home, but the school life seems to stifle her."

"How do you mean?"

"Meredith has to do everything from within. The rigid regimentation of school the last two years seems to be thwarting all that is precious in her. That is one reason I think that she got sick."

"She probably has genius," said Charles. "Edison did everything that way and the teacher called him a dunce. His mother resented the insult, took him out of school, taught him to read, gave him some tools to play with, and he created for us a new world."

"It depends largely on the teachers," said Arthur Wainright. "Two years ago she had a Miss Ruth McMaster, a woman of great understanding and spiritual discernment. Meredith simply throve under her leadership. Last year she had a crabbed Miss Swenson, and all her spontaneous originality simply dried up. This year she has a Miss Gertrude Long who sometimes blows hot and sometimes blows cold. As a result she is thwarted again. What can I do for her?"

"I have sometimes wondered," said Charles, "what Jesus would do about our educational system, and about children like little Meredith especially."

"Belle and I would appreciate it, Parson, if you would make that a matter of prayer. We find it harder to pray for persons close to us than for persons farther away."

"Naturally," said Charles. "Physicians never treat their own family. Why shouldn't we invite outsiders to pray for ours?

Well, Arthur, you can count on me to do a lot of praying for little Meredith. Now that God has saved her life, I'll tell the good Father it is up to Him to see that it has been saved for something very worth while."

"Thanks a lot." And Arthur's big hand all but crushed the hand of Charles Maxwell. As he turned to his wheel he called over his shoulder:

"That was a great meeting of men today. If we keep it up we may make Raymond a City of God yet."

CHAPTER 14

"My sheep hear my voice and I know them, and
they follow me. And I give unto them eternal life; and
they shall never perish, neither shall any man pluck
them out of my hand."

CHARLES FOUND it had come to be a habit to go back into
the church after saying farewell to the last member
Sunday mornings, and follow the old sexton around as
he picked up bulletins and put song books back into their place.
It often ended up in their sitting together for a few minutes in
the front seat and talking.

The sermon always seemed to unlock the sexton's tongue and
make his wisdom flow. At such times Charles found flashes of
rare intuition always at hand. Sandy's understanding of character was uncanny, his knowledge of scripture was remarkable.
One day Charles asked him how he came by this remarkable
knowledge of the scriptures.

"My Scottish faither made me an' ma' brither tak turns
readin' the Gude Buik tae him Sunday afternoons," he replied,
shoving back his unruly white hair. "Sometimes he would fa'
asleep an' we'd try tae sneak awa', but the moment we stopped
readin' he woke up an' made us continue. I hae got what they
call a photographic memory. I remember whole chapters. I
never went to school mae than three years. It was na till I was
nineteen that I left Scotland. But I never regretted na goin' tae
school. Everythin' I got was ma ain. I am what ye wad ca' a
'natural.'"

"A 'natural'?" Charles smiled at the term. "I never heard that word used that way before. What does it mean?"

"If ye want an example of it leuk at Miss Page," MacIntosh grew more animated. "Ye hae a gran' choir, Parson, but yer sparkplug is Miss Page. She is what I wad ca' a 'natural' if there ever wes ane. Only she dinna ken it, an' her trainers dinna ken it, and she's been weel nigh spoilt in the makin'."

"What do you mean, spoiled?" Maxwell straightened up in the pew and turned towards the older man.

"Parson, did ye ever see a piece o' fine wood—oak or walnut, say, wi' the finest natural grain that the forest could produce, a natural design that only needs a touch o' varnish tae bring it out—an' then some fool painter com alang an' slaps on sae mony coats o' paint that a' its natural beauty is obscured?"

"I see what you mean. But how has that affected Frances' singing?"

"Only ane thin' she lacks. When she gets that, I'm fearfu' ye wull lose her tae Grand Opera or radio. For if she gets that, she wull bowl 'em ower like ninepins, believe me, lad."

"What does she lack? I thought her voice seemed meticulously trained," said Charles, defensively.

"That's it. Tae weel trained. Tae much veneering for a little piece o' wood. Yes, sir, tae much trainin', na enough soul. She disna hae that 'somethin' plus' that her gudemither haen."

"That sounds pretty harsh, Mr. MacIntosh," protested Charles.

"But it's true!" and Sandy's gray thatch nodded emphatically. "She has bin ower-trained i' voice an' under-disciplined i' soul. I'm fearfu' her soul is na powerfu' enough tae tak control o' her voice!"

"I think she has lots of soul," said Charles, remembering the evening when she had visited him shortly after the suicide of the Japanese boy.

"Parson," old MacIntosh fixed Charles with a keen eye, "I hae noticed that ye like her singin'. Ye always turn ye head an' a licht com's intae yer een when she begins—but that's because ye are on her beam. Ye see somethin' i' her the rest o' us dinna see."

"What do I see in her?" asked Maxwell.

"Ye see what Gude sees, Pastor. That's because ye are a gude man. But I see a spoilt bairn. A sweet, dear, little spoilt bairn— but spoilt, just the same. Beginnin' wi' her grandparents, that fine auld couple Mr. and Mrs. Rollin Page, her family always has bin looked up tae. They hae bin tae Raymond what the Royal Family hae bin tae England. An' their only lad, Egbert, is a prince o' the royal line. An' noo as President o' the College he is adored by auld an' young alike, an' he deserves tae be!"

When Charles did not speak, Sandy went on reminiscently. "When I began in this kirk as a young man, next tae yer ain grandsire, wha wes ye micht ca' a saunt o' the town, cam Mrs. Rollin Page, wha wes beloved by maist everybody. I' fact people liked her sae much that onythin' she wad ask wes just like a command. Her lad, Egbert, though he's a big imposing man, has a' her sweetness, alang wi' his strength, an' ye wad be surprised how a request frae him is received as a law, especially be everyane i' this particular kirk.

"Sae frae the time Frances wes a little lass, she acted like she wes the crown princess o' this whole community. Among ither things she seemed tae think that the preacher wes her family's private property. She wad often drap i' on the study on her way home frae school an' ask him tae preach about this or that the next Sunday. Quite bossy for a wee ane, I suld sae."

"Now, Sandy," soothed Maxwell, "that might have been earnest seeking—an honest attempt of a little girl to get the gospel into her little mind."

"Micht be, micht be," mused the sexton, nodding his head. "She aince got yer auld grandsire tae gie a series o' sermons on fairy tales an' Mither Goose rhymes."

"Well, well! I'll bet they were the best sermons he ever preached!" exclaimed Charles delightedly.

"The bairns fae a' ower town crowded in tae hear them. The ither preachers got awfully jealous ower his 'robbin' their cradles' as they ca' it. He maist wrecked their Sunday Schools that month."

"I almost wish she would select my topics for me awhile."

"Dinna worrit, she wull, if ye gie her half a chance. But she is nae as bossy as she used tae be since she hae bin engaged tae young Eton. If anyane can break her wull, it's that young tycoon. If she wes spoilt as a lass, he wes spoilt before he was born. They are the tae maist obstinate snobs this town ever ken."

"You are far too severe," expostulated Charles. Then, emphatically, "Her aggressive demands on the minister sprang from her desire to find God. It's her soul on a quest."

"That wad be true, Parson, if it wes na that its only wi' her brain she gaes aseekin', na her soul. Just lissen tae her sing next Sunday. Overtrain' in music, undertrain' in soul. When she gets thae i' balance she will be a Gude-inspired 'natural.' But it wull tak a miracle tae change her. She knes a' the stops an' starts, a' the sharps an' flats. But she winna be a great singer till ane o' tae things happen tae her."

"And what are these?"

"When either ane happens she wull be the greatest singer i' this country next tae Lily Pons."

"What are these two things?" persisted Charles.

"A great sorrow—"

"God forbid!"

"Or a great lo'e." concluded Sandy with a sage look on his grizzled face.

"She *is* in love. She's engaged to be married," Charles objected.

"She's engaged, a' richt, an' she thinks it is lo'e—but I doot it. She's tae smart tae fool hersel'. He's a' brains an' efficiency, an' thoroughly stuck on himsel'. She selected Arnold i' the first place because her mither wanted her tae. I' the other places, because he's handsome, because he's rich, because he has a strang wull. He is drawn tae her because he tires quickly o' namby-pamby critters that are putty i' his han'. She is drawn tae him

116

because she hates tae be managed an' yet she wants a maister."

"Well, isn't that falling in love?" insisted Charles.

"She has com tae the water's edge," continued MacIntosh. "She's stickin' in her wee toes an' playin' wi' the idea. But she hasna plunged i'. Dinna fool yersel'."

"And when she does?" Charles smiled at the vehemence of the little sexton.

"Nae audience can stand before her voice!"

"Really? Then we'd better speed their love affair."

MacIntosh stared thoughtfully at him. He took a pipe out of his pocket, looked at it, tapped it, wrapped it in his handkerchief, and placed it in his other pocket. He arose to go.

"Na, I think we'se hae tae depend on a great sorrow," he said cryptically, and went out.

"He's uncanny," said Charles to himself. "That last remark makes me uneasy. Is that a premonition?"

The next Sunday he found himself unconsciously studying Frances' singing. It *was* meticulously correct. MacIntosh was right. Not a single flaw in it. But as Charles listened, power seemed somehow to have gone out of it.

After the service, when all handshaking at the door was over, he went to his study. He was surprised to find Frances waiting for him there.

"What did you do to me this morning, Mr. Preacher?" she asked abruptly, eyeing him sharply.

"I?" he stammered, "I? Are you asking what did *I* do to—to you?"

"Yes, yes, and don't you try to get out of it, either."

He wished she would take her beautiful unblinking eyes away from his.

"You, or somebody, let me down terribly this morning, Mr. Maxwell."

"Sit down," he said, pointing to the window seat. "You are a strange girl. I don't know what you're talking about. Sit down and explain yourself!"

"Perhaps I should," she said as she sat down, a half smile appearing on her face as though she found some amusement and relief at the sight of the blush on his face. "Perhaps I was a little abrupt. But if you knew how I look forward each week to the joy of singing to the back of your neck on Sunday, and what a tremendous pull or something the mere seeing you sitting there does for my singing, you would forgive my outburst."

"Pull!" he said, completely at a loss. "And what did I do today?"

"There was no pull. You simply turned off the power. I don't know what you did. But you must have done something. For it was like singing against a closed door. Please, Mr. Maxwell, is there something that I have done that doesn't please you?"

Charles sat down opposite her. At last he understood, and was ashamed. In his heart was a writhing impatience with MacIntosh. If he hadn't planted that poisoned judgment in his heart this might never have happened! The acute intuition of Frances Page put him on the spot. He didn't know what to say. He felt like a convict caught in his crime. He lifted his eyes from the floor and met her clear blue eyes still fixed unwaveringly on his.

"What a guilty look you have, Mr. Preacher. Come, confess the truth. What have I done to hurt you? I will do anything to make amends. Please tell me."

"Well, I'll confess. Perhaps I did turn off the power, as you say, but I must insist that I didn't know any power was there or I wouldn't have turned it off."

"And why did you turn it off? That is what I want to know."

"Well, all these Sundays I have listened only to the soul of your singing. But today I thought it was my duty to focus on your technique. And lo, and behold, your technique was so good that it absorbed *all* my attention. In the process I forgot to listen to your soul. I must confess that I missed something in your singing. If I *am* to blame, my dear lady, I am the one who should apologize to you, not you to me."

"Then I really haven't offended you? Oh, I am so relieved!" Suddenly a frown replaced her smile. "But my technique—you say it absorbed you so much you forgot my soul. Perhaps that is my fault. Maybe it is a bigger fault than I have dreamed. Is it a fault, Mr. Maxwell, my technique?"

"Well," Charles here saw an opportunity for an entering wedge. Perhaps MacIntosh was *half* right, after all. "If I have *any* criticism to offer you it is perhaps that you are *too* good a singer, if such a thing is possible. So you see, my only criticism is really a form of praise."

"Oh, you don't have to explain!" she interrupted. "I know. I am all technique—nothing else. But I had begun to hope that there *was something* else—ever since you came. I mean, ever since you made me try to do what Jesus would do—ever since you—"

She broke off abruptly and rose from the window seat. Her eyes were on the open doorway behind him. Charles turned and saw Arnold Eton standing there, hat in hand. His eyes, cold and stern, were on Frances. He did not speak.

Charles arose and said politely, "Frances wasn't satisfied with her singing this morning. Didn't you think it was all right?"

"Never heard her sing better in her life," he snapped. "But you will be late to your dinner, Frances, if you don't draw this post mortem to an end."

And as they left Charles said to himself, "How much of our talk did he hear? Then, "But I'm glad Frances and I got to the root of her singing." And as he gathered up bulletins with MacIntosh he wondered if there would be new soul in her singing next Sunday. Finally he said aloud, "What shall I do, MacIntosh, to make my neck shine more brilliantly?"

MacIntosh laughed loud and uproariously. "That's a gude ane, Parson! I never heard that ane before. A little rum on the i'side can mak the nose shine on the outside. But I am fearfu', Parson, it will take somethin' a lot stronger than rum tae bring out the shine in the back of yer neck!"

CHAPTER 15

"I am the Way, the Truth and the Life."

CHARLES MAXWELL answered his telephone one sunny November day to hear the voice of Egbert Page, President of Lincoln College.

"Mr. Maxwell, will you be willing to speak to the Lincoln students next Friday morning at their regular chapel hour?"

"I should say I would!" answered Charles Maxwell.

"It is only fair to tell you," the voice went on, apologetically, "that this is the week of the big Homecoming football game, and everything is demoralized, so you may have a poor hearing. But it's the only time we can get you in before Christmas."

"I understand how those things are," Charles replied heartily. "It all comes from having a wonderful team!"

"To put it very mildly," said President Page, with a laugh, "the school has gone football mad. It eats, sleeps and talks football morning, noon and night. You are partly to blame because, according to Coach Wainright, it was your counsel and your inspiration that led to our winning the first and most difficult game of the season. And I am sorry to add," Page cleared his throat hesitantly, "that you will have another hurdle to face, because they have all heard of your new *In Jesus' Steps* Crusade and they are on their guard. You know how students are—as skittish about high pressure evangelism as a horse is at a newspaper blowing across its track. Paul at Athens didn't have a harder job than you will have next Friday."

"Well, Mr. Page," replied Charles, "it will require lots of

prayer, that's all! So if you will pray about it at your end of the line, I will at mine. And send me a little dope about the team! It will all help."

"I think you are on the right track," laughed Page. "A combination of grace and gumption is what college students need. Either one alone won't do it. I'll mail you a copy of the college paper. It may give you an idea of the kind of gumption my students are used to."

When the college paper came—the *Lincoln Log*—Charles found the edition was all football. The editorial, however, was on another line. A student signing the name Murray was making an appeal for "Less Religion in College." Although a cynical piece, it was well executed.

"This is a brilliant piece of writing," thought Charles. "It will take all I've got to meet that challenge."

When Friday arrived, Charles Maxwell entered the campus through the low-pillared red stone gateway. His eyes were bombarded at every step with brightly painted banners: "Stop the Audubons!" "Annihilate Audubon!" "Luck for Lincoln!" "This is V. A. Day!" "Victory over Audubon!" Walking briskly up the long walk beneath elms whose branches spread as he never had seen elms spread before, to weather-beaten old stone MacGregor Hall, he found President Page waiting for him in his office.

"We have about ten minutes yet before you are to speak," Page told him. "There are a lot of noisy preliminaries before your talk starts."

When President Page finally escorted him to the platform, the cheer leader was concluding the last pep talk of the morning.

"Get aboard the Lincoln Locomotive," he chanted. "Now—all together . . . !"

Slowly, methodically the yell got underway to the beat of the leader's hands and the rhythm of his swaying body. Gradually the deafening chant accelerated until with one final leap of the cheer leader pandemonium broke loose. Then waving jauntily to the roaring crowd, the boy turned with a grin to the President, now seated behind him on the platform, and went down to his vacant seat among the seniors.

Charles found himself seated on a platform that jutted out far into the chapel. The chapel was wider than it was long, and Charles had the sensation of being literally surrounded by students.

"It's a major crime to ask you to talk against a tide like this," apologized Mr. Page behind his hand while waiting for the turbulence to subside. "If you and the Lord will forgive me this time, I'll never ask you to do it again!" Then stepping to the front of the platform he began:

"Men and women of Lincoln College, you will now have the privilege of listening to Reverend Charles Sheldon Maxwell, pastor of your own First Church of this city. Reverend Maxwell," turning to him, "this is my college family—a real live bunch, as you can easily see. Go to it."

Charles had to raise his voice to be heard above the dull monotone of a hundred whispering voices. Hardly a face was turned his way.

"My friends of Lincoln College," he began against the storm of whispers, "I want to talk to you about the greatest player on your team—a player that some of you may not be as well acquainted with as you should. He is in your backfield—the greatest triple threat player the world has ever known."

Faces began to turn towards him. The whispering died down. Charles knew he had caught their attention, and went on enthusiastically.

"I understand that you have a wonderful backfield at Lincoln this year—the greatest in your history—and you are depending upon that backfield to win for you the championship. From the talk that I hear, I wonder if they are better than the famous quartet of Notre Dame known as the Four Horsemen!

"The player I refer to came from a small town. He led a quiet life but He was in constant training for the great season on ahead. He selected a team and trained it Himself. He had an

122

all-star backfield. Their names were Peter, James and John. He took these three with Him to the healing of Jairus' daughter, to the Mount of Transfiguration, and to Gethsemane—whenever He wanted to make a touchdown He took that trio with him. Together with Jesus they made the greatest four horsemen that ever carried the ball."

Three husky boys on the front seat with monogramed letters on their gold sweaters were now giving him very close attention. Charles thought to himself, "If I hold those three I may keep the attention of the rest." Then aloud:

"Peter stands for Faith; James for Hope, John for Love. Faith calls the signals, Hope is the right halfback who clears the way, Love is the left halfback who carries the ball, and Christ behind them all is the fullback or tailback or whatever you call the key man who usually makes the touchdowns.

"Your center is Meekness. Your guards are Temperance and Patience. Your tackles are Goodness and Gentleness. The ends are Joy and Peace. You will find this team described in Galatians 5:22 as 'the Fruits of the Spirit; against such there is no law.' For our purpose I shall call them 'The *Team* of the Spirit, against whom there is no *defense*.' Just listen to that—this team, this All-American team—this All-Eternal and All-Infinite team— nothing can stop!"

Charles could see amazed looks being exchanged all over the auditorium, and a little flurry of whispers went through the air.

"Jesus was, as I said, the greatest triple-threat player of all time—He could plunge, pass and punt, that is, preach, pray and penetrate to the very heart of God.

"He plunged when He gave the Sermon on the Mount and led His disciples and the people, through precept and example, along the solid paths of righteousness.

"But when He was blocked on the line of scrimmage, the line of ordinary endeavor, or when He could not reach the persons because they were too far away, like the nobleman's son and the Syrophenician's daughter, He reached them by the forward pass of prayer. Jesus was the greatest forward passer the world has

123

ever known. He tuned in to the Father, took careful aim, and always reached his man.

"If you take Him as your coach, you, too, can learn how to plunge and pass and punt."

Charles walked around the speaker's stand to the edge of the platform and took an easy stance, resting one elbow on the stand.

"Suppose the signal is to plunge. You will find an opening straight down the field if you let the guards, Temperance and Patience, protect the way, and if the tackles, Goodness and Gentleness, remove the opposition.

"If the need is to pass—your prayer will be perfect and complete if it falls into the waiting arms of the ends known as Peace and Joy. If your prayer is followed by no sense of Peace or Joy, it is probably an 'incompleted pass' and you will have to pray again.

"But supposing you are in a position where neither preaching nor praying seems to work—where the plunge of action seems to be without avail, and the passes of prayer fail to reach the arms of Peace. Suppose all the forces of evil seem about to take over. There is always a way to out-defeat defeat itself, and that is to send the ball spinning down the field in a glorious punt."

From the expressions of rapt attention on the faces of the young people before him, Charles knew they were with him completely now.

"To punt is to relinquish personal ownership of the ball for a season. To punt spiritually is to relinquish the fulfillment of your prayer if God so wills. Abraham was a great relinquisher when he gave Isaac back to the Father. Remember how he took him to the mountain top to relinquish him to the Great Adversary, Death? And you remember how the enemy fumbled the ball? The enemy always fumbles the ball when the relinquishment is complete enough. Abraham's punt was such a gloriously unselfish, spiralling, sacrificial relinquishment that Isaac was restored to him to become the father of a great race. In modern times Gandhi was our greatest relinquisher. He called it renunciation. Thru renunciation he won the liberation of his people. But the greatest relinquisher the world has ever known was Jesus, Himself. When an enemy slapped Him on one cheek —instead of retaliating He turned the other! On Golgotha He relinquished His body entirely into the hands of His enemies, and His spirit utterly into the hands of his Father. The greatest punt in the history of the world was made in the Garden of Gethsemane. 'Not my will but Thine be done.' Some teams, you know, have famous punters that can spin the ball so far into the enemy territory that they gain more ground by giving the ball away than by everlastingly hanging on to it. That was Jesus' greatest secret—relinquishment. Greater even than His practical services and His prevailing prayers were His sacrificial relinquishments. Skilled in all three, He was invincible."

Charles paused for a moment, walked a few steps to the side, then back in front of the stand. "I shall ask you now to imagine a team beaten back to its own goal-line with the score against it and only a few minutes left to play. What shall they do? It is too late to plunge, too far back to pass. The ball is shot back to the star punter behind his own goal-line and he punts clear down the field to the opponents' goal. The spiralling ball is hard to handle, the adversary fumbles and the victory is won.

"Now exchange that picture for another one. Behold Jesus hanging on the cross. To all outer appearance nothing but defeat looms before Him. He is being snatched out of this world at the age of thirty-three, an age when most men are just starting their life work. All the leaders of His time, both religious and political, have turned against Him. The common people are railing at Him. Even His closest twelve have deserted Him. The weakest of the twelve has betrayed Him, and the strongest has denied Him. Only one stands by Him—and he is a cousin.

"As He hangs there, does He say to Matthew, write a book about me; does He say to Peter, build a church in my honor; does He say to Stephen, fill a treasury for me? No. His thoughts in those closing minutes are not on what He can *get* but on what He can *give*. And what does He have to give?

"He has no home. 'The birds of the air have nests and the foxes have holes, but the Son of Man hath nowhere to lay his head.' He has no wealth. He could say with Peter, 'Silver and gold have I none, but what I have give I unto you.' Even his last garment is being gambled away at the foot of the cross.'

Suddenly Maxwell became aware of the complete stillness in the assembly clear back to the farthest rows. In slow and rhythmic cadence he went on:

"And there with nothing to give, the man on the cross turns and gives three precious, imperishable, priceless gifts. To His mother He gives a son; to the thief, Paradise; and to His accusers, forgiveness."

And now Charles' voice raised to a powerful climax.

"You cannot stop a man like that. If there were no other proof of Christ's divinity that alone would be enough. And in return for that outward tide of irresistible, selfless giving there is now flowing back to Him such tides of love and loyalty and devotion as were never given before to anyone who ever walked this earth.

"Yes, in the final minutes of the game, beaten back to His goal-line, this great Champion of the hearts and souls of men sent the ball spiralling far into the opponents' territory, so far that the adversary fumbled the ball, the stone was rolled away, and the resurrected Savior of Mankind rose to proclaim for us the triumph of Love and the assurance of Life Everlasting."

The contrast between the atmosphere when he began and when he ended was almost unbelievable. "Now," Charles concluded in a friendly voice, "after the game is played Saturday and the football season for this year is over, I should like to invite as many of you as are willing to enroll in a Team of the Spirit to consider together what our lives might become if we let that All-Star Player within us take complete charge of the game."

CHAPTER 16

*"I have compassion on the multitude because they
continue with me three days."*

BEFORE THEY LEFT the platform President Page announced
to the student body that Reverend Maxwell would be
available for one hour in the Dean's office for conferences
and personal problems for those students who might desire it.
He also announced that all who wished to follow up these ideas
were invited to attend a special meeting of young people Sunday
evening at First Church.

President Page conducted Charles Maxwell to the Dean's
office, which opened on his own. Hardly had he entered and sat
down when a pale young man, tall and thin and slightly stooped,
walked in.

"I am Jerry Grey," he said, "I have a problem that I hate to
bother you with, but I just can't solve it myself. Would you
mind if I told it?"

"Not at all. Take a chair." As Charles pulled a chair up closer,
he added with a smile, "Well, what shall we do? Plunge, pass or
punt?"

"I guess it will have to be a pass, Reverend, in more ways than
one. For I've tried every plunge I've known, and if prayer
can't solve it, I'll have to pass right out of school."

Charles sensed real desperation in the boy's voice, and urged
him to go on.

"I used to work for my room at a Mrs. Collins, and have done
evening press work at the News office. Two weeks ago I got
drunk, and when I say drunk, I mean drunk. I was down and

out for a couple of days—dead to the world—in some flophouse. Mrs. Collins wouldn't take me back. I've traipsed all over town and I can't find a room anywhere."

"Can't you get into the men's dormitory?"

"No, it's full, and a waiting list besides. But maybe they wouldn't take me anyway. I don't know what to do." The boy's voice broke, and he put his head in his hands.

"See here, Jerry," said Charles briskly, "I have a big house and no one in it. It's the same manse in which my grandfather brought up a family. You might just as well take one of the vacant rooms."

Jerry's head jerked up, his eyes unbelieving. "Could you let me work for my room?" There was real eagerness in his voice. "Could I help you?"

"I'll let you help some if you want to. You could take off the screens this week, rake the leaves next week. When December comes you could shovel snow off the walk. And every morning you can get our breakfast, if you like."

"I can cook, Reverend Maxwell," Jerry exclaimed. "I'll get supper, too—and wash dishes."

"No, a Mrs. Bailey comes in to get the supper every afternoon and stays and washes the dishes for the day," interrupted Charles. "She does the washing and ironing and cleaning, too. If this suits you it's all right with me. Bring your things over tonight and I'll help you settle."

"Thanks! Thanks, Reverend Maxwell!" said the young man. "I can't tell you what this means to me, and coming just now when I was about to give up—it's too good to be true!"

Charles rose and took the lad by the hand. "Yes, Jerry, you have a chance to make a touchdown yet."

Jerry's face clouded suddenly, and he moved away from Maxwell. "But maybe you didn't hear what I said—about me getting—getting drunk. That's why no one will have me. Mrs. Collins spread the news all over town—all the kids know. I don't know why I did it. Why would you want me around, knowing that?" The boy's eyes widened, and he made an effort at a belligerent tone as he said, "What if it happens again?"

Charles Maxwell put an arm around Jerry's thin shoulders and said thoughtfully, "Yes, I heard what you said, Jerry, and still want you. It doesn't matter what Mrs. Collins or anyone has said about you. I know you're a good boy, an intelligent boy —too good and intelligent to be wasted. And about its happening again—well," Charles smiled straight into Jerry's haunted eyes, "we'll see what we can do about that. Quit worrying—remember, you said you were going to relinquish! You'll have to relinquish your worries as well as your dreams to do the job right."

Jerry smiled waveringly, muttered, "See you tonight" and was gone. A chill of premonition came suddenly over Charles, but three more students were waiting to see him and he could not pause to consider the matter of Jerry Grey any longer.

When Charles had seen the last one, President Page came in.

"There are three things I wanted to talk with you about," he said. "One is Jerry, the first chap you saw this morning. He is a dangerous boy. Not when he is normal, but he is a periodical drinker. When this comes on him he is a fiend incarnate. Suicide or murder is in the cards if we don't watch out.

"My second concern is the college. My biggest problem is the terrific congestion of students this college is burdened with, and the necessity for starting a campaign next spring for a new dormitory to meet the need. But the immediate problem before our college and one I want your special help on, is regarding a jarring note in our student body named Murray Edwards."

"Don't worry, one student can't do much harm," smiled Charles.

"But it's a serious jar," insisted President Page, "for this student is exceedingly influential. He is so popular that he will probably be elected President of the student body next year when he becomes a senior. Young Murray is an out-and-out atheist, a brilliant debater, popular with the students and chief editorial writer on the *Lincoln Log*."

"*Lincoln Log?* Oh, yes, that is the weekly you mailed me last week."

President Page smiled, "Yes, Lincoln was a log-splitter, you remember." Then his face clouded, "Murray's editorials are masterpieces of satire and invective. Voltaire and Thomas Payne and Robert Ingersoll combined couldn't do better."

"You are right," said Charles. "I was impressed by an article of his in the copy you sent me."

"Recently he has started going around with a girl in his class, Florence Bowen."

"Florence Bowen!" Charles exclaimed, "She is the life of the Young People's Society in my church. I certainly do know her! I met her the Sunday that I first met your daughter Frances. They were leaving the church together."

"Yes, they're inseparable. That is how I happen to have all this inside information. Florence is a unique combination of deep spirituality and tremendous vitality. I can see how she would be the life of the young people's work at your church, for she is the life of every party at this college. I have been counting on her and Harlan Douglas to be the chief leaders in the follow-up after your talk this morning. If a big turn-out greets you Sunday night, it will be due to the efforts of these two!"

"Bless their hearts," said Charles.

"They'll succeed," said Mr. Page, "if they aren't blocked by Murray Edwards. But what I am most concerned with is the influence he may get over Florence."

"My impression was that Florence doesn't give a rap about the boys."

Again the President nodded agreement. "And it's all the more surprising when she is such an attractive girl. But here is her point of danger: When she does go in for a thing she goes in with all her might. The only kind of lad that will interest her will be some unusual chap who will be mighty hard to get. Murray Edwards is a very unusual boy. The mill-run sort she dismisses with the mitten. What concerns me about Murray is that he isn't a bit sentimental and therein lies the danger. The very fact that he is so audacious and debonair and unsentimental makes him very alluring to her. He is exactly the kind that she might fall for. And if she ever falls she will fall hard." President Page shook his head.

"But you said just now that he has no religion," remarked

Charles, puzzled. "Do you think she will fall in love with a chap that is so openly atheistic as he is? That is, unless she converts him first!"

"That is another point of danger!" exclaimed Mr. Page. "His very atheism puts her on her mettle to convert him! I wouldn't be surprised if she brought him to your meeting Sunday. And if he comes it will not be because he is in love with her, but for some deeper, more devious reason of his own. He will use her as a screen behind which he can work his plots and schemes. He is all out to smash everything he can. He reminds me at times of a cattle rustler riding head-on to change the course of a herd of galloping cattle."

"And what's the herd?"

"The whole young people's religious program in both the college and the church."

"Do you think he is plotting so ambitious a program as all that?" asked Charles.

"If he can deflect the leader, and that is Florence, he might send the whole herd over the precipice. And he now has his sights trained on you."

"On me?"

President Page nodded. "Ever since you started your crusade about "What Would Jesus Do?" you have been like a red rag to him. He's a perfect replica of Saul of Tarsus, 'breathing out threatenings and slaughter against the disciples of the Lord.' He is definitely committed to undermining your work."

"When there are two strong wills pitted against each other like Florence's and Murray's," said Charles calmly, "there is one other force that can enter in and turn the balance. Let's you and me bring that in to the best of our ability."

"You mean—"

"Prayer."

The next day was Saturday. Lincoln won the game, and with it the State championship. Charles walked home tingling with the excitement of the stands, the joy of the day, and the renewed memory of his own football days.

The sun was going down infilling all the western sky with

glory. There would be a beautiful afterglow, he thought, as he watched three gold-tinted clouds drift across the sky. Thanksgiving wasn't too far away. Why not pour out a little Thanksgiving tonight? Pushing open his front door, he paused to take one final look at the heavens. When the melody first reached him, he frowned in disbelief and shook his ears to clear their ringing. But the notes lingered on the current of warm air and he knew with amazement that they came from the piano in the living room. He had never heard it played. The door was slightly ajar and he pushed it open silently and stood on the threshold.

Jerry sat alone at the piano. His brown sweater was missing a button and his black hair fell tousled across his forehead. His face was in shadow but the light from the curved student lamp fell full upon the empty music rack. Charles tried to recognize what he was playing, a soft, dreamy melody. A log fell in the fireplace and Jerry looked up quickly.

"Hello," he said, with a nervous smile. "Didn't know I was so talented, did you?"

"You hadn't told me you played at all," said Charles. "What was it?"

"I am pretty good," and he grinned devilishly, "but I'm torn between women and my musical career."

"How're they coming?" smiled Charles affably, leaning on the piano.

"The women are going," Jerry said. "The sexy type are clear off the stage making room for the intellectual type. Well," he winked at Charles, "us geniuses are born to live alone."

"We do have our troubles, don't we?" said Charles. He tossed his coat on a chair and sank onto the sofa. "What were you thinking about when you played that dreamy piece?"

Jerry closed his eyes in reverie. "A two inch steak smothered in onions, topped off with the kind of Bourbon served only to men of distinction."

"Some imagination!" said Charles, falling in with his repartee. "Guess you won't get it here, though."

Jerry laughed and touched the keys again.

"That was Chopin. My mother used to play his nocturnes. She loved music but she had to work too hard to play much."

The smile on his face flickered and vanished and his fingers moved slowly over the keys. To Charles the noisy stadium was now a vague memory. He felt a warmth in his chest and a deep love for the slim boy with the tousled hair.

"Where do your parents live, Jerry?" he asked.

"They're both dead," he replied quickly. "Dad died when I was a kid. I don't remember him. Mom had it easy for a while but had a couple of bad years just before I went into the Army. Those years were sure hard on her. She worked like a dog but she was never too tired to talk to me. She wanted me to be somebody, I guess. Not president, but just somebody—a good, solid citizen was her highest hope for me. She didn't read much but she loved flowers and music." He paused a moment, then continued, "I can remember as a child leaving my bedroom door open at night to hear her play. I used to think of her a lot when I was stuck in that hole in the Pacific. There was a lot of time for thinking. A fellow gets full of ideas about what he's going to be and do at first. I worked out the next five years of my life in a rough way, figured where I'd get started. I even wanted to read some! There's a lot in the world to know. I think I had some re-forming ideas—making the world a better place to live in. But the war dragged and dragged—you got so bored you didn't give a whoop about anything. Then it was hot as fire and I started drinking the stuff they had all around, whiskey and beer. Beer never knocked me out completely—just made me feel terrible—but I found whiskey could sure wipe out the world. I guess I lost everything I ever had. Mom died a year after I got out of the Army. It broke her heart to see me drink like that." He dropped his head on his hand and stared at the keys. "You see, her brother threw away his life like me. He's a derelict," he said, thickly. "Thank God Mom's dead."

133

Chapter 17

*"Whoever shall confess me before men, him shall the
Son of man also confess before the angels of God."*

WHEN THE YOUNG PEOPLE assembled in the church parlor the following evening, Charles gave a sigh of relief when he saw Florence Bowen enter without Murray Edwards. After an opening song and a prayer, Harlan Douglas stepped up to the front of the room.

"You will be surprised to find me acting as Chairman of the meeting, but I am under orders and Mr. Maxwell says that he is only the coach, and so he plans to sit on the sidelines and let us play the game for him tonight.

"Now, folks," and Harlan straightened up and looked over the entire group. "Most of you heard Mr. Maxwell's Chapel talk last Friday about the team of the Spirit, with a backfield made up of Faith, Hope and Love, with Jesus Christ the bright and shining star who could plunge and pass and punt. All of us who want to make the team must learn how to do these things. So the program tonight will be divided into three parts.

"The first part will be a plunge. It will be a ten minute talk by Florence Bowen. The second part will be a pass consisting of a period of prayer. Then we will end the game with a punt that we hope will clinch the victory. The first speaker will be Florence Bowen."

"This will be a sort of plunge in the dark," said Florence when she had risen to face the audience. "Bear with me if I stumble a bit. First of all, I want to turn back to Mr. Maxwell's grandfather's sermon, given in this church fifty years ago. It started

out something like this, 'I want volunteers who will pledge themselves, earnestly and honestly for an entire year, not to do anything without first asking the question, 'What would Jesus do?' "

She related some of the experiences the people in that day
went through in carrying out that pledge, and then ended with
a call for all who would be willing to try to follow their example
to raise their hands. Over two-thirds of the young people
present responded.

"This is better than I expected," said Harlan, as Florence
took her seat, her face flushed with elation over the splendid
response. "But I don't believe the game is completed yet. Now
let us try a pass. Dorothy Calvert will now take over."

Dorothy Calvert was hardly the one that Charles would have
chosen for this round. She was too shy, her face too serious, and
he was sure she was going to make the prayer period too solemn
an affair.

But a moment later he was happily surprised.

"If I asked for some oral prayers," she said, "only a few would
take part. All the rest would sit by with their minds on lots of
things besides God. When a man makes a forward pass he has
to look at the one he throws the ball to, at least that's what
Harlan told me. You will all find a blank card in your seat. You
are to get still for a while and know that God is present, and
then write down spontaneously on one side of the card the
prayer you would like to give Him. Then get still again and with
spontaniety write on the other side anything that comes through
to you from God."

Charles thought he had never seen anything more rapt than
the expressions on the faces of the young people as they con-
centrated in this two-way conversation with God. After fifteen
minutes the cards were taken up and without giving the names,
a few of the best ones were read by Dorothy. Their simplicity
and genuineness lifted the spirit of the meeting, and created the
perfect atmosphere for Harlan to step into when he rose to
conduct the final round.

"To punt," Harlan began, "means to relinquish the ball, or to

135

give up the very thing you hoped to win the game with. There are a lot of things with which we hope to make our mark in the world. And how tightly we cling to them! Our pride, our vanity, our prejudices, our possessions, our addictions, yes, our selfish ego and all it represents. Who of you in this crowd tonight is willing to give your ego a big swift kick and send it flying down the field? Here is the time in the game when a real punt is called for. Who will be the first to send your old self flying through the air?"

To Charles' amazement, half the group stood up. The contagion of Harlan's words, and the manner in which they were uttered, must have taken them by storm.

"One at a time, please," continued Harlan. "Fill these front vacant seats if you want to, but wait patiently for your turn."

A tall, slender girl with sharp features and serious face, faced the young people.

"The one thing that has kept me from making a touchdown is my habit of criticism. I criticise people behind their back. I criticise the bad things they do, and I criticise the good things they do. If you will pray for me, I will try to kick that little demon out so far that he will never come back again."

As she moved to a seat in the back of the room, tears formed in the corner of her eyes.

Almost immediately another girl leaped up, facing the audience, and exclaimed:

"I am Martha Wells, the girl Betsy criticised most of all. I am a chain smoker and I know and you know and everybody knows that Betsy Cain hates chain smokers, and I, in turn hate the prudes that hate us. But when I saw Betsy's tears just now, and when she asked us to forgive her I wanted to beat her to it and ask all you goody-goody's that don't smoke, to forgive me and pray for me, and with God's help I'm going to beat this habit, or bust in the attempt."

Tuffy Sullivan, the captain of the football team was now standing before them. "In a psychology questionnaire this fall there was a question, 'What do you put first?' and I wrote down

Football. I am going to change that now. From here on I'm going to put Christ first."

He hardly took his seat before Ed Jones, star guard on the football team took his place.

"Fellow students of Lincoln College," he began, "I have a real confession to make. I think I am to blame for our team losing most of its games last year. I wanted to be captain and was so sore I wasn't elected that I kept out of tune with the whole squad all season. I discovered this year that a team can't win games where there isn't harmony. So while everybody blamed Coach Wainright for our poor showing, I was the discordant note that caused it. So if you want a goat for last year's poor record, I am the goat."

A heavy-set boy rose and faced the group. "Folks," he said, "what keeps me from making touchdowns is impure thoughts. Please pray that I can keep them out and let Christ in."

After he sat down a silence ensued, broken finally by a small lad who said, "I am going to buy four different pictures of Jesus tomorrow to take the places of four other pictures that adorn my room, that I always take down when I know my mother is coming."

The good natured laughter that followed was broken by a comely girl with dimpled cheeks.

"It isn't only you fellows that are bothered that way," she declared. "If we girls would spend more time thinking of Jesus' hand on our heads, and less time thinking of some mug's arm around our waists, it would be a lot better for all of us. I confess before all of you that I have done my full share in trying to draw you fellows on. I want to ask God's forgiveness and your forgiveness and put Christ first from now on."

Another girl rose, "My fault is I've been too exclusive—too picky and choosy,—too high hat. Oh, you know what I'm trying to say. Nobody rates with me unless she is in my very special clique. I could only love the lovely—no time for wall flowers. Please forgive me, kids."

A boy arose. "I cheated in examinations and got away with it.

I am beginning to see that cheaters don't cheat anybody but themselves."

Charles, sitting in a back seat, was thinking to himself, "I have never seen anything like this before. The Holy Spirit is certainly at work tonight."

One by one the stream of testimony poured forth. It was almost eleven o'clock when they finally came to an end. Harlan now took over.

"Remember this, fellows and girls," he began. "If we are sincere in all this it means some real work lies ahead. We didn't win the football championship by one afternoon's practice. It takes training, it takes drill, it takes persistent practice. Get some books on prayer and spiritual living. Dust off the Bible your mother gave you when you left home, and start reading it again.

"And now before you go, how many of you will take the pledge that for this next year you won't start anything without first asking 'What would Jesus do?' "

Every hand in the room went up.

"Praise the Lord!" said Charles, rising from his seat.

"God bless you all."

Chapter 18

*"They that are whole have no need of the physician,
but they that are sick: I came not to call the righteous,
but sinners to repentance."*

CHARLES MAXWELL had just completed a conference with
a young couple who had come to consult him about
details of their wedding and was bidding them goodbye
when the door was flung open and Jerry Grey staggered in.

"Mishter Magswell," he mumbled, as he fell into the nearest
chair, "you're a good man. I'm a bad man. That maksh ush all
even, don't it?"

"Jerry, Jerry!" exclaimed Charles. "Just tell me how I can
help you."

"Take me home—no shir, no shir—I have no home—I'm jush
a loushy bum. Take me to your home and lock me up. Shut the
dirty likker away from me. Let me have jush one last drink. I'm
jush startin'. Jush give me three more drinks. Money all gone.
I'm all gone." Maudlin tears rolled down his cheeks. "You don't
call me a sinner, do you, mishter?"

"I'll tell you, Jerry—you're a sick man. Not a sinner. Just a
weak man—and an awfully sick one."

"A sick man"—holding his head between his hands, the sobs
grew more noisy, punctuated at regular intervals now with loud
hiccups.

With a heavy heart, Charles dialed the city hospital.

"I've got an alcoholic here," he explained to the matron in
charge. "He is in the beginning of a tailspin. Proper medication
and care right now might save him."

139

"Sorry," came the curt reply, "we just haven't room for alcoholic cases. We are simply flooded with calls from them. If we took in all that called we'd have to dismiss all our other patients." And she hung up.

Charles looked despairingly at the boy whose sobbing didn't halt his ceaseless monologue.

"A sick man, shure, shure, and a weak man—awful weak," and he touched with the long forefinger of his right hand each of the fingers of his left, one by one, as he continued, "I'm a hammered-down, pigeon-toed, knock-kneed, cross-eyed, son-of-a-gun, and, and—what else?"

"What can I do?" asked Charles worriedly. "The city hospital won't take you."

"I shay, I gotta be locked up—unless you lock up all the likker in town. You gotta build a fence, I shay, or I'm a goner." Suddenly a look of terror twisted Jerry's sallow features, and he flung an arm across his eyes. "I can't stand this—snakes!" he screamed. "I see 'em coming!"

When Jerry had quieted a little, Charles continued. "Locked up—you mean you want to go to jail?"

"Jail's all right, mishter, but jail is too blue-stockin' for me. They won't take me no more than the hospital would. I'm a lost soul—even the jail won't take me."

"Oh yes, surely they will," and Maxwell quickly dialed the police station.

"We'll send a wagon directly," he was told.

"No, even the jail-birds won't take me, brother. Wait and see." Jerry rose, threw his arms clumsily about Charles and rested his head on his shoulder. "I can't even qualify for the high and mighty honor to reshide in the county jail even for one night. Brother, behold your own kith and kin—at least I'm your kith, ain't I, even if I ain't your kin? Behold me, the once-famous All-American knock-kneed, pigeon-toed, hammered-down, cross-eyed, son-of-a-gun who now hash to stand on his tiptoes to touch the bottom of hell. How the mighty hash fallen!" His sobs suddenly turned into hiccups. Charles was startled

140

by the unearthly siren of the police wagon approaching. When he went to the door he was aware of curious faces peering out of windows all along the street. Crowds of children returning from school soon were clustering around the paddy-wagon. Two magnificent-looking young men clad in resplendent uniforms of the law descended from the car.

Charles Maxwell and his "patient" were at the entrance awaiting them. Jerry had ceased his weeping, but his hiccups were continuing unabated, and his unnaturally bright eyes had a look almost of amusement in them as he watched the men approach.

"Where's your man?" the policeman asked.

"Here he is, officer. As you see, he is very drunk."

"How drunk?" One officer eyed Jerry skeptically. "Come down here in the yard and walk across the grass."

Jerry walked a remarkably straight line.

"Try it again," commanded the officer.

Again the patient walked across the grass, wobbling only slightly.

"Sorry, we can't take him. We only take them when they have committed some crime or are dangerously violent," said one of the officers, and started back to the car. Charles grabbed him by the arm.

"I thought it was your business to lock up men like this," he protested.

"In prohibition days we did. But now there are so many if we took in one fourth of them there would be no room for anyone else." They slammed the car door and sped away.

"Shee—snobs!" snorted Jerry. "Nothing but snobs. Shee me, Mishter Magswell, I can't even touch the bottom of hell," and he sat down abruptly on the sidewalk, helplessness in every angle of his thin frame.

The school children with eyes and mouths wide open still stood gazing and snickering. Maxwell thought to himself, "Suppose he had been a T.B. victim. Would they leave him in the gutter like this?" Then, lifting Jerry to his feet, he said briskly,

"Come on, Jerry. Your room in the manse is waiting for you. We can pretend it's a hospital. It has a strong door."

"And a lock? Remember, lock up your likker, after just two more drinks? Got a lock? Got a key?" Jerry raised hopeful, though bleary, eyes.

"Yes, I have a key to the room and I promise to keep you locked up for three days. You must promise you won't fight and you won't get mad. Please, my young friends, clear the way."

"I'll promise! I'm a hammered-down, knock-kneed, pigeon-toed—" and his monologue continued without pause until they reached the house.

As Maxwell entered the house with Jerry, his housekeeper, who had arrived early to prepare dinner, met him at the door.

"Some distinguished guests," she whispered excitedly. "Mr. Eton and two men from New York. I put them in the front parlor." She broke off and stared aghast at Jerry.

"Tell them I'll be with them in a minute, as soon as I get Jerry upstairs," and Charles held open the door for the latter to walk in. As Charles turned to close the door, Jerry suddenly quickened his stride and followed Mrs. Bailey straight into the parlor where she had gone to notify the guests. When Charles over-took his patient, he was shaking hands pump-handle style with one of the bewildered guests from New York.

"Pleashed to meet you, your highness," Jerry was saying to the newcomer. Then he turned and suddenly embraced Arnold Eton and patted him on the cheek. Arnold's face went white and the cold look came over it that Charles had never been able to forget after seeing it for the first time. Charles looked away before its steel shaft was leveled on him.

"Pardon my friend," Charles addressed the two astonished strangers. "This is my college boy helper. If you will excuse me for a moment I will take him to his room."

And slipping his arm in the arm of Jerry he escorted him to the stairs. When Charles got him to his room, Jerry slumped down on a chair, his legs sprawling out in front, acute suffering on his unkempt, bloated face. The radio had been left on, and the announcer was saying, "This is the Mutual Broadcasting System, Station WQQ: Here's the news, but first a word from the sponsor—Drink Antonelli's Vermouth. It makes your cocktail the bright spot of the day."

Even the air waves are organized against him, thought Charles. Not even in his own room, in a minister's home, is Jerry protected against the greed of the liquor interests.

When Charles returned, the guests were still standing, not having resumed their seats. It was as if they had been frozen on their feet by the sudden onslaught they had just experienced. Eton's crisp voice broke the silence.

"Mr. Maxwell, this is Dr. Caxton, director of the Ministerial Retirement Fund of New York City." Knives shone out of the eyes Arnold fixed upon him. "And Dr. Parkham, who is to address the union meeting of the churches Sunday afternoon on the theme, 'The High Place of the Church Today.' I thought it better taste not to introduce them until your—your helper was disposed of."

"Be seated, gentlemen," smiled Maxwell, cordially. "I am honored to meet you."

"Rather a strange employee you have," continued Eton sternly.

Back in his mind Maxwell heard the old phrase singing: "He mingled with publicans and sinners."

"Yes, strange and unusual," said Charles gravely. "Now can you tell me the purpose of this visit?"

"We wanted to know," said Reverend Caxton, clearing his throat nervously, "if we could use your pulpit Sunday morning, and your auditorium for a mass meeting in the afternoon?"

"Gladly! Gladly!" was Charles' quick response.

"That is all we wanted to know," said Eton, as he rose to leave. The others followed.

The following Sunday Dr. Caxton gave the morning sermon and Dr. Parkham addressed the afternoon union meeting which was also held in First Church. Arnold Eton attended both these services. But he never set foot in that church again.

CHAPTER 19

"Blessed are the meek, for they shall inherit the earth."

FOR THREE DAYS Charles managed to care for his "invalid." Whenever he left the house he locked Jerry in his room as he had promised. The meals he prepared were very simple —but for dinner each day when Mrs. Bailey came to prepare the meals they both fared well.

Saturday night when Charles gave her the week's wage, however, she told him abruptly that she had found another place.

"When I offered to get the suppers for you, Mr. Maxwell, I thought I was coming to a manse and not an alcoholic ward," was her only comment, but her pursed lips and averted eyes told Charles more than her words. "Mrs. Eton offered me good wages for full time work so I'm going there."

So the Etons were not only leaving his church—they were taking his housekeeper, too, Charles thought in good-humored despair.

"How about it, Jerry?" he asked after Mrs. Bailey had gone. "Can we make out alone?"

"Mr. Maxwell," said Jerry seriously, "I'm going to be very frank with you. Old John Barleycorn has got me down deeper than you know. If I hadn't come to you three days ago I would have jumped in the river. In three days you have pulled me out of that tailspin. Now I'm O.K. And to prove it I am going to the class play tonight. I can help you now, and I am going to start by ceasing to be an invalid. I know Mrs. Bailey left on account of me, and I'm awful sorry." His eyes brightened. "But I'm swell now, really."

"But I thought you said it would take a week to get the alcohol out of your system," Charles protested. "Hadn't I better play jailer for three more days and be sure? In case of doubt, you know, it's always better to play safe."

"But there is no doubt! I *am* safe!" the boy's eyes gleamed.

"But, Jerry!" Charles began, and then hesitated. An inner voice deep inside was shouting to him, "The boy is play-acting. Don't trust him."

"See here," Jerry exclaimed, gripping Charles' arm. "You believe in the power of faith—why don't you practice it on me?"

"All right," said Charles, relenting, but still inwardly dubious. "Go ahead. I'll trust you."

"Am I a softie?" he asked himself when the door had closed. "Poor fellow. I hope he has a good time tonight. What a fight he is making! Good Lord, do protect him!"

At two o'clock that night Charles awoke. A strange uneasiness filled him. He put on his robe and went to Jerry's room. The bed was untouched. He shivered from head to foot as he returned to his room. Why had he let him go! Why?

By morning he had asked himself the question a thousand times. Just as he was sitting down to a scant breakfast, Jerry staggered in—dead drunk.

Charles got him to his room and helped him to bed.

"I am sorry, Jerry," he said, "but I'll have to keep you locked in for a whole week, I guess."

When Charles got back from his calls that evening Jerry wasn't in shape for supper. He was still in a stupor, sprawled motionless across the bed, his breathing heavy.

Charles stood for a long time looking helplessly down at the boy, as worries began to pile up in his mind. After all, he knew next to nothing about the care of alcoholics—did they always sleep like this? Should he call a doctor? Could it be something worse than liquor—maybe dope—that had so extinguished Jerry's consciousness?

Ineffectually he smoothed the tousled black hair back from Jerry's forehead, tried to straighten the pillow and sheet. Jerry turned restlessly at the touch, and flung an arm up, only to let it fall limp again off the edge of the bed. Charles straightened, encouraged somewhat by this slight response. Then abruptly he knelt beside the rumpled bed and prayed in the silence. "Father, this is your child—your child—"

He was aroused from his meditation by the shrill sound of the telephone. He hurried downstairs to hear the soft and urgent voice of Frances.

"I am on the beam for you tonight, good and strong, praying for the right kind of housekeeper to come quick. I was at Eton's this afternoon and found Mrs. Bailey is working for them. I can't get you off my mind."

"Why be concerned about me?" he returned with a feeble attempt at badinage. "Remember I am not really alone."

Quick as a whip came the reply, "You and your college boy help! Such help! It's nonsense, running a house without a woman's touch. Remember, you belong to the church, and don't have any business—"

"See here!" he broke in. "Don't you slam us men-folks like that."

He rather expected her to return his banter. But she didn't. He was surprised at what he next heard. There was a momentary pause and then:

"Charles Sheldon Maxwell, I mean it when I say you have no business to be alone with that college boy. I mean it when I say I am praying for you to find the right housekeeper. Now you pray hard. Please do. Be on the beam. I know God will answer it. Please, please!" And the receiver clicked.

Charles looked at his watch. It was seven o'clock. He went to his room, knelt down and prayed. When he retired that night he lay down with a great sense of comfort and peace. It was nice, being watched over, yes, prayed for. He knew God would answer that prayer.

The snow was falling softly outside the window when he awoke the next morning. After breakfast the kitchen doorbell rang. Puzzled, he went to answer it—the milkman usually came without ringing. When he opened the door he was confronted by a face, positively shining in its blackness. The moment he looked squarely into the bright, glowing eyes he realized that the shine came only partly from the face itself.

"Is you Dr. Maxwell?"

He returned the infectious smile, caught the contagion of something in her eyes, and replied in a mischievous, very undignified way:

"I sho' is!"

She clapped her hands with delight.

"I'se glad you's human!" she exclaimed. "From what they say of you on 'tother side of the tracks, you is a sure saint! Fact is, that's why I'se comin' here."

"Coming here?" he inquired.

"Yes, I'se been sayin' to maself ever since I heerd you was fixin' to follow in His steps, I'se said to maself, 'Melissa,' I says, 'you work for that man. There ain't agoin' to be nothin' you won't do for a man like that.' Now can you tell me, sir, where should I begin?"

"So you up and came?" commented the puzzled Charles. Then a thought struck him. "When did the idea come to you?"

"While I was clearin' up the supper dishes las' night 'bout seven."

"Seven o'clock!" Charles exclaimed, remembering Frances' call.

"Yes, siree, I suddenly remembered a colored family that couldn't find a house to rent. My brother who works as a porter at Union Station, now that he's on the night shift, said he'd found a room nearer his work than when he stays with me. And it sure woulda been a waste—me in that house by maself when other folks needed one so bad! So I said, 'Lord, You's pushin' me right out on the outside and I'se got a deep wish on the inside. Now Lord, when you knock on the outside and pound on the inside at the same time, I knows You mean business.' So I

147

says, 'Thank You, Lord. I'll jest pack up and ask that man that's walkin' in Your steps, does he need a cook and someone to do the scrubbin' and washin' and cleanin' fo' him?' So here I is." The smile widened on the black face as the bright black eyes scanned Charles hopefully.

"Come right in," he exclaimed heartily. "At the top of the back stairs you'll find a room. In the kitchen you'll find this morning's breakfast dishes and last night's supper dishes. The rest of the house you'll find in a mess. Start in anywhere and anyway you wish." Charles paused, regarding the woman thoughtfully. "You're right. God must have sent you."

"I'se all ready to start," and joy was in her rich Ethiopian voice, "but I won't move in totalitarian till tomorrow when my brother will help bring my things over, if you don't mind."

Charles reassured her,—then went on hesitantly, "I have a— an invalid college boy staying with me. It has taken a lot of time looking after him—that's the reason for the mess."

After he had explained the lay of the kitchen to her she said,

"Now, Mr. Maxwell, just tell me things you like to eat and I'll do the marketin', the plannin', and the cookin'. You give all your time to walkin' in His steps. I can't tell you how glad I is I come here." She grinned up at him. "You jest go on about the Lord's business."

As Charles went into the front room he was filled with a great peace. As he sat down to read the paper this new peace seemed to fill the room. He laid the newspaper down and closed his eyes. "Thank You, thank You, thank You, dear Father!"

Fifteen minutes later he aroused himself from the deepest and richest meditation he had ever had. He looked down at the floor where the paper had fallen from his hands.

"I must drop this paper. I must reserve this precious morning hour for prayer and meditation. The world news can wait till evening. I *must* start every day with God."

From the kitchen came the rich, contralto notes of a born singer. Full-throated and free, the voice rose, subsided, rose again, filled the house.

"Strange," he thought, "how a Negro's voice carries overtones and undertones no other voice can carry. And this is an unusual voice—a wonderful voice!"

It was a spiritual he had never heard before. She and her brother evidently must not have been long out of the deep South. Only there did one hear such a song as this:

"Oh brother, you should have been thar,
Oh brother, you should have been thar,
Oh brother, you should have been thar,
When His Love comes atricklin' down.
Oh, ask, ask, ask and ye shall receive,
Oh, knock, and the door shall be opened
Seek, seek, seek and ye shall find,
When His Love comes atricklin' down."

There was a pause as he heard her piling up plates.

"I wish she'd sing it again," he thought.

"Oh sister, you should have been thar,"

And so the song ran on and on with "mother" next, and then "cousin" and then "preacher."

"This is wonderful!" he thought as he walked to the church. "Some way I must contrive for her to sing that to my church. What will Frances think? She's gotten herself a rival!" Frances' beautiful face seemed to fill the room. "Bless her sweet heart. Her prayer surely worked! I must call her the moment I reach the office." And he could hardly wait till he could get her on the phone.

After breakfast each morning it became his habit to straddle a kitchen chair and rest his arms on its back and talk with Melissa a while as she washed the dishes.

"Yes, sir, I should say I do come from the deep South—down Livingston-way, Alabama. We knows hundreds of spirituals you folks never heerd up no'th, I reckon. I could sing all day and nevah run out. My Grandmammy taught me. I don' know where she got 'em. From her mammy mos'ly, and othe' colo'd folks all 'round." Melissa chuckled warmly, "Mos'ly they was born in her, I reckon." Charles' smile encouraged her to go on.

"I was a troublesome chile. I had temp'ament. But after I growed up and my young man lef' me a grass widow and I was alone without a chick or chile, I knew I had to get close to God. Yes, I got religion, but not in the shoutin' way we do in our church down thar. I learned a lot 'bout practicin' the presence of the Lawd."

"You did what?" asked Charles, puzzled.

"Yes sir, practicin' the presence of the Lawd Jesus," she went on. "It isn't a noisy thing, but a quiet thing—leastways, to me it is. 'Course, they is lots of rhythm to it, and a heap of singin' will help—but the real down-to-business practicin' is a quiet, every-day thing. It's somethin' nobody hardly ever does—least of all the ones who talks most 'bout it. And that's why when I heard there was a preacher who was really practicin' it I says, 'He's the man I'm workin' for.' "

"You embarrass me by such high anticipation—"

"Don't get embarrassed, Mister Maxwell,—I'm not really workin' for you," she replied matter of factly. "You is only His deputy. The Man I'm really workin' for is the Man Upstairs. But as long as you's tryin' to walk in His steps, you'se got first call on my time and work. That's been what I'se been tryin' to do for a long time—walk in His dear steps."

"Would you mind telling me how you do it?" asked Charles, deeply interested.

Turning to face Charles, and leaning against the sink as she dried her hands, she said slowly, "Well, after hearin' all the preachers tell me how to be good and follow Him—I found so many ways of followin' Jesus that my heart got all filled up with the confusion of it. So I jest forgot all the things the preachers said and the books said that was confusin' me and jest gave my-self wholly to God and asked Him to take away my sins. I tole Him I'd always be slippin' and fallin' if He didn't holt tight of me. I jest gave Him all my love and He tole me over and over that He was right beside me, hoverin' over me, yes, right inside me."

Charles was silent, held in the spell of her expressive voice and face, her child-like sincerity.

She folded the towel carefully and hung it up, then turned to gaze out the kitchen window at the first snowfall of the year. "Sometimes He's so real and so close right while I'm workin' that it's an interruption when I go to church. Then when everybody is singin' and a half-dozen is shoutin' they found the Lawd, the Lawd Himself is driven out of maself. Now I learned to go to church and rejoice in everybody's way of findin' God." She turned away from the window and faced Charles again, the infectious smile brightening her broad features. "But I finds Him best in washin' the dishes and pans."

CHAPTER 20

"Verily I say unto you, I have not found so great faith, no, not in Israel."

M ELISSA SEEMED to be the right doctor for Jerry. Her good cooking was the best possible medicine for his body, and her singing the best possible music to reach his soul. Often when Charles returned after an evening meeting he found Jerry at the piano while Melissa filled the air with song. Between her deeply religious spirituals and the spiritual atmosphere of the manse, the boy seemed to have recaptured his grip on himself. And to Charles' delight, all his spare time he gave to his studies, making up for lost time.

With a great sense of well-being Charles was working in his study at the church one blustery afternoon in the last days of November, as the whirling snowflakes fell outside his window, when President Egbert Page entered unannounced, dusting the snow from his shoulders and shaking his hat against his side.

"Another emergency call, Mr. Maxwell," said the President urgently as he took the chair Charles indicated. "This time it's not a football rally, but a football casualty. Young Harlan Douglas got a scab torn off his knee in the last game of the season from a wound that he thought was nicely healed, and now infection has set in in its most virulent form. They've taken him to the hospital with blood poisoning, in a very serious condition. The doctors say it must be amputation or death. And the last report was that he is not in condition to stand the shock of amputation."

"What are they going to do about it?" anxiously queried Charles.

"Nothing," sighed Page, with a hopeless gesture. "It is now out of their hands. They told Mr. and Mrs. Douglas that it is only a question of time, and this afternoon they told Harlan himself exactly what his condition is. I've been to see him just now. He says he is willing to die if that is the Lord's will. 'But before I give up,' he said, 'I'd like to talk to Mr. Maxwell.' Then he added, 'Remember Mr. Maxwell's talk? When you are pushed back against the goal-line and it's too late to plunge or pass, you can always punt. If he would only come and see me right away and just give me another little pep talk, I'm sure I could get the old fight back again. Do you think he would come?' I said, 'I'm sure he will.' So here I am!"

Charles leaped to his feet, seized his hat and coat, and said, "You drove, did you?"

"My car is right out here," Page exclaimed. "And the engine's going."

They disregarded all speed laws as they sped through the swirling blizzard.

"The only hope lies in prayer." President Page had to speak loudly above the rattle of the windshield wiper. "The entire Lincoln student body will be prostrated with grief if he dies. It will be a terrible shock."

"It will be a shock to the students if he doesn't recover," said Charles thoughtfully as the car hurried on, "and it will be an equal shock to some of my church members if he does recover. I have been told by some that I must put an end to this healing business!"

"Will that knowledge affect you any in this case?"

"None whatever," said Charles firmly. "If the boy lives it will be no work of mine but of the Father who sent me on this errand."

"Isn't it strange," said Mr. Page, shaking his head sadly, "that there are some so-called Christians who would be shocked to have any of the teachings of Jesus questioned, and as equally shocked to have any of them practiced?"

"I am a little surprised," said Charles, "that the doctors told Harlan he was going to die. Do they do that usually?"

"The doctors so admired his courage that they knew that was the way he would want it. And they were right. He said he could take it. But he says he has a sneaking idea that God wants something else." Page took his eyes from the road for a moment to smile confidently at Charles. "So instead of making his will he is sending for you."

"Are his parents there?"

"Yes, they have been at his side night and day."

"I should like to see them for a few minutes alone first."

"That can be arranged. They're anxious to see you."

The waiting-room of the hospital was filled with silent college students, their grave faces making a strange sort of lane for the two men to walk between. Charles noticed many faces brighten as he passed.

At door 102 Mr. Page halted.

"I will bring the parents out to see you first," he whispered. A moment later the father and mother, their drawn faces plainly showing the strain of the past two days, stood before him.

"Could we go into some side room?" asked Charles in a quiet voice.

"I think it would be all right for you to use the superintendent's office," said the nurse who stood behind them. "He will be out for another hour."

It was an office rather than a sanctuary, but it gave the privacy Charles wanted.

"There are three ways in which you parents can help," he began at once. "First, you can love the boy, and love is a tremendous thing. But in this hour of supreme crisis you must love him in a very high way. You must put his highest good first, and foremost—not your own little good. If the glory of heaven and its new opportunities is the supreme good for your boy, you must be willing to let him go into that bliss. Are you?"

154

Mrs. Douglas nodded, stifling her sobs, her face on her husband's shoulder while her right hand clutched at the lapel of his coat. Mr. Douglas grimly stared straight ahead and gave a slight nod also. Tears glistened in the corners of his eyes.

"Now because all of us believe Harlan has some real work for the Kingdom to do on this earth," continued Charles, "will you two agree together that if God wants him in the Kingdom you will do your best to make your home as much of an expression of the Kingdom of heaven on earth as you possibly can, so that in giving him now to the Heavenly Kingdom the Lord can choose whether to take him there or leave him here? Will you?"

Again they nodded, and Mr. Douglas ejaculated in a thick voice, "O God yes, yes!"

"That means there must be perfect harmony and love between you two."

Mrs. Douglas' eyes opened very wide.

"Strange you should say that. There hasn't been that perfect harmony always—in the past—has there, Bill?" She took his hand and clasped it between her two hands. "But there is now, complete. This trouble has seemed to sweep away everything that used to separate us."

"There is no couple that love each other in such loyalty as we do now," said Mr. Douglas, putting his arm around his wife.

"All right, you love your boy, you release him. There remains one thing more. Can you trust him utterly in God's hands?" Charles picked up his Bible and opened it to the 91st Psalm, as the eyes of the couple followed his every move.

"Now I am going to ask you to lay your boy—lay this situation—right now—on these promises of God. Just lay your hand upon this open Bible—but don't lay Harlan here if you are going to take him up again," he cautioned. "Can you leave him here on the promises, say, for this night—can you go off in peace and trust God for just one whole night?"

"We can try," said Mrs. Douglas. She was not sobbing now. As she wiped her cheeks with her handkerchief, Charles saw that the beginning of peace had come to her.

"Good, good!" exclaimed Charles, holding out the Bible. Each laid a hand upon it and all three closed their eyes and bowed their heads.

"Now God," prayed Charles aloud, "You have the burden entirely. We have given Harlan back to You, and You are capable of doing what is best for him. We trust You completely, Father, to take care of Your child. Yours is the love and the power and whatever happens, Yours will be the glory. Amen." Raising his head, he smiled at the couple who stood in each other's arms, heads bowed, as if each leaned equally on the other. "All is well," he thought gratefully.

"Now you stay here and rejoice. I'll go in and see your boy alone."

When he entered the sickroom, a pretty nurse was mechanically freshening up the flowers in the vases on the table and window seat.

"I'm so glad you came," said Harlan, breathing heavily. "I'm counting on you, Pastor."

"Do you remember my talk in chapel last month?" asked Charles, smiling.

"Do I! I think it won the game for us."

"Well, we're going to play the real game right now, my boy, the biggest game you ever played. Are the teams ready? All right—kick off—let's go!"

Harlan's eyes were on Charles. They seemed to be catching a new light.

"I'm awfully weak, Pastor. Won't you just keep talking—about the game—let me listen. It puts the old pep back in me."

"All right, my boy." Charles took a relaxed position in the bedside chair. "We are up against our own goal-posts—our backs to the wall. Harlan Douglas is called back to punt. It's fourth down and ten yards to go. No chance to plunge, dangerous business to pass—all we can do is punt. Remember what I called punt? *Relinquish.* Let go and let God. Let go and give over. You are not giving up, mind you, my lad, you are just giving *over.* Give yourself completely over into the hands of the Father to do whatever He knows is best for you. Trust Him completely, utterly, perfectly."

Charles paused for a moment to let the thought penetrate, then leaned forward in the chair, his eyes on the distance as if he really saw what he described.

"There goes the ball—a beautiful punt! The most perfect punt I ever saw. Just see the ball go sailing down the field! Remember,—the opponent is weak, has no power except the power we give him. He has no power to destroy except as we give him power. He has no power in himself. Give him the ball and see him drop it. Now close your eyes, and I'll put this all into a prayer."

The nurse who had been listening, motionlessly, to these words, now started to leave, then instead, closed the door and walked over to the other side of Harlan's bed and knelt with arms folded on the coverlet, head on her hands.

"Dear Lord," began Charles, "we avail ourselves this hour of Jesus' promise that wherever two or three come together and agree asking *anything* in His name it will be done. We agree, O Father, in asking for Harlan's complete recovery. We feel that he has important work to do for the Kingdom. But Father, we leave it all up to You. He is Your son, not ours, and Your love for him is greater than any we could bestow. Your power is infinite, unlimited, it could easily bring him back. And so, Father, we relinquish him utterly into Your power, to do with him as You please, in *any* way You please, either in heaven or on earth—all for Your Kingdom, Your power and Your glory. Amen."

After a long silence Charles said, "It seems that the Lord is telling me to place my hand upon your leg. I never had such a strong compulsion before. Would you mind?"

"Go ahead," Harlan whispered. He feebly started to remove the sheet.

"No, I'll reach right under it."

Then he noticed that the nurse was still kneeling. She had not moved a muscle.

The touch of the fevered flesh caused Charles momentarily to start. Then he slid his other hand under the sheet and held the leg gently in both hands. In ten minutes the fever seemed to be lessened. In a little while the flesh seemed normal. Harlan had fallen into a sound sleep.

Charles rose. The nurse smiled at him, her eyes radiant with tears.

"Please forgive me for staying, but I felt such tremendous faith when you first began speaking that I *knew* I wouldn't bother you. Did I?"

"You were a great help, dear girl."

She spoke in an awed whisper. "I never felt the power of God so close before."

She went toward the door, then paused with her hand on the doorknob. "Won't you come someday and—and talk to the nurses? I don't know of anything that could happen to this hospital that would be more wonderful!"

CHAPTER 21

"What went ye out into the wilderness to see? A reed shaken by the wind?"

CONDENSING AND "DEHYDRATING" of the crime news and relegating it to an inside page of the *Raymond News* had not materially reduced the list of its subscribers. The spiritual features, chief of which had been the prominent place on the first page of the meditation and prayer for the day, and the two full pages each Monday morning given to generous reporting of the sermons preached the day before, and above all, the human interest stories of sacrifice and heroism, had actually tended to increase circulation rather than diminish it.

But now Editor Norman announced in a startling editorial that he was going to embark upon a policy that would put to a final test whether a newspaper edited as Jesus would run it could live without going into bankruptcy in a modern world.

The new policy, Richard Norman announced, was the printing of the news behind the news. He promised to keep away from personalities. He assured his readers that he was not turning his paper into a scandal sheet. He wanted facts behind the facts and the real causes behind the effects. The Nuremburg trials, which were then beginning, furnished him the first opportunity to test out how this new policy would be received.

The American reporters who were permitted to be on hand at these trials found all outgoing reports were censored and the most significant parts of the reports could not reach the public eye. Through his various journalistic contacts Norman had plenty of avenues to receive the inside information and when he began to publish it a veritable cyclone broke around his head. One of the sensational reports was that the German army leaders had committed most of their atrocities under orders, whereas those who made all these deeds possible, the men who actually financed the whole movement of Hitler, were so interlocked with British and American industries that they were going to get off scot free. One startling statement was that Neville Chamberlain, prime minister of England, had almost a million dollars invested in the Krupp Munition factories. Similiar actions following other wars had made present wars possible. Another item of news that had not been allowed to reach the American press was a frank statement of the utter cynicism that pervaded those watching the proceedings. The Americans and British present all knew of atrocities inflicted by Russians, and Russians knew of similiar ones, inflicted by Anglo-Americans that were almost as deserving of punishment as some of those inflicted by Germans. Norman himself was told by a marine how his corps had found it necessary upon invading some islands in the Southern Pacific to shoot every man, woman and child, because they never could tell which little child might be concealing a hand grenade to blow them up.

"The real criminal is War itself," wrote Norman, "and the tragic irony in the whole affair is the way the conscientious objectors who opposed this real criminal, War, have been treated as only real criminals should be treated. We, a so-called Christian nation, have levied on the young men of belief far longer sentences in prison than on persons convicted of traffic in white slaves or the peddling of narcotics. And yet we call ourselves a land of freedom."

In an editorial on the Four Freedoms he opened with this statement: "The war is over, but we don't know yet who won it. We fought to win four freedoms: freedom from want, freedom from fear, freedom of speech and freedom of religion. If there are any persons still in prison because of their religious beliefs, if there are any persons starving for food, if there are any persons living in fear of another war, if there are any persons not allowed to speak their convictions—then we have not won the war. And as we look about us in our own country, and take an occasional peep abroad, we are convinced that never in history was a war so completely lost as this one we entered into December 7, 1941."

He followed this with a startling statement: "I think as a matter of fact that the world would have actually been better off if our nation had stayed out of both wars entirely. Twice in one generation we have let ourselves be pushed and pulled into foreign wars. The world is infinitely worse off today than if they had never been fought. The condition of the world is vastly more precarious than it would have been had the United States maintained her neutrality in both conflicts.

"The United States is today pouring one billion, three-hundred million dollars into 'bridgeheads' around Russia, including two little worthless islands in the Pacific, Saipan and Okinawa, arming them like giant pistols aimed at Russia's only warm water port on the Pacific. Then why are we surprised that Russia doesn't trust us?"

The editorial ended as follows:

"If our government took the one billion, three-hundred million dollars they are sinking into holes of hate, and turned it over to the training and sending of emissaries of love to all the Asiatic countries, including Russia, and if these men were trained to render service in agriculture, medicine and education, such a bridge of friendship would be built that no war or even rumor of war with the United States would ever stir their hearts again. Just recall the gift that the United States made to China when they returned the Boxer Indemnity of twenty-million dollars, on the interest of which China has sent two hundred chosen students each year to be trained in American ways of life. This tiny gift, only one-fourth the cost of a battleship, only one-third of one percent of the sum we are sinking into arming these two tiny islands, has rendered the United States more immune from attack from China than if we had a thousand battleships patrol-

161

ling the Pacific Ocean and a million troops on constant guard along the Pacific coast."

Articles and editorials of this kind against war in general and the last war in particular aroused such resentment among those who prided themselves upon their patriotism that they cancelled their subscriptions. It became a common rumor that Norman must be receiving money from the Kremlin.

The loss of over one-fourth of his subscribers was a serious blow, but he could still weather that storm financially. When it came to advertising, however, the real financial blow fell. The three department stores in Raymond that were the leading rivals of Jonathan Wright, all controlled by New York capital, immediately ceased all advertising. Many locally-owned stores followed suit. Although great pressure was put upon Jonathan Wright from influential Eastern friends, the Wright Department Store continued its advertising and even added an extra page or two from time to time. To keep from going to the wall, Norman reduced the paper in size. Thanks to the endowment Miss Virginia Page had left, he was not forced to lower salaries. During the prosperous years of the *News*, Edward Norman, the original owner, had used the income of this endowment for promoting other charities. Now when the need was calling, his son felt justified in using the full income to protect his work. Whether it would suffice to weather the storm was still to be seen.

The fireworks really began, however, when he started attacking the seats of corruption in Raymond itself. Norman began with the slot machines, gambling halls, and illicit sale of liquor and drugs. The big explosion came when he went into a detailed analysis of the hidden machinations of the last city election.

"The Tax Reduction League, which was established by the managers of our three New York-owned department stores and is now presided over by the president of our garment factory, was able this past year to get their entire slate of aldermen elected. This could not have been possible had it not been for the heavy support of the redlight districts. All efforts by forward

162

looking citizens this year to increase the taxes upon downtown property, in order to increase the salaries of teachers, have been frustrated because of the solid front of the mayor and board of aldermen who took office at the last city election. The *News* has just discovered the under-cover work by which this unexpected election result came about.

"Our present city government came into power through an unholy alliance between the Good Government League, which is the self-righteous name chosen by the owners of two-thirds of our taxable real estate in the business district, and the notorious leaders of the underworld. 'There is something rotten in the state of Denmark,'—and equally rotten in the city of Raymond! If you don't believe it, just keep your eyes open, and see if a real orgy of crime won't soon burst upon the city."

The *News* mentioned no names but everyone knew that the president of this League was Arnold Eton, president of the Garment Works and part owner of an entire building block in the city.

Anonymous letters began to come to the editor after that, all carrying threats. Not only was the life of the *News* in peril, but the life of its editor as well. "It seems," said Norman to Charles, "that we both stand in need of prayer."

CHAPTER 22

*"Flesh and blood hath not revealed it unto thee, but
my Father which is in heaven."*

WHAT'S 'A MATTAH with you this mornin', Mistah
Maxwell?" clucked Melissa one Sunday shortly
after Christmas, as she removed Charles' almost
untouched breakfast from the table. "You's as broody as a
settin' hen! You ain't comin' down with somethin', is you?"

Charles smiled into her worried eyes as he put down his coffee
cup and rose to go. "Now, Melissa, don't you worry. I'm not
sick. I'm just—broody, like you said—heavy with some idea—
a great idea, I hope. I need to be alone and quiet—very quiet."

Melissa's eyes crinkled as she grinned back at Maxwell. "You
jest go on and be as quiet as you pleases—maybe you'll hatch
a whole nest-full of ideas!"

He went early to his church study and restlessly read over his
sermon. He had it well in hand—no need to be concerned about
that. But somehow it didn't satisfy him.

"Sawdust," he muttered as he crossed out one entire para-
graph. "Not enough life-blood in it."

He laid the sermon aside and leaned back in his chair, aglow
with a great yearning.

"Give me a spiritual blood transfusion this Sunday morning,
O Lord," he called. "Let Your love flow through me today. Let
Your thoughts speak through my lips. Take me completely cap-
tive to You.—As broody as a broody hen," he mused, smiling to
himself as he remembered Melissa's concern, "Oh, that some-

thing great and grand might be hatched into birth this morning!"

Then he knew he could not preach the carefully prepared sermon lying before him. The real sermon might rise from its ashes; no doubt the living coals smoldered within or from whence rose the present warmth? But his was not the living breath to touch the coal to incandescence. Only the Holy Spirit could do that. He knew that the right words, the living words, would come to him only as he stood before the congregation. Succeed or fail, he knew that he could not preach in any other way that day.

"Be not anxious how or what ye shall say, for the Holy Spirit shall teach you in that very hour what ye ought to say."

He was in that mood, listening, waiting, open to the very thoughts of heaven when the choir leader came in to tell him it was almost time to begin. Charles looked at him in amazement. Where had the hours gone! How long had he sat there!

Still he did not rise; the sense of something greater than himself still possessed him.

"I will join you presently. I must be alone a few minutes longer. Pray for me as I preach this morning. And Henry," he called as the choir leader turned to go, "I see Frances is down to sing a solo this morning from one of the Bach oratorios. Will you ask if she will sing 'The Holy City' instead?"

The other stared at Charles.

"But, Mr. Maxwell, Miss Page *never* sings without long and meticulous practice," he protested.

"Ask her anyway," interrupted Charles, with a smile. "It would do wonders for my sermon. Tell her I asked for it."

As Charles looked out upon the congregation a great love flowed out from him to all of them. Every man, woman and child seemed bathed in glorious light that Sunday morning. Everyone seemed tremendously important, everyone, even the little children, appeared absolutely indispensable, everyone seemed ecstatically beautiful. All seemed to be caught up in the light that shone through the great window where Jesus gathered His happy lambs about Him. What a wonderful world God had made if we only could see it as it truly is—a veritable heaven right here on earth! And still he did not know what he was going to say.

Yet he had no concern. If ideas failed him, he could fall back on his written manuscript. No—he could not preach those written words today, those words written in cold ink! The only words his lips could utter today would be words flowing like warm blood propelled by a heart on fire. Because his yearning was so great he *knew* that God would send him the words when the time came.

And now the time was practically at hand! Frances was about to sing the solo that was to precede his sermon. "Jerusalem . . ." —no! What was she singing? It was the Bach oratorio. Well, perhaps the choir leader hadn't told her. It would have been an imposition anyway, he realized, to ask a singer to change a song at the last moment. Yes, at the *very* last moment. And how well she was singing the solo!

As the voice rang on he paid no heed to the words. He was listening for another Voice—a Voice from Above.

"What shall I preach this morning?" he asked the Father.

When the song was over, while the notes of the organ were slowly dying away, he arose and opened the Bible to the passage that ended with the words, "Blessed art thou, Simon Bar-Jonah: for flesh and blood hath not revealed it unto thee, but my Father which is in heaven. And I also say unto thee, that thou art Peter, and upon this rock I will build my church; and the gates of Hades shall not prevail against it."

"I find myself led this morning to speak of the Eternal Value of Life as the Creator of all the little values," he began. "Eternity begins here and now and goes on forever if we but keep our eyes on God." And then, to his surprise the sermon flowed effortlessly from his lips:

"One day Rip Van Winkle on his way to the Catskill Mountains tarried in the tavern bearing the coat of arms of George the Third. After a deep sleep on the mountain, he returned to find the tavern now bore the coat of arms of George the First— first in peace, first in war and first in the hearts of his country men. When he inquired why the change, he discovered that he had slept through a revolution.

"Today we are sleeping through four revolutions: an economic revolution in Russia and parts of Europe; a racial revolution in the awakening of the dark races; an educational revolution in the campaign of literacy by Frank Laubach; and a scientific revolution in the release of atomic energy. Unless we in the United States awake, the world will leave us behind. The only way we can catch up and harmonize all, is for the Church of America to start a fifth revolution—a revolution of the spirit. If we make Jesus the coordinator of all these revolutions, then instead of chaos crashing down upon us, we shall find the King-dom itself has come."

From that point the sermon preached itself. A passage from the Bible, a reference to recent history, an example of a great saint of the past, all mingled and rolled together in his mind and came forth braided together in a pattern of beauty and power. For a sermon to build itself as it came from his lips in that fash-ion, thrilled him. He felt as though he could go on forever, and was startled when he found he had talked his time out.

He did not go out to shake hands with the congregation that morning. The "broody hen" feeling was still too heavy upon him.

"There is still something to be born, a little residue that didn't come out; something greater than any words could express, than any sermon could bring forth. I must be alone a little longer," and he quietly closed his study door and sank into the big leather chair behind his desk. "Sometimes when the atmosphere is heavy with moisture," he thought, "the mere discharge of a firecracker is sufficient to precipitate the whole sky to pour down in rain. Lord, send the rain."

The church was now empty. Out there alone in the empty pews he could picture the old sexton gathering calendars and readying things up. Alone—in an empty church.

Then the door to his study slowly opened and Frances stood before him. He had never seen her eyes so wide—and so beautiful! Great sorrow and great yearning were in them, each striving for the mastery. In those eyes was contrition, pleading. Charles raised his hand as if to ward off a light too strong for his eyes to bear. Then he could see that Frances mistook the gesture.

"Please, please, don't wave me away," she begged. "I was never more crushed in my life. And to think how I failed you—failed you in the greatest hour since you have been here!"

"Failed me? My dear girl, how did you fail me?" Charles rose and led her to a chair.

"The song! The song you asked me to sing and I refused. In the pride of my voice which must be shown only for its own glory—not for the glory of God!" Sobs shook her slender body as she lifted her head and looked straight into his face, the tears rolling down her cheeks. "Will you ever, ever forgive me?"

"Frances, my dear, there is nothing to forgive. I shouldn't have asked—"

"And to think," she went on, ignoring his words, speaking as a child would speak when no one was around, "and to think that all these weeks I have been longing, longing—till I thought I could hardly stand it—longing to put my hand in yours and climb with you up a high mountain. Today you offered to take my hand and I refused. And you went up the high mountain alone! The highest privilege that ever came into my life I threw away!"

She rose and moved slowly toward the door.

"If there is any way I can ever serve you, I promise I will never fail you again. Never! And when I say never, I mean never!"

Charles' eyes rested upon her. That precipitation he had been waiting for had come. A great, overpowering flood of God's love, a great, impersonal love for this rare girl was on the verge of breaking. He rose slowly and took her by both hands. They were soft hands but firm and very cold. New tears flowed down her cheeks. She swayed toward him. Then collecting herself with an effort she drew away and was gone. The brooding heaviness that had rested on Charles was gone, too. It was as though something had actually been born. Something in her and something in him.

A great sorrow or a great love!

Presently the sexton came in, cleaning up. He paid no attention to Charles, who leaned back in his chair and gazed at the ceiling, still deeply moved by the scene in which he had just been a participant.

"Ay," the sexton said softly as if murmuring to himself, "thae was life-blud i' that sermon—lots of life—it twae a livin' thing."

Not until he prepared to go did he seem aware of Maxwell's presence. Then he turned at the door and said:

"Say, Parson, I believe Miss Frannie is goin' to put heaven into her singin' come next Sunday. I saw her ee when she went oot just now."

"Eyes!" murmured Charles. "He saw heaven in her eyes! Heaven!"

CHAPTER 23

"If they have persecuted me they will also persecute you."

CHARLES MAXWELL was awakened from a sound sleep by the shrill ringing of the front doorbell. Dazedly rubbing his eyes, he turned on the bedside lamp and peered at his watch. Two A.M.! Who could be calling this time of night? The prolonged ringing ceased. Loud pounding on the door followed.

Suddenly wide awake, his heart beating fast, he slipped into his bathrobe and slippers and hurried downstairs. The light at the top of the stairs projected his long shadow before him. It touched the front door like a bobbing ghost. As he swung open the door, the figure of Richard Norman staggered in, blood covering one side of his face.

"My God, man!" exclaimed Charles, aghast. "What happened! I'd better call a doctor!"

"Doctor, hell!" said Norman. "This is only a scratch. But oh, the bump on top of my head! I was knocked silly for free. Ugh!"

Charles helped him to the big cushioned chair in the sitting room and hurried to the kitchen, returning immediately with basin and towel.

"When you've washed my scratch, lay that cool cloth on the top of my head," Norman mumbled as Charles gently washed the blood stains from his face. "It must have been a big club they used on me. It certainly was lights out for awhile."

"Tell me what happened." Charles had discovered the cut below the temple. "This might have been serious," he muttered.

"A mob attacked my plant tonight—about midnight. Broke all the windows, overturned presses and scattered type to the four winds. Lucky the paper is small now!" he laughed bitterly.

"Who were they?" asked Charles, as he dipped the towel in the basin.

"It seems there was a meeting somewhere and Arnold Eton addressed it on Patriotism and the American Way of Life. I don't think he deliberately stirred them to action, but he certainly didn't hold them back. He said some nasty things about you, too."

"How do you know? Were you there?"

"One of my reporters was. He said Eton branded us all as Communists. He said this love-way we were preaching was worse than appeasement—it was treason. He called me a fellow-traveller, and suspected that I was receiving my orders from Moscow. That I was out to destroy the American Way of Life." Norman winced as Charles continued to bathe the wound, but went on excitedly, pausing after every few words to get his breath. "Before he had told me half of what Eton had said, the mob began storming the place. But they especially accused me of attacking the one clean city government we ever had!" Suddenly he dropped his head against the back of the chair and closed his eyes. "Say—if you don't mind I believe I will take the davenport for awhile."

When Charles returned with fresh water, Norman thanked him profusely, his face unnaturally pale against the dark pillows of the couch.

"But I haven't told you yet the thing that disturbs me the most! I called the police when I heard the windows breaking—" he paused for breath.

"What about the police?" Charles dampened the towel again.

"They laughed at me. The more I pleaded, the more they laughed. I think there was some collusion there."

"In that case," exclaimed Charles, "it is time to take off our coats and roll up our sleeves."

"The old Yale Spirit, eh?" Richard Norman grinned, some

of his ruddy color returning. "That makes me feel better already. When shall we begin?"

Just then the telephone rang. It was the worried voice of Andrew Marsh. "Pardon for calling at such a gosh-almighty hour. I just heard that a mob broke into Norman's plant and played the dickens with it. One of the foremen called me up just now and said that Norman was badly beaten up, and now he has disappeared. He's afraid of some foul play."

"Rest easy," Charles broke in. "Norman escaped and is here right now. He is in bad shape, that is true, but he needs a doctor more than a lawyer. Come over, if you can."

"Sure, gosh, yes!" and the receiver was hung up with a bang.

But when Marsh arrived Norman was too fagged out to talk.

"Get me to bed," he whispered, "I'll do my talking tomorrow. I'm too tired to think."

The two men helped Norman up stairs. There they removed his coat and his shoes and tie and unloosed his collar and tucked him in the spare bed for the night.

"I think it's only a slight concussion," said Charles when they came downstairs again. "He'll sleep it off. His pulse is almost normal. Now tell me what you know."

"Well, I went to the Good Government League meeting that started all this off," and Marsh sank back in the chair Norman had occupied when he first came in. "It was a vicious thing from beginning to end. Several speeches were made, but Eton's was worst. He laid it on thick. Everyone who opposed the profit system was a Communist. The unfortunate part about it was that one thing Eton said was true, and this gave the illusion that everything else he said was true."

"What was that?"

"The true thing that he kept reiterating was that the crime wave predicted by Norman hasn't broken forth. He was right when he said that the past months have been more free from crime than any similar period in the city's history."

Charles nodded. "That puts Norman in a pretty poor spot as a prophet, I admit."

"Let us drop Norman for a bit," and Marsh rose from his chair and took two long steps over to the mantel. After two futile attempts to strike a match, a flame finally burst forth and he lighted his cigar. Then turning to face Charles who had relaxed in his large chair, he said between vigorous puffs. "I, too, have felt the flattening power of the steam roller. I don't know if you knew it, but I have been in line for some time for the presidency of the railroad I have been serving for so long."

He withdrew his cigar and folded his arms and looked down at Charles under knitted eyebrows.

"Well, Maxwell, that balloon has burst, and Arnold Eton was the moving influence that made it burst. It seems that young tycoon is a bigger figure in the financial world than most of us have realized. It is amazing what a tremendous interlocking of capital interests he inherited from his old man. It appears that among other things he has the dominating control of banking syndicates which controlled this railroad during the long period following the last depression. It seems that my support all through this period of Norman's newspaper program was to him the height of red radicalism. If it had not been for what the board of directors considered a highly creditable record of long service behind me, he would have effected my actual discharge from the company. As it is I have just been demoted."

"Demoted?" exclaimed Charles, amazed. Things were worse than he had dreamed. This news affected him more than what had happened to Norman.

"I am thinking seriously of resigning and going into politics," Marsh went on. "Babcock said he would back me for governor or even for senator. He thinks we have some very weak sisters representing us in those offices right now. Norman would back me with his newspaper,—if there's any newspaper left," he added with a wry face. "I have quite a following already throughout the state."

"Your political plans interest me tremendously," said Charles. "It sounds like putting Christianity into politics."

"All we need," concluded Marsh, seating himself heavily in a chair opposite Charles, "is a fourth man to make up our team, a man who knows the game of politics from the ground up, a veteran who could steer us past the breakers that amateurs might be wrecked by."

"I see," replied Charles, nodding, "I suppose you get your hunch from Jesus' description of the wise steward who was wiser in his field than the 'children of light' were in theirs! Whom do you have in mind?"

"The perfect example in this city of the wise and wily steward Jesus described is Bill Peters."

"Bill Peters!" exclaimed Charles, aghast. "You don't mean the man that Jonathan Wright discharged from his company?"

"Exactly," replied Marsh. "It appears that all the while he was vice-president in charge of operations of the Wright Department Store, he was also ward chairman in his district and a power behind local politics. So, like the wily steward, when he found his job was in danger, he quietly pulled the strings and got appointed chief of police of Raymond. And now by some uncanny power that the rest of us can't explain or account for, he has in the short period of his control, built up the best city police record the city has known. It is already a common saying around the Court House and City Hall that anyone who crosses swords with Bill Peters is committing political suicide."

"Bill Peters!" Charles gasped. "I can hardly believe it!" And long after Marsh had left, Charles was still pondering over the mystery of this strange news.

"I have seen Jim Long changed into a loyal co-worker and supporter of Jonathan Wright," he mused. "Why couldn't I pray for a miracle like that to happen to Bill Peters?"

CHAPTER 24

*"They bind heavy burdens and grievous to be borne
and lay them on men's shoulders."*

WHEN MORNING CAME Norman had recovered sufficiently to be driven to his home. "I'm mighty glad
my wife was away when this happened," he exclaimed. "Unless the Associated Press plays this up she may
not hear about it till she comes back. By then we will be running
full speed again."

That evening at the close of the midweek prayer meeting,
which had been preceded by a splendidly attended church supper, Charles Maxwell was in his study reaching for his hat and
overcoat when he heard Sandy MacIntosh open the door and
enter.

"Ye told me ane day na tae knock when ye haen the jitters,
but tae walk richt i'," the old sexton began, "and as yer door
was closed and I ken ye were alane I walked richt i'. And I do
hope, Parson, that ye dinna hae only jitters tae-day."

"I had them last night, Sandy, but right now, after that grand
prayer meeting I feel as renewed as the eagle. Wasn't this about
the finest witnessing for the power of prayer we have had all
year?"

"Ye're richt, Parson, what I heard o' it. The reason I wes late
wes for exactly the opposite reason. While ye were upstairs
witnessing tae the power o' Gude I wes doon i' the basement
listenin' tae the power o' Beelzebeb. While ye were gettin' cured
o' the auld jitters, I wes gettin' an attack o' some new anes."

Charles sensed something very strange in Sandy's manner,

175

noticing for the first time the unusual brightness of his blue eyes.

"Explain yourself, Sandy. Stop talking in parables."

"Best ye throw off yer overcoat, Parson, and sit doon." Old Sandy shuffled back and turned the key in the door. He drew up a chair beside the table behind which Charles was seating himself, watching the old man's every move with intense curiosity. What on earth did Sandy have on his mind? Sandy lowered himself stiffly into the chair, as the reading lamp made sharp shadows in the lines of his face. When he began speaking again it was in a husky whisper.

"This is verra confidential, Mr. Maxwell, and a lot o' harm wad come tae the man wha tald me if onyane knew whar it cam frae, but I ken I can trust ye and I think ye suld ken about it."

"Fire away," said Charles, leaning attentively closer to Sandy. "Nothing will pass beyond this room."

"Weel, we hae a new policeman on our beat, perhaps ye noticed. He used tae be ane o' the squad that warked the red licht district. Tae-nicht after the kirk supper wes ower, he drapped in for a little han'-out ane o' the ladies haen promised him. While he drank coffee and ate ice cream he bubbled ower tae me. Everyane else haen left the basement and gaen up to the meetin'. Noo remember—ye're na tae tell onyane."

"I remember."

"And especially ye're na tae tell Norman or Marsh. That wad be dynamite."

Charles put both elbows on the table and stared right into the other's eyes.

"What are you uncovering now?" he asked. "Spill it out quick. Of course I will keep your confidence."

"I wull trust ye, Parson. It's about this policeman. He feels demoted, lat doon and is awfu' sore wi' Bill Peters, the new police chief. He says ane month after Bill took charge he shifted narly a' the red-licht squad intae ither parts o' the city, and has been puttin' men there wha are nae better than the people they are tae watch. He says a hale new criminal gang is already

176

comin' intae that district. If it keeps on it wull be a regular sanctuary for the criminal elements o' the hale state."

"What!" exclaimed Charles. "I can't believe it!" Then, puckering his eye-brows he added, "And I suppose you are telling me that we should keep the church carefully locked from now on." One of Charles' bones of contention with the trustees was his insistence on keeping the sanctuary doors unlocked and open to the public day and night, and on this point alone had MacIntosh sided with the trustees against him.

"Na," said the sexton solemnly, "noo the kirk wull be safer than ever."

A cynical smile was Charles' only response to this sally. "Pretty good, Sandy! I suppose you mean that churches will be the safest places. Gangsters will keep far away from them. But won't there be an awful outburst of crime in our city?"

"Just the opposite. We are i' for the safest time, the best-protected time the city wull ever hae. We hae already been havin' proof o' that the past six weeks. Under Bill Peters' regime the city wull be mair crime-free than i' a' its history."

"Quit your joking."

"Na, I mean it," insisted Sandy.

"How can you explain that?"

"I wull let the policeman explain it. And remember, ye're na tae tell on him. 'The criminals o' the State are goin' tae fin' protection here!' he says. 'Protection costs money,' he says. 'Wha gets that money? I do na believe i' hot money,' he says, 'sae I am na ane tae be trusted in that district. That is why I wes moved. Peters is positively uncanny,' he says, 'i' selectin' men. But tak' ma word for it, the little fellows get only the drippin's,' he says. 'A new millionaire wull be i' Raymond i' tae years—a better racket than personnel manager in the Wright Store. And a new kin' of police wull be patrolling the red-licht district, gettin' a lot of extra dough, while I and a lot of honest guys are out.' That is the upshot. That is what I heard while ye folks were prayin'."

"So that accounts for Raymond's crime free record," mused

177

Charles. "Blood money! How can we stop it? What is the next step?"

"Na anither Town Meetin', Parson. That wad blow the roof off. Nather onythin' in the newspaper. A' Norman got for poppin' off wes a smear. If ye got intae this, ye wad wreck the kirk. If ye made ane peep, ye wud be responsible for the murder o' this policeman. He is ane of the disgusted anes; he is already under suspicion, and he is on yer beat."

"Peters wouldn't dare!" Charles asserted vehemently. The picture of the dead Kamada, hostage to fate, came floating before his eyes. One more violent death in this vicinity was unthinkable.

"Peters in na fearfu' o' onythin'," was Sandy's dry rejoinder. "He has everythin' water-tight. The only leak is this Irishman wha told me. And he is scared tae death les' the gang fin' out he talked. A shot in the back and a private lot six-feet lang and six-feet deep wad be his reward. Sae be awfu' carefu', Parson. Peters wad do onythin' for money. I can just hear the protection money rollin' in."

"But Peters' income tax will show it," protested Charles.

"I' can be got around. Treasure buried in a field, if na ither way opens. But his safest bet is his partnership wi' the Tax Reform League o' the city, headed by young Eton."

"Do you mean to tell me that Norman was actually right in his editorials?"

"Aye, a' that rumor wes true about that group of men wha are movin' heaven and earth tae keep the Board of Aldermen loaded with a majority tae block the tax increase on doon-town property urged by the school teachers wha are sae scandalously underpaid. Noo wi' Peters' control o' the red-light district, combined wi' young Eton's control o' the conservative business leaders, they can block thae proposals till doomsday and as reward for this service the influential men i' the city wull squint at ony mistaks Bill maks and insure him protection. Aye, Bill has things stacked sae he could get awa' with murder."

"Not literally?"

"Aye, literally. If he shot this policeman t'morrow his lawyer wad stack the jury wi' some rank 'insiders'—a' respectable business men—and they wad bring i' a verdict of sel'-defense or at maist a little fine o' some kin'."

"Impossible!" ejaculated Charles, aghast.

"Impossible, naethin'! But remember, keep yer mouth locked and yer hoose and kirk unlocked. That is what we a' are goin' tae get under this lily-white administration—protection!"

"But the rest of the world? Where will be their protection?"

"Aye, whar wull be their protection?" Sandy agreed solemnly.

Both sat silent for a moment, the parson staring at the sexton and the sexton staring at the parson. The sexton was the first to break the silence.

"Weel, Mr. Maxwell, I guess when a' the ither doors are locked, the best door tae tak is the door that leads tae Gude."

"Bless you, Sandy," cried Charles. "That is the way we shall surely take—the way of prayer."

CHAPTER 25

"The younger son gathered all together and took his journey into a far country."

ONE MORNING Charles found Jerry packing up all his belongings.

"What are you doing?" he exclaimed. "You aren't leaving me, are you?"

"Yes, Parson," said Jerry, concentrating on what he was doing. "I am sorry to say I am," and he took special pains to avoid the other's eyes. "My pal at the printing plant has an extra cot and wants me to come." His tense voice didn't ring true, somehow. "I thought I had been a care to you long enough, Mr. Maxwell."

"You aren't a care when you are master of yourself, Jerry." Charles checked himself suddenly and seized Jerry's thin shoulders. 'You aren't on a verge of another tailspin, are you? Look at me, Jerry, answer me."

Jerry tried to pull himself loose, then with a shrug of his shoulders, still held in the vise-like grip of the young minister, he stared into his eyes and exclaimed desperately, "I won't have you always, Parson. I've got to stand on my own feet sooner or later, and if I ever do it, now is the time."

"Please, Jerry, stay till the year is over," Charles pleaded, everything in him crying out for the boy to stay. "You aren't a bother. Look what Melissa's cooking is doing for you!"

"No, dammit, let me go!" Tears suddenly welled up in the boy's eyes and he hung his head. "Pardon me, Mr. Maxwell, I wasn't swearing at you. You are the one good man I know—

too good." He sank down on the bed, dropping his head into his hands.

Almost instantly he was up again. "The devil was in me for a minute, Parson, but he's gone now. I am clear and know exactly what I am doing." He now was looking straight into Charles' face, calm and at ease—an almost unbelievable metamorphosis.

"And you still think you should go?"

"I have thought it through and my mind is made up, Parson. I am *sure* I should go. A fellow of my temperament can't stay long in one place. I am more likely to blow up here than I will be if I move."

"You are sure of that?"

"Yes, positive. Your influence, your spirit is wonderful. But you are so high and I am so low it just hurts me to hurt you. Just the *fear* of a tailspin might bring it on." Jerry's eyes seemed to beg Charles for understanding.

"I get you," said Charles. "Some Alcoholics Anonymous men who have been through the mill like you could help you more than I." He gazed wistfully into the other's eyes. "Just a little boy," he thought, "just a little lonely boy." Half an hour later when he saw Jerry leave the house, loaded down with two heavy suitcases, that old sinking at the heart came upon him that he had felt once before.

"I feel all is not well. Why did I let him go? Why, oh, why?"

At one o'clock that night he awoke with the same premonition he had felt the night he found Jerry's bed untouched. "Why?" he found himself saying to himself over and over again, "Why, oh why?" The heavy weight upon his heart almost stifled his breathing. He tossed restlessly for hours. It was not till four o'clock that he finally fell into a fitful sleep.

That morning after breakfast Charles went to the corner drug store to make a purchase. As he waited for the cashier to make the change, his eye fell on the headlines of newspapers stacked on the glass counter.

"A war veteran and senior at Lincoln University committed suicide last night. The body of Jerry Grey was found by his room mate on a cot in the back room of the Roberts Printing Company at 1:30 A.M."

"Take another nickel for this paper," Charles exclaimed, and paper in hand he hurried to the church study, reading as he went. "In Jerry Grey's pocket," the newspaper story continued, "the police found a suicide note that read: 'I was dumped into this world with two strikes against me. Damned unfair, I call it. Been trying to dodge the third strike all my life. I hate the world. All it throws is third strikes—with curves on 'em. Sorry but I struck out.'

"His roommate, Harry Percival, said he knew what he meant. 'The fellow was born unstable, that was the first strike. He had a bad boyhood environment. That was the second strike. But the third strike that struck him out was the newspapers, magazines, motion pictures, billboards, and radio stations that kept old John Barleycorn throwing curves at him night and day. He couldn't open a magazine without liquor ads staring him in the face. He couldn't go to a movie without finding liquor glamorized. He couldn't turn on the radio without hearing the bottle and glass clinking together. This immense advertising,' said Percival, 'was too much for him to withstand. He wasn't as strong as the next guy. He went to the wrong movie last night. And so poor Jerry struck out.' "

The death, the coroner reported, was caused by sleeping powders, a very undramatic form of taking off. Before the day was over the campus was all astir about the tragedy.

Charles kept the telephone line busy trying to locate relatives. An old uncle in a home for inebriates in a distant city was the only relative. Over the phone the old man evinced very little interest.

"Poor kid," was his only comment. "He's better off where he is. Handle the funeral any way you want to. I can't be there," and he hung up.

A consultation with President Page resulted in plans for a simple service later in the week.

When the *Evening News* came out that afternoon, Mr. Norman discussed this incident in detail in a blistering editorial entitled, "Propaganda for Profit."

"Propaganda is the instrument that Greed plays upon to spread its nefarious trade. The immense consumption of liquor would not be possible were it not for the newspapers, magazines, motion pictures, billboards, public carriers and broadcasting companies, which join to forge the link of liquor advertising and propaganda. *The advertising of alcoholic beverages is the greatest cause of our present liquor problem.*

"The time has come to unite our forces, to move as one against the greatest contributing factor in our liquor problem—the liquor ads. It is the huge alcoholic beverage advertising and propaganda program which is teaching old and young in greater and greater numbers to drink.

"In the last World War when there was a great shortage of ships to carry soldiers and supplies to the seat of conflict fast enough, there was always storage space for liquor. It was a common sight to see great wharves laden with barrels of rum and beer awaiting shipment, while thousands of boys in the burning heat of the Southwest area complained because soft drinks were not available and alcoholic drinks always were. Thousands of boys who had never touched a drop in their lives, returned from the War confirmed alcoholics. That was where Jerry formed his habit. No, all the war casualties did not get into the papers. Hundreds of mothers have wished that their boys had died on the battle field rather than returned to the hell which Jerry returned to. Congressmen tell us that no lobby is more powerful than the liquor lobby in Washington, and that no saloon is as active as the Senate Bar.

"Can't we do something to prevent this continual flaunting of liquor drinking, this glorifying of it before the eyes of our boys and girls? This insidious propaganda backed by men who put profits above lives is the 'third strike.' Even Alcoholics Anonymous can't always beat that. Only an aroused American citizenry can."

CHAPTER 26

"You cannot serve God and Mammon."

THE TRAGIC END of Jerry weighed heavily on Charles' heart. Two suicides in one year—and both young men! One overcome by war, the other by alcohol. "My prayers have helped to heal the sick," he brooded, "but war and alcohol are two sicknesses that prayer alone can't heal." Then he recalled the story of Kagawa. While he was "saving the soul" of a young man in Tokyo, Kagawa discovered that this young man's sister was being sold to a geisha house to keep the family from starvation. When he inquired into the causes, he discovered that economic conditions were causing souls to be lost faster than the overworked missionaries could save them. Thereafter Kagawa went about saving souls on the one hand while spreading cooperatives on the other. "Perhaps prevention is the solution," thought Charles.

As the days went by he found himself set on fire with a new message—the America that is to be. If the world was going through four revolutions all at the same time, his own beloved country must not stand still. But where should it go from here? What direction should it take?

He broached this subject to Sandy one morning when the sexton came in to clean his church study.

"How would it do," Charles began thoughtfully to the old Scotchman whose gnarled fingers were emptying the waste basket into a bushel basket, "yes, how would it do to consult four old men who have seen much of life, and hear where they think America should go from here? In that case, suppose I begin with you?"

"Dinna ask the auld anes," grinned Sandy, "the young anes hae the forward leuk."

"But it's neither backward nor forward looking that is going to save America. It must be the upward look."

"I dinna ken whether I am a gude up-leuker but I'm a mighty gude doon-leuker," he smiled, "an' what I see is that we're nae buildin' on Gude's Foundation Stones."

"What are those Foundation Stones, Sandy?" Charles' eyes followed the old man intently as he went on about his work.

"We hae been neglectin' ane o' the maist important laws o' science and that is, it is dangerous for a sore tae heal on the outside before it heals on the inside. We think we won this war, but we dinna," Sandy finished emphatically, setting the basket down with a bang, as if to underscore his statement.

"What do you mean, we lost the war?" asked Charles, astonished.

"We licked the enemy but we lost the war," went on Sandy, unperturbed. "The loser hae to pay reparations, dinna he? Weel, we wull be payin' reparations for mony years."

"I see what you mean," mused Charles. "All because we healed the sore on the outside before we started on the inside?"

"Sure, sure," and Sandy took his pipe out of his pocket and shook some tobacco into it from a well-used soft leather pouch. "Churchill and Roosevelt said 'We wull win the war first and then we wull discuss our war aims; we haena time tae do baith at the same time.' And sae we lost the war. Haen the war aims been clear,—haen the four freedoms meant the four freedoms for a' nations and a' races, the war wad hae ended at least a year earlier and millions of lives wad hae been saved." Sandy shook his head wisely. "Na, na, you canna heal a sore richt till you treat it frae the inside first."

"How about China?" Charles asked.

"Same mistak, same mistak!" Sandy shook his head dolefully. "Tak Chiang Kai-shek. He was asked tae cast out the graft in the government and plan some land reforms. He replied, 'I canna do two things tae aince. First I wull defeat the Communists, then I wull gie attention to reformin' our graft-infested government.' If he continues this policy I forecas' that he never wull owercome the Communists but that the Communists wull owercome him. You canna owercome ane form o' rottenness wi' anither form o' rottenness. You can only owercome evil wi' gude."

"That's an old viewpoint, freshly put," said Charles, pulling out his notebook. "Let me jot that down. Got any other ideas?"

"Na," replied the other, "but I wull tell you some ane wha does. Gae to old mon Babcock. If ye want a young viewpoint he is the youngest ane I know. He wull gie you some sidelichts whar America is gaun."

That very evening Charles went to the mansion of the old financier. "While the trail is hot," he thought, "it is hard to keep a hunting hound on the leash."

Mr. Babcock was pleased to see him. He was still more delighted when he heard the purpose of the call.

"So you want to build a sermon, young man, around the theme 'Where is America going from here?' Yes, that sounds exciting. What do you want from me?"

"I want to hear your diagnosis of our greatest weakness. From what spot must we move?"

"Greed!" exclaimed the old man, his false teeth clicking as if to lend special emphasis. "Greed and nothing but greed. It is the poison oak that must be dug out root and branch or it will exterminate us."

"Greed in business? Wall Street?" Charles asked.

"Greed everywhere," snapped the old man. "It has got into our politics, into our churches, into our schools. Everywhere! Today we spend one-half-billion for churches, one billion for schools, two billion for cosmetics and candy, three billion for movies, four billion for tobacco, six billion for alcoholic drinks, fifteen billion for crime and twenty-five billion for war! What a wonderful world we would have if we just reversed this process and spent twenty-five billion for religion, fifteen billion for schools and only one billion for crime, and nothing for war! Why don't we? *Because there is profit in war and in crime and in alcohol, but no profit in education and religion.*" Babcock paused to let that thought sink in before he continued grimly, "Until we can take the profit motive off the pedestal and put God and human welfare in its place, all our minor reforms are just scratching the surface. Not until then will the world be safe."

At this moment the door opened abruptly and Andrew Marsh walked in. "Am I interrupting something?" he said, surprised as he saw Maxwell, who rose with Babcock to greet him. "Hello, Parson, I never knock when I call on Babcock."

"You're not interrupting anything," said Mr. Babcock. "This young man here talked about Four Revolutions last Sunday and he has asked me what our nation's place is in this whole situation." When the three were comfortably seated before the fireplace, Babcock went on, "As I see it, our nation is standing like a pioneer cabin of free enterprise in the face of a great prairie fire of Communism that is sweeping down upon us. The only safe thing to do is to start a backfire. But we shouldn't neglect to remove the refuse in our door-yards first, the tinder that will invite that fire."

"What is the tinder in our land of free enterprise that invites the fire of Communism?" asked Mr. Marsh.

"Monopoly," snapped the old man. "In Europe monopoly has been the vestibule of socialism. The cartel is private monopoly. When cartels took control of Europe, free enterprise was kicked out. The only monopoly people approve is the public monopoly. Let any monopoly grow big enough and the public insists on taking it over."

"Aren't labor unions monopolies?" asked Charles.

"Of course they are. And if they get too cocky you will see government taking them over. Some people believe that the American Medical Association is another monopoly. Let the charge 'medical trust' be believed and 'socialized medicine,' no matter how the doctors dread it, will soon be here."

"So you believe," said Charles, "that the monopolist brings upon himself the socialism he fears?"

"I certainly do. Monopoly is bad for all concerned—for the monopolist and for the monopolized."

"But, how can you stop monopolies?" asked Charles.

"I would recommend a Christian brand of cooperative free enterprise to neutralize the atheistic brand of Communism that is threatening the world. Denmark, Sweden, Norway, Holland and England have done something like that, and they are the only nations in Europe that are now safe from Communism within their own borders."

"Can you suggest such a form?" asked Charles. "One that would fit our American way of life?"

"I think I can," said Andrew Marsh. "Would you like to hear it?"

"Sure, sure," said Babcock, leaning forward eagerly. "Go ahead!"

"It may sound a little radical," Marsh began, "but I think we all agree that the surest way to be engulfed in the most dangerous form of radicalism is to be overconservative. You can't hold down steam by sitting on the safety valve."

"Go ahead," urged Charles, "we aren't asking whether your plan is radical or conservative. All we want to be sure of is whether it is truly good for mankind."

"Well, then," said Marsh, "I shall tell you how I think it could be done. As a railroad man, I think of our economic system as one that has never progressed beyond the old choo-choo, single track era, while all the rest of the world has gone streamlined. Remember how it used to be when trains crossing the continent on single tracks met other trains; they were switched off on sidings where they would have to wait until the other trains passed them. Well, that is the point to which our economic system advanced—and then stopped. Production runs one way and distribution runs the other, and both are trying to use the same track, the track marked 'Profit Unlimited!' Consequently, when production comes down the track too fast, as it does every ten years or so, it has to be side tracked in what is called a 'depression siding' until distribution can come up to the point that production has reached. The only thing required to end our economic problems would be to build a double track which would enable distribution to go ahead just as fast as production; and production need never stop and wait for distribution."

"Hold on a minute!" Charles exclaimed. "You make it sound so simple. Just how can this be done?"

"Exactly the same way trains are run today," replied Marsh matter-of-factly. "By a planning board which can watch the schedules and see that all are run in perfect relationship to all the rest with no collisions on the one hand and no delays on the other."

"But that is regimentation," objected Charles. "Won't it destroy free enterprise?"

"I can hear the engineer who runs the locomotive say the same thing," replied Marsh, with a broad smile. " 'Confound those traffic managers,' he exclaims, 'who schedule this train to leave Los Angeles at ten o'clock this morning and insist that I reach Ogden at three o'clock tomorrow morning and Omaha at eight the next morning. I want to exercise my free enterprise today and reach Ogden when I darn please.' Of course, it is regimentation, but it saves people's lives. Think of the joy and comfort of the travelers who go to the railroad station knowing they can count on the train to leave on schedule."

"That should not be impossible to arrange," said Babcock. "Procter and Gamble have discovered that eighty-five percent of the goods used in this country are consumed evenly, but they are not bought evenly, and therein lies the cause of the recurrent depressions that gives our economy its bad name. The principle you are stressing is that we must produce to the consumption line instead of to the buying line? Is that it?"

"Certainly. It would not be difficult to determine how many shoes would be needed each year,—how many automobiles. Why, insurance companies can foretell within ninety percent of accuracy just how many people will die each year."

"Do you believe," said Charles, "that ending monopolies and balancing production with consumption would end wars?"

"Yes, if done on an international scale," said Marsh. "As long as European countries exploited underprivileged peoples the colonial empires amounted to nothing more or less than trade monopolies. Whenever they discriminated against the trade of other nations, including Germany and Japan, that started wars."

"Give an example of that discrimination," said Charles.

"When a tariff wall was erected in British Malaya whereby for every piece of Japanese goods 110 pieces of British goods could enter, we learned the truth in the adage that when goods can't cross boundaries, soldiers will."

"Thank goodness," said Babcock, "the day of the Colonial Empires is going."

"But with its going," said Marsh, "the standard of living based upon the monopolies they furnished the European Empires will sag. Mass poverty will haunt Europe until the nations thus bereft reweave the strong fibre of faith and good will into the fabric of the common life. When they learn that the best form of mutual security is collective prosperity, and that discriminative tariffs lead to impoverishment and not to prosperity, when, in short, they establish something like an economic United States of Europe, then all will be well."

"In what way should the United States change her policy?" Charles asked. "What should be our first step to take toward preventing another war?"

"We should take immediate steps to remove all causes for fear," said Marsh. "America is making a big mistake in basing her foreign policy too much on fear and not enough on faith and mutual aid."

"Can it be," asked Babcock, "that the United States is out of step with the onward trend of the world?"

"In one respect, yes. We missed the boat when we allowed our gold to be used to defend the European Colonial dictatorships in Asia; it is high time for us to learn that Asia, not America, is the main determinant of the world trend," and Marsh got up and walked to the fireplace, "and the trend is nothing more than the adjustment of exaggerated contrasts. Two-thirds of mankind are shouting, 'We are going to raise our standards of living. Help us if you will, but obstruct us or exploit us at your peril.' Those four revolutions you described last Sunday are carrying the world toward that goal like the four wheels on a car. But there is no safety in this journey, only peril, unless there is that fifth wheel you mentioned—a spiritual revolution—to serve as a steering wheel in the hands of One who knows the way."

See page 16 7

He paused while he lighted a cigar.

"Go on," said Charles. "This is what I came to hear."

"The steering wheel alone can't do it." Marsh took a few long puffs from his cigar and took it from his lips and faced Charles. "That would be mere idealism and will lead only to futility. The four wheels alone can't do it. That would be mere materialism and would lead only to destruction. Not until all five wheels operate as one will we all roll down the road to peace and prosperity."

"Then the United States should get busy furnishing that fifth wheel," exclaimed Charles. "As long as we defer doing that, and as long as we obstruct the forward movement of any of the other wheels, we are not only delaying world peace but we are putting ourselves in the line of danger. Isn't that true?"

"It certainly is," said Marsh. "The purpose behind all these revolutions is to establish equality and balance where for centuries there has been terrible inequality and terrible unbalance in the world. If the United States should contribute generously to the world of her *surplus* in products, and of her *'know how'* in technical knowledge, and of her *love* in Christian compassion, our superiority in wealth and power instead of creating envy and hate and fear, which are the seeds of war, would create admiration, gratitude and love, which are the seeds of peace. That is absolutely and positively the only way we can make our land safe from war."

"Thanks, men," said Charles, rising to his feet. "You have given me what I wanted. This is a Christian nation, and if we lived up to our name we could insure peace. If Andrew Marsh were president I can just see him converting our battle ships, now practically obsolete in this atomic age, into food ships to carry our surplus wheat and potatoes to all the hungry people of the earth."

"And if you were the arch-bishop of America," added Babcock, "I can see you gathering together all the men America sends abroad, whether they go as ambassadors, salesmen, technical advisers or missionaries, and training them to love and pray as true Christians should."

Charles smiled as he picked up his hat. He looked straight into the eyes of Marsh and asked, "Do you honestly believe that democracy and totalitarianism can live peacefully side by side?"

"There is no need to waste any time trying to reconcile democracy with totalitarianism," exclaimed Marsh. "That is not where the conflict lies. Our political differences can very easily be resolved but our economic antagonisms, as they stand today, can never be reconciled. By taking one definite step toward ending the day of Monopolistic Capitalism, and marshalling all the resources of this nation in ways that will bless other nations, we would end all occasion for quarrel between Russia and the United States. Russia would then come more than half way to meet us."

"If we can prevent war we can stop Communism," said Babcock. "War is the parent of Communism. Above every thing we must prevent war. The first World War brought Communism to Russia; the second World War brought Communism to Asia and half of Europe; a third World War will bring Communism to the world. Democracy, on the other hand, thrives on peace because it is the child of the church and the school."

"Thanks again," said Charles, as he turned to leave. "We must stand behind the church and the school. As to the next step for America, you have started me thinking. Pray that the Lord will continue where you two have left off."

"We will pray that He will do that in your sermon next Sunday," said Marsh.

"If you don't mind," said Mr. Babcock unexpectedly, "why can't we have that prayer right now?"

CHAPTER 27

"Fear not. It is your Father's good will to give you the Kingdom."

CHARLES MAXWELL spent a restless night. "How can I put all this into a sermon?" plagued him hour after hour. He was wrestling with a mammoth problem: How can greed be eliminated? Will this drastic method suggested by Marsh be necessary? Isn't there an easier way?

"One thing is certain," he resolved. "I *must* speak out boldly. No matter what the remedy, some remedy must be found. I shall lash out against Old Man Greed—and I'll lash out hard."

Giving up sleep, he donned a warm robe and sat before his bedroom window, looking out on his quiet street, made almost as bright as day by moonlight on the new snow, and still his thoughts ran on. "Even to talk about Greed," he meditated, "has its perils unless one clothes his words in generalities and platitudes. The moment I step into the field of controversy that moment my influence as a minister of the gospel is gone. The true, the beautiful and the good get befogged so easily, the emotions are so tied up with the old patterns of life that anyone who steps out and offers new ones is labelled as a crackpot, unless—unless he does so in poetry, parable or platitude."

He was still pondering over these three alternatives when finally he returned to bed and fell into a deep sleep. When he awoke the next morning these three words were still echoing and reechoing through his mind: poetry, parable or platitude.

"I am not a poet," he thought, "and I refuse to talk in platitudes. Jesus' way would be the parable way. It is God's answer!"

he exclaimed, as the solution to his problem suddenly came clear and whole into his mind. "Thank you, Lord!"

When he mounted the pulpit the next Sunday, he again had the broody feeling of some great idea about to hatch. But unlike the other Sunday, when the sermon was born as he spoke, this time he knew exactly what he was going to say before he began.

Before he turned to his pulpit chair he caught the eye of Frances and it seemed filled with wistful apprehension. He felt the sense of suspense and concern of the entire congregation. He noticed in the full sanctuary before him there were some new faces. When the anthem was finished, he rose and went to the pulpit and spread out some papers.

"I had a dream a few nights ago," he began, "and I shall try to relate it as it came to me." He cleared his throat and went on.

"I awakened from a deep sleep that seemed to have covered an interminable length of time. Someone was shaking me. 'Wake up, Rip Van Winkle, wake up.' I opened my eyes and looked into a face I seemed to recognize.

" 'How long have I been sleeping, Andrew Marsh?' I asked. 'Every bone in my body seems ten years older.'

" 'You have been sleeping fifty years, old grey beard—it is now 2000 A.D.—and I am not Andrew Marsh. I am his grandson, Jim. Now that you are awake at last you better go to the barber.'

"I gasped when I looked into the mirror. Long white locks and a beard that reached half-way to my waist! Rip Van Winkle, if there ever was one!

"My face felt clean and free when the beard came off but I was amazed at the number of wrinkles. When we emerged from the barber shop Jim said, 'Your clothes are all out of date, old man. Let's stop into this store at once.' At the men's haberdashery I was fitted out with an entirely new outfit. Jim bought a new shirt for himself and calmly threw his old one in the waste basket. To my horror he did the same with mine.

" 'Hold on!' I cried. 'My shirt had more wear in it and yours was as good as new.'

" 'Nonsense,' he said, laughing at my distress, 'shirts today are made out of cornstalk fiber in enormous factories. The finest ones cost only ten cents. It would cost twenty cents to launder them, therefore why bother? There is abundance of cornstalk fiber. You don't dream how streamlined we have become since your day. It makes travel mighty easy—nothing much to carry. Buy a new change of clothes wherever you happen to be. I see you have a lot to catch up on. Let's take a little flier over to the Rocky Mountains this afternoon and talk it over.'

"He pulled a little 'walkie-talkie' from his pocket, dialed his mother and told her he was off to the Rockies over the weekend. He stopped in his office and pulled out some apparatus that looked like two sets of wings with a small streamlined engine attached. We climbed out on the roof, he adjusted a set on me, gave me a few simple directions, and we shot through the sky at amazing speed till we landed before a beautiful little bungalow cabin high on Long's Peak.

" 'Sit down,' he commanded, while he started a cozy wood fire in the cabin, 'and I'll tell you what it's all about. You act a little flustered.'

" 'Flustered!' I exclaimed. 'I'm positively flabbergasted.'

" 'You see, it's this way. Like Rip Van Winkle, you slept through a revolution.'

" 'A revolution!' I exclaimed. 'It must have been a hundred revolutions.'

" 'You are right,' he replied, 'but they were peaceful revolutions. The diagnosis the ancient doctors handed down to us about your strange sleep was that it was a sort of self-induced hypnosis—an escape from a world that lacked moral and economic leadership. You felt so sure that the blind were leading the blind that you fell into the ditch before the leaders even got there themselves. The new insignia that you will be confronted with if you were passing by a familiar tavern as Rip Van Winkle did would reveal that you have awakened into a nation that is first in political democracy, first in economic democracy and first in moral leadership.'

" 'Eureka!' I cried. 'Too good to be true!'

" 'Hold on,' he continued, smiling at my excitement. 'I see I shall have to break the good news to you gradually. First we shall start with the little things, for instance, how we got to the Rocky Mountains just now.'

" 'Little things, indeed!' I exclaimed. 'This journey is one of the colossal things that astonished me.'

" 'Scientists,' he went on, 'have finally found the secret of overcoming gravity. Years ago Einstein proved that gravity, electricity, heat, light and sound all belong to the unity of the plane of matter. We can turn on heat and light and sound so why not turn on and off gravity? That is exactly what we did a little while ago. Everybody now has his private flying apparatus. We don't need to carry fuel—we merely tune in to the wave length of the central power plant.'

" 'This central power house must be immense.'

" 'No, not very large. You see, it is run by atomic energy.'

" 'Atomic energy!' I exclaimed. 'When did that come into use?'

" 'Oh, a long time ago. It was the core of the economic revolution. Indeed, one of the most revolutionary facts involved in applying atomic energy for general uses, a fact almost entirely overlooked by the general public at the time under the first shock of this amazing discovery, was that public control through the government was taken for granted. This was almost as revolutionary as the discovery of the atomic principle itself. In the past, social adjustment to new inventions always lagged behind the inventions themselves. Never before in history had this principle of control of a source of energy by the people been accepted or adopted at the outset in our country. It was not done with electricity or with gas or oil or steam.

" 'Now coal and gas for heating purposes are almost things of the past. A ten-dollar atomic unit placed in a house keeps it warm all winter and cool all summer. When an automobile leaves the factory it is equipped with a ten-dollar atomic unit which runs it for the life of the car.'

" 'This is unbelievable,' I gasped. 'But now tell me about yourself. What is your business? How could you just walk off and leave it for a trip like this, how——?'

" 'Now you are getting into a new field. These days no one has to work more than four hours a day, four days a week. This is Friday and I am free till Monday. My hobby is painting. Having all afternoons free and these long weekends and two-months' vacations each year besides, as we all do, I have plenty of time to do all the creating I love and will soon become so recognized that I will qualify to devote all my time to painting. Our nation never knew what free enterprise really meant until the peaceful revolution came!'

" 'Tell me what you mean by the revolution.'

" 'One day the whole nation woke up, like you and Rip Van Winkle did, from a long nap, as it were, and realized how silly it was for a third of this great nation to live in want on a continent simply overflowing with plenty. A planning board equal in character and influence to our Supreme Court was appointed, made up of leading citizens, business leaders, labor leaders and economic experts—the most capable men in the world—and they acted on the premise that if persons were allocated to the professions and vocations of their choice and that if all men worked four hours a day, four days a week, for ten months of the year, no one would need to halt his education till he was twenty-five and no one would need to work after he was fifty-five unless he wanted to, and every individual, yes, every member of the family would have the equivalent of $10,000 purchasing power a year as long as he lived.'

" 'It seems impossible,' I said. 'And no taxes?'

" 'No taxes,' he replied. 'All government employees from the president down receive the same buying power. Immediately after this system was adopted inventions and discoveries simply poured in. We were amazed at the vast number of patents for improving our instruments of use, which had been suppressed by the monopolies to prevent loss to the stockholders. For instance, electric light bulbs that had to be replaced every few years now last fifty. Safety-razor blades that were good for ten shaves now last for ten years. Automobiles—'

" 'Stop!' I said again, 'I get the point. But what about all the leisure the people have now? Isn't it producing a lot of delinquency and crime?'

" 'Just the opposite. The moment all profits were taken out of alcoholic beverages and tobacco the demand for them was reduced by two-thirds. The moment people lost all fear of unemployment, of old age, half the mental hospitals were closed for want of occupants. People set free from worry turned their minds to creative things—and the chief purpose of all education changed overnight into the training of children and adults in the fine art of making the most creative and constructive use of leisure time.'

" 'And how about that war with Russia that everyone predicted was coming so soon? Didn't you have it?'

" 'Of course not. When all private profit was taken out of oil and munitions and all our giant monopolies ended, the Russian "cold war" on us ceased. And when we adopted something so much better than anything Marx ever dreamed—a form of free enterprise with all the evils taken out of it, the Soviet satellite nations began to imitate us and not long after, Russia herself followed suit. We now have a world living in peace and plenty.'

" 'And how did this all come about? What shook people out of the old system? How did the peaceful revolution start?'

" 'Well, my grandfather told a parable of the single track and the double track railroad. . . .' " Here Charles repeated the illustration he had heard Marsh give.

" 'But strange to say,' went on young Jim, 'that did not make much impression except to bring down torrents of criticism and abuse upon grandfather's head. When our entire economic structure was staggering under the tremendous load of trying to keep the economic wells of Europe primed while our own wells were beginning to run dry; yes, when we were at the very precipice of another depression even greater than the famous one of 1929, and hovering over the brink of another world war greater than the war of 1941–45, then the nation in desperation began to give some serious thought to my grandfather's theories. But I am not sure that all these calamities combined would have been enough if at that moment Paul the Piper hadn't arrived on the scene.'

" 'Who?'

" 'Oh, we just call him that. He is still living. You must hear him someday. He is a mixture of Frank Laubach, that great Apostle of Prayer, and of Will Rogers, the Apostle of Humor, both of your time, I believe. He believed in what he called the "therapeutic power of laughter." He went from city to city hiring the largest auditoriums—his fame as a comedian filled them to bursting. An advance man preceded him, who spent a week training "choruses in laughter." '

" 'In what?' I exclaimed.

" 'In laughter. Haven't you learned that the easiest way to get rid of unnecessary evils is to laugh them away? Well, when the big night came, Paul the Piper would hold the audience in the hollow of his hand with a mixture of high philosophy and contagious humor. Finally he would say, "Now it has come time to pray. Let us first pray for God to avert all war. We have been told that there will always be war, that it is the brute in man. How absurd! Brutes don't kill each other. Lions don't kill lions. They merely kill their meat. We turn that job over to Swift and Armour and Cudahy. Now let us ask the Lord to lift mankind up to the level of the intelligence of brutes. We mustn't ask Him for too much for His hands are so full, you know. Just this we shall ask, that we be lifted up to the intelligence of brutes. Folks, can't you just see the Lord leaning over the parapets of heaven, laughing at us? Before we pray, let us join in the laugh with Him." That was the signal for the "laughing choruses" to start. First the high school girls' "giggling choir," then the young men's choir trained in the "horse laugh," and by the time the "hysteria choir" of old ladies joined in, the whole auditorium was in pandemonium. As fast as the laughter started to die down the choirs would pump it up again until the entire auditorium finally was so rocking in mirth that the windows rattled.'

" 'Then he tackled the economic problems. In a few short sentences he told of the absurdity of anyone being in want in a land of plenty and ended with this statement: "On a monkey island, as long as there was one cocoanut left, no monkey would starve. Now let us pray for the good Lord to lift us up to the level of the intelligence of monkeys." Then the laughter would start all over again. During a respite for breath he recited the following soliloquy of the monkeys:

"Three monkeys sat in a cocoanut tree,
    Discussing things as they're to be;
    Said one to the others, 'Now listen, you two,
    There's a certain rumor that can't be true
    That man descended from our noble race;
    The very idea is a disgrace!

'No monkey ever deserted his wife,
    Starved her babies and ruined her life;
    And you've never known a mother monk
    To leave her babies with others to bunk,
    Or pass them on from one to another
    Till they scarcely know who is their mother.

'And another thing, you will never see;
    A monk build a fence 'round a cocoanut tree,
    And let the cocoanuts go to waste,
    Forbidding all other monks a taste.
    Why, if I'd put a fence around a tree,
    Starvation would force you to steal from me!

'Here's another thing a monk won't do,
    Go out at night and get in a stew;
    Or use a gun, a club or knife,
    To take some other monkey's life;
    Yes, man *descended*, the ornery cuss,
    But Brother, he didn't descend from US!' " *

* Author unknown.

200

" 'News of these sensational meetings preceded him everywhere and as a result Paul the Piper found crowded auditoriums waiting for him all over the land. He visited all the larger cities and spoke every night for nine months. And slowly the nation woke up. Yes, they rose to the intelligence of monkeys. All the evils in our single-tracked economic system were removed—the crash was averted—Russia held her hand—and within ten years prosperity had come to our people such as they had never known before and we all awakened to an era of peace on earth and good will to men.'

" 'Hold on, Jim,' I cried. 'Did this all actually happen or was it just a dream?'

" 'It really and truly happened,' he said. 'If you don't believe it I will fly to New York with you to show you the back files of the *New York Times* for the last fifty years.'

" 'This is almost too much,' I said. 'I'm getting dizzy!'

" 'Yes,' he said. 'It was a big dose to give you all at once. You'd better lie down and rest awhile.'

"I was relaxing and my eyelids were getting heavy when he leaned over me and whispered in my ear, 'If it hadn't happened, Mr. Maxwell, if it *were* just a dream, I and all the other descendants of your friends in the First Church of Raymond would not be here in the year 2000 A.D. If these reforms hadn't come about, the world would have plunged into the worst war of all history—a war that would have destroyed civilization from the face of the earth!' "

Charles Maxwell paused. The congregation had sat so still he had almost forgotten they were there. The eagerness in their eyes seemed begging him to go on and on.

"You look as though you wish I hadn't wakened!" The ripple of laughter that greeted this broke the tension.

"That is all," he said with a smile. "I just remembered that I forgot to give you my text: 'Your old men shall dream dreams, your young men shall see visions. Joel 2:28.' " He pronounced the benediction and the service for that Sunday was over.

CHAPTER 28

*"Moreover, if thy brother shall trespass against thee,
go and tell him his fault between thee and him alone."*

ONE EVENING, tucked away in the "condensed and dehydrated" crime page of Richard Norman's *Raymond
News* Charles read of two serious hold-ups in neighboring towns. When he went to bed he couldn't sleep. He spent
most of the night trying to determine where justice began and
mercy ended, attempting to weigh the validity of a solemn
promise against the dead certainty of an innocent man losing
his money or possibly even his life. And all the while one question and one question alone stood out uppermost in his mind:
"What would Jesus do?"

How could he keep the solemn promise he had made to Mac-
Intosh not to reveal the information he had received, and yet
be true as a man of God to the people of the state that were being
preyed upon by an evil system at work right under the shadow
of his own church?

It was toward morning when he was almost exhausted with a
night of wrestling with the problem, that the answer came. Once
settled to his own satisfaction, a great peace came to him—a
peace so profound that he was able to roll over on his side and
fall into as restful sleep as a little child.

It was four o'clock when he fell asleep, and eight when he
awoke. To his surprise, he was completely refreshed.

There is nothing more destructive to peace and rest than
hanging on the two horns of a dilemma where no possible solution presents itself. In contrast to this, Charles discovered that

there is nothing so soothing and healing and peace-giving as the sudden appearance of a miraculous solution to that dilemma at the very moment when an adequate solution has seemed absolutely impossible.

A hot bath followed by a cold shower, a light breakfast, then his customary half-hour of Bible reading, meditation and prayer, and Charles was on his way to the City Hall.

The office of the Police Commissioner was on the fourth floor. The old Irishman running the elevator eyed Charles carefully when he told him his destination. Charles Maxwell was well aware that a Power greater than himself was going with him and giving him strength. He was moving in a cosmic rhythm that he didn't want to break. He had an absolute confidence that he would find Bill Peters in. He did not entertain a single doubt. If, for any reason, he would be greeted with the announcement that Peters was away on a journey, or even that he had not arrived yet from his home, would that have broken the rhythm? He did not permit himself to face that question. As long as the momentum which began with the flash of light that came to him at four that morning continued to propel him onward, he knew that what he was doing was exactly right for all concerned—was positively in accordance with the will of God.

"Yes, Mr. Peters is in. Go right into his office. No one is with him."

The tall, angular woman opened the door for him. She made no announcement. Thanking God silently, he walked in and heard the door close behind him.

Bill Peters was sitting at his desk. At the sound of the door opening and closing he swung slowly around and took a long black cigar out of his mouth with his left hand as he automatically reached out his right to take the hand of Charles, a mere flicker of the eyes betraying any surprise he might feel at this unscheduled call.

"Reverend Maxwell, I believe. What can I do for you?" The cigar went back into his lips at an oblique angle.

Charles sat down, knitting his fingers, and smiling across the immense desk at Peters. "This is going to be the most unusual conversation you ever sat in on, Mr. Peters, perhaps the most unusual that anyone in the world ever sat in on."

The cigar came out between two strong fingers, and two eyes under knitted brows, half in apprehension and half in defiance were fixed upon Charles.

"Fire away." Peters' tone betrayed no concern, but the cigar was back in his mouth again and the teeth were clamping on it.

"Mr. Peters, I have been informed by unimpeachable authority exactly what you are doing. I know of the protection the police of this city are giving the criminal element of this entire section of the country, and the reward they are receiving. I know and as a citizen appreciate the immunity from crime our own city is receiving, but I don't claim to know the amount of blood money you and your friends are receiving as your share of the rake-off for sheltering those committing crimes in other parts of the country. All I know is that it is plenty, and that in receiving it you are partners in those crimes."

The cigar, badly chewed, was between two strong fingers again.

"You can't prove a word you say."

"I don't need to prove it," Charles stated calmly. "It is there. It is the truth and you know it. But here is where the unusual part of this interview comes in. As far as I know, I am the only responsible person with any power to act that knows this, and I don't intend to breathe it to a single individual beside yourself."

"Oh, blackmail, eh? And what do you expect to get out of it? Want to horn in on the profits? Shame on you, Parson." Peters' face was disfigured by a leer that would have done credit to Mephistopheles himself.

"It reached me by the grapevine route straight from the underworld itself. If you try hard enough, you might be able to trace it back to the source. I can assure you that this information will not spread. That is, if you promise me and keep your promise that if you *should* find the source of my information you would do no harm to him. I also will keep my promise and inform no one of what I know."

"Sounds reasonable." The cigar was back in the mouth and puffing fast.

"You may know, Mr. Peters," Charles continued humbly, "that this year I am making a special effort to do only what I think Jesus would do, and getting as many of my friends to share with me as I can. You may have heard about it?"

"And how! That's why I happen to be police commissioner. Chain of events, you might say!" In the laugh there was a ring of relaxation and a relief, as if the assurance just given had hit the mark.

"Because I have promised you that I shall tell no man, I am a little like a teakettle filled with steam," continued Charles. "I have to let it out somewhere and that place will be God. Just you and God share the secret with me. So if you don't mind, I want to talk to you a few minutes about God."

"Fire away," Peters said, as if he were humoring a child.

"Now, you may think the laws laid down in the Bible are all—what shall I say?—just fairy-tale stuff, kindergarten, Sunday-school twaddle. Is that so, Mr. Peters?"

"A better word than any you are trying to use is 'hooey.' But see here, Mr. Maxwell, I am not a moron just because I happen to be seated in this police commissioner's chair. I am a reader and I've studied a lot, even though I don't pretend to be a gentleman. But like a lot of scholars, I am a skeptic, and agnostic, perhaps an atheist. Ever heard of Solomon Richter? Sure you did. I believe with him that the laws of the Bible are 'a set of scruples imposed on the framework of humanity to keep it from functioning naturally and normally.' "

For a moment Charles stared at the man before him. The job he had undertaken was going to be harder than he had anticipated. An arch skeptic, fortified with arguments of defence and offence, might bring this whole expedition, so well-intentioned and prayerfully prepared, into disaster.

"Prayerfully prepared!" That was the hope. "God, don't forsake me now," he prayed inwardly. "I need You more than ever." Then aloud: "Mr. Peters, I see if this descends into a debate you are well armed to defend your side of the case. So I am going to remove it from the field of argument and place it where it belongs: in the field of life.

"What I have to say will therefore be brief. These laws of Christianity are written in the Bible and if that were the only place where they were written, I would have to go into a debate with you on the authority of the Scriptures. That might take hours of talk followed by months of research. But these laws are also written in the moral order of the universe, and this moral order has the final word. Though *we* may choose, the moral universe decides the results of our choosing and those results are inexorable. We do not break the laws of God written into the nature of things, we break ourselves on them. If you leap from a tenth-story window you will not break the law of gravity, you will only illustrate it."

Charles saw that Peters was following him with close attention. As he rose and reached for his hat, he continued:

"Now you are breaking those laws, Mr. Peters. That is all I came to tell you. It doesn't matter whether you have faith in God or in the Bible or in the words I am saying. The tides are not concerned with one who ignores them. They merely act according to laws inherent in their nature and drown the one who disregards them."

Mr. Peters took his cigar from his mouth and rose uncertainly from his chair, a strange mixture of expressions in his small eyes as they met Charles'.

"You say this is a secret conversation just between you and me?"

"Between you and me and God," Charles replied gravely.—"Don't forget the most important One of the three. You and I have said some words, but don't forget, He will have the last word."

When he had left, Charles went straight to see his one clearest, most comforting adviser, the saintly friend of his grandfather. Rachel Page herself greeted him at the door.

"You know that I have many problems of people to deal with," he began when they were alone in her private study, "and some of them are big problems, some are awful problems."

"I am well aware that the task of a Father Confessor is not an easy one," Rachel spoke in her understanding voice.

"And you are aware, of course, that personal problems cannot be divulged to others."

"Of course, Charles."

"Well, today I have had a strange interview: a problem that I cannot reveal and yet one that involves so many lives beside the one whom I had the conference with, that I need *all* your prayers behind me. I can tell you no more. You are the only one I feel that I can safely intrust this much to."

"Can you give me just a clue to the general direction toward which this prayer should be directed?"

"That I can, and perhaps there we can find a fulcrum for our leverage. Pray for God in His own good way to bring an end to the crime wave that has been sweeping this section of the country. If we two agree asking that in faith, Jesus will be in our midst, and we can turn it all over to Him."

After a short period of silence, Charles stumbled through a little oral prayer.

When he finished he turned to Mrs. Page.

"The words I uttered with my lips just now were my feeble attempt at a prayer. I felt a sense of great power just now, but the power came not from the prayer but from the faith behind the prayer. Your faith joining my faith made a bridge that led straight to the throne of heaven."

"Did you feel it, too? I wondered if I was just imagining it."

"No, you were not imagining. You were simply touching with your inner radio system the most real Power in the universe. If something happens it will not be our prayer that caused it—our prayer merely turned on the switch. It won't be even our faith that caused it. Our faith, yes, our combined faith, was merely the wire that bridged the gap between God and us."

"Not faith—not prayer?" asked Mrs. Page, wonderingly.

"Only God and His great cosmic laws of the Universe," Charles spoke with finality. "Whatever is done, He and He alone will do it. We without Him are helpless. God alone is that Infinite Power. But we can tap the Source of that Power. Little tiny taps on our part, but how wonderful is His Power to respond! Let us trust Him to respond to this request with tremendous power!"

As Charles left, Rachel Winslow Page went quietly with him to the door.

"To show my gratitude in being given the privilege of helping in this, I shall spend the entire day in meditation and prayer. God bless you!" she said.

CHAPTER 29

*"Not everyone that saith unto me, Lord, Lord, shall
enter into the kingdom of heaven; but he that doeth the
will of my Father which is in heaven."*

D AVID PAUL, principal of Crocker School, watched his
teachers file into the eighth grade room for the customary bi-weekly teachers' meeting. Somehow, as he sat
behind the desk doodling on a large blank sheet of paper, a
habit of his when waiting for things to happen, he felt as if the
whole gathering were unreal. Women, women, women! In they
came. Dressed as teachers garb themselves. Dressed as teachers
ought to dress, perhaps would be putting it better. Good, well-
meaning women—but oh, such uprooted lives! The offspring of
an artificial civilization, he thought. In a more primitive society
all of these would have had mates. His eye fell on Marguerite
DeFoe—young, full-breasted, always animated, warm, mag-
netic. "She will get a husband. If she doesn't, she will be a
problem woman someday. And who is to blame?"

But there is crabby, sour-faced Martha Swenson, showing
age in every line of throat, snappy in voice in spite of her double
chin. Some man was lucky who didn't get her—the man she
says she turned down. How did she ever get a chance to turn
any man down? But Martha never told lies. Yes, Martha had
lots in her favor. She was sour, but so was clabber. She was the
most dependable woman on his staff.

And there was Gertrude Long, young, bright-eyed, but how
rebellious! Some bronco-busting cowhand with skill in the use

of the lariat might have a chance with her, but not a mild man like me, thought David Paul.

And then Ruth McMaster came in, white-haired, motherly, a vindication of every tribute ever paid a teacher. No, this is not, no, this need not be, an artificial, machine-made vocation for frustrated lives—it can be, it is, a real vocation, as sacred a calling as motherhood itself; yes, as sacred as the priesthood! Somehow, with white-haired Ruth in the room with him, he would dare to do the audacious thing he had in mind. Would the aura around her sweet face spread wide enough to soften the hard skulls, the conventional brain-sets of the others?

"Fellow teachers," he began, when the hum of conversation lulled, "I was reading the words of a famous educator that what is needed in our school system is more religion. Business executives say our product is not dependable. The output of our schools can't be trusted either as to honesty or as to accuracy.

"But we are a public school system. We aren't allowed to read the Bible in the classrooms, and we aren't allowed to teach our separate creeds. I personally have a church creed. But I know I have no business to propagate my own special denomination. However, I also have a spiritual conviction that runs across all creeds—that does violence to no one's beliefs. And I would like to suggest that we try an experiment along lines that will at least open doors for every boy's and girl's religion to function in its own way right here in Crocker School. Would you like to hear it?"

The white locks of Ruth McMaster nodded vigorously. The bored sleepy look in the other faces seemed to change a little. Eyes began to open wider.

"I was impressed to find at the Wright Department Store a room set apart for silent worship. Now you know and I know that most of the great things come out of silence. Most of the great religions make a place for silence. Why can't we, too, have a silent room, a room set apart with soft rugs, a little altar perhaps, some pictures of religious significance, and a few books of spiritual nature adapted to children's age?"

"Oh, I think that would be gorgeous!" exclaimed Marguerite DeFoe, her shapely arms coming together in an embrace over the idea itself.

"It certainly is a lovely thought," spoke Ruth McMaster.

Gertrude Long rose abruptly, her brown eyes flashing. "I'm against it! Our people will call it just one more of those sugar-sweet, sentimental gestures that make religion the laughing-stock it has become. In the first place, no pupil will ever go to that room. No pupil will invite ostracism from his fellow pupils —he'd be called queer. We teachers, on our part, never will have *time* to use it! Nobody will use it. It will be just one more empty room when we don't have rooms enough as it is. It will be one more expense when we don't have money enough for legitimate things. If you want some real religion, increase the teachers' pay! Gosh, that's where real religion begins. Don't spend money on the knick-knacks until we see some of it on our bread and butter!"

Mr. Paul felt as though he had been slapped in the face. He looked down at the doodling on his paper, pictures of little brownies and cupids. A silence filled the room. No one spoke in answer to that Long spitfire. He hadn't intended to let his proposition get into controversy.

"I hadn't thought of this as a knick-knack. I thought of it as the bread of life," he said quietly. "But we don't want to start anything of this kind unless it has the complete, unanimous support of all. Let us proceed now to the regular business of the day. Will Miss Callen please read the minutes of the last meeting?"

As the meeting broke up an hour and a half later, Gertrude said to Marguerite, "Gosh, I didn't intend to smash the whole thing without a fight. Why didn't that softie fight back?"

"You know Mr. Paul. He never fights."

"No, darn him! But if a man has a conviction he should fight for it. I have no use for these wishy-washy men. He's as innocent and starry-eyed as his ideas. Neither one has any backbone!"

The next morning before school opened Ruth McMaster came into David's office.

"I loved your idea yesterday, Mr. Paul, and just wanted to say, don't give up. Let me talk to some of the teachers quietly and bring it up again sometime. I know several were very much in favor of it. A little more talking with the teachers in a quiet way may do it."

"And a little more talking with God in a quiet way will help still more," said Paul, smiling his gratitude for her encouragement. "I feel guilty of not doing enough of that. Keep the matter in your prayers, won't you please?"

Outside her classroom, Ruth McMaster met Gertrude Long hurrying by.

"Just a minute," said Ruth. "I thought you were a little snappy yesterday the way you spiked Mr. Paul's idea."

"Snappy! I sure was, and I sure intended to be. But I didn't spike it. There is only one way to spike a thing—and that is to try it out. If old man Paul is too soft to try it, I will."

"What!" exclaimed Ruth.

"You heard me. I'm going to see if his idea is tough enough to stand hard roads or if the rubber in it is so thin that a tack could explode it."

And she hurried on down the hall, leaving Ruth McMaster speechless with surprise.

As her pupils settled in their seats, Gertrude Long began:

"This morning we are going to try something. You all have different religions. You all pray differently. Perhaps some of you never even pray. Some people say one can do better work if he prays. Personally, I have my doubts. As an honest matter of fact, I don't pray. But sometimes I do get still and then sometimes guidance comes through. A Power bigger than myself speaks through me. Now I suggest you all get still for five minutes. After that you can do anything you want to do—study your next lesson, write, or even draw pictures if you want to. How many would like to try this thing?"

A dozen hands went up, but most of the young faces wore puzzled expressions.

"Perhaps I didn't make it clear," she said patiently, after a pause. "How many tune in your radios and get music?"

All hands went up.

"Well, this idea I have in mind is to try to use our bodies and minds as radio sets. Tune in and see if any message comes through. Would you like to try that?"

All hands went up, and a ripple of laughter swept the room, as if Teacher had suggested a funny new game.

"All right—are you ready? It will be for five minutes, remember." The smile Gertrude gave her boys and girls was radiant with love and enthusiasm, and the young eyes watched her as she bent her head and whispered, "Let's see how quiet—we—can—be!"

CHAPTER 30

"Suffer little children to come unto me, and forbid them not."

A T THE NEXT teachers' meeting of the Crocker School there were few things on the agenda to be taken care of, and an early adjournment seemed in order. When Principal Paul called for the motion, Gertrude Long exclaimed, "Before we adjourn I'd like to call for an old motion to be taken off the table."

"Motion—what motion?" asked Paul, plainly mystified.

"The motion to have a quiet room."

"Why, that," and he cleared his throat to conceal his amazement, "was never moved, much less seconded."

"Oh yes, it was. You moved it, and I want to second it right now."

Again Mr. Paul cleared his throat. Then a smile lighted his face in response to a light in Gertrude's face—a light that was more beautiful to him than any smile could have been.

"I will gladly bring the subject before the group again—I certainly will. But technically we can't call it taking an old motion off the table. That's what I wanted to make clear for the sake of—"

"Technically I am all wrong," interrupted Gertrude impatiently. "Technically I'm always wrong, but I don't give a darn about Robert's Rules of Order. To be honest, I'm usually religiously wrong, too. But this time I'm awfully glad that I am only technically out of order. Ethically I'm in awfully good order and I want to report about it."

A ripple of laughter spread around the room. When Gertrude

turned and made a grimace at the others they burst into gales of laughter. The wrinkled brows and tired faces of a grilling day in the schoolroom had suddenly found an outlet. But it was a joy-filled, expectant laughter.

When it had subsided, Gertrude Long turned toward Mr. Paul.

"Well, this is my report, honored sir. I tried your quiet room treatment on my pupils and the cock-eyed idea worked! Since then I've used it every day and whenever I miss it my pupils clamor for it."

"What!" Principal Paul's exclamation was purely involuntary. "Pardon me for interrupting, Miss Long, but did I hear you right?"

"I'll say you did. But steady your ears; you 'ain't heard nothin' yet.' When I put this up to my pupils only a few responded in favor of it, but when I likened it to radio they all wanted it."

A ripple of laughter amid the amazed and smiling teachers gave Principal Paul opportunity to interrupt again.

"Radio?" he asked, now completely at sea.

"Oh, I suppose you religious people would call it 'tuning in.' Have it your way, if you wish. Well, we 'tuned in,' and ever since we've been tuning in every morning and—here's my report all in a nutshell—everything in my room has been going on twice as well ever since. That's all."

"No, it isn't all," broke in Ruth McMaster. "She's told me some things privately that I think it would do us all good to hear."

"Would you mind telling us some of the things Miss McMaster is referring to?" asked Mr. Paul.

"Oh, I don't want to tell things that might sound show-off, and you all know I'd die before I'd do anything that would sound sentimental!" Gertrude protested.

Mr. Paul's backbone stiffened. He was generous, patient and humble, but not the "softie" that he was acutely aware Gertrude Long thought him to be. In that hour she knew it as she had

215

never known it before. While everyone looked at him expectantly he said firmly and with quiet dignity, "No one will accuse you of being 'show-off,' Miss Long. Nor is there anything sentimental about it. What you are talking about is practical realism. It deals with the very issues of life. The home and the school have been remiss. We have been too compromising and cowardly to face the real issues head-on. So you tackled the situation. I'm proud of you. And how did it come out?"

"Well, to make a long story short, the first day nothing much happened. But the second day when I called for a quiet time one of the girls folded her arms across her desk and put her head on her arms. One by one everyone in the room did the same thing. When I asked if anyone got a message one little boy, a very poor worker, told me that God told him to work harder and get better marks. Another boy, a giggler, said that God told him not to be so silly about little things. One little girl said, 'He told me to be more obedient to my parents and to help more.'

"Another time when we had a quiet time, I told the children that we would take the last ten minutes at noon to talk about it. One little girl who talks a lot said that God had told her not to whisper so much, and that she tried not to all morning. A little boy who had been dishonest in correcting his papers, corrected his papers honestly that morning because he said God had told him to be honest.

"One morning I felt they should think of God talking to them not only about school work, but also in their relationships with each other, and we had the quiet time just before recess. The captain of the girls' team said that God told her it was up to her as captain to play fair and to help everyone else on the team to play fair.

"Then I began to wonder whether this experience was carrying over into the children's home, so one day we talked about it. One little girl said she did cheerfully a task her mother asked her to do and later heard her mother say to her father, 'There certainly is a change in Patsy!'

"One of the boys told me that his mother thought listening to

God is a very good idea and that she would try it, and other children report that their parents are glad the children are learning to do so. And in several instances the parents are following the children's lead in it."

Gertrude Long's lively voice had slowed, and there was a hint almost of tears in it as she continued hesitantly:

"I'll admit this sounds like baby-talk, the last thing I ever thought I would be telling the world. But my kids are just babies—or were, a few years ago. But until now they have been the wildest little bunch of cops-and-robbers and cowboys that ever came into this school. Even now they aren't exactly eating out of my hand, but this has changed the whole atmosphere of my school-room.

"I had become terribly bored with teaching. I felt I was moving day after day in the same old ruts. I found I was dreading to face my pupils. Then you made that silly suggestion about a quiet room. The reason I fought it was because I was worn to a frazzle and I was ready to fight anything—except a raise in pay. I had come to the place where the only thing I was interested in was pay-day. Then on a dare I started this thing. It was a gamble. But with it came the pay-off. More interesting than pay-day! While the kids tuned in, I tuned in. God made several suggestions to me, I took them, and now I am convinced that teaching is a most challenging opportunity! I've been given a plan for living beyond my own ambitions and desires, and I am given strength, wisdom and grace to live in that plan. Now every day is an adventure!"

She sat down as abruptly as she had begun.

For a moment it looked like she was going to cry. But after two choking gulps and a little cough she regained control of herself. No one had ever seen Gertrude Long cry.

Ruth McMaster slid her arm around her, and their eyes met. Both were smiling.

Principal Paul slowly rose from behind his desk. Everyone in the silent room had a changed expression as she waited for him to speak.

"I don't know when anything has moved me like this. Just the hearing of it seems to have changed the very atmosphere of this room. If all of you would adopt some similar method I don't know whether we really will need that quiet room! Perhaps it is better to have a little dose of this somehow taken into every room. I think we will adjourn at this point so we can carry with us for the rest of the day the spirit that this has brought us."

CHAPTER 31

"Joy shall be in heaven over one sinner that repenteth more than over ninety and nine just persons which need no repentance."

EASTER CAME early and went quickly. Spring was in full dress. The orchards were filled with bloom. The gardens shook out color and fragrance on the air. Automobiles filled the country roads on Sunday afternoons. Church attendance had begun to fall off. But Charles Maxwell's heart was singing every day and all day long. He had never dreamed that living constantly in the presence of God could bring such continuing sense of peace and joy.

On one of these spring days he received two letters in the same mail inviting him to be the chief leader in two summer conferences.

One was an invitation from the Young Men's and Young Women's Christian Associations of the state to be their leader at a week's Student Conference at a lovely lakeside camp grounds, early in August.

The other, the one that thrilled him most, was an invitation to be the chief leader at a five-day district gathering of ministers at another beautiful camp grounds, the first part of May. There would be probably over a hundred ministers coming to the May meeting, the letter explained, all of whom were especially eager to learn more of his experience in trying to walk in the footsteps of Jesus.

According to the Y Secretary who sent the other invitation, the young college people of the state were also very eager to hear his story. Both letters closed with an identical sentence: "We sincerely hope you will find it possible to accept."

He immediately sent acceptances to both.

Having sent these replies on the same day that the invitations arrived, Charles knelt in the little chapel for a long period of prayer. He then took his way to the home of the Pages and had a long prayer time with Rachel Page. After that he felt strengthened and fortified for any responsibility the Lord wished to lay upon him.

"Isn't it wonderful," was Mrs. Page's comment, "that you can meet with these two strategic groups in such a significant way! First, the ministers from all these neighboring states. Second, the young people of this particular state. I know God will bless you every step of the way!"

He was busy in his church study one day making outlines of the kind of talks he should have to give at these camps when Bill Peters walked into the study. He didn't have a cigar in his mouth. He didn't have the defiance that marked his appearance when Charles had interviewed him four weeks before in the court house.

"Mr. Maxwell," he burst out, hardly waiting for Charles to greet him. "You are the straightest shooter I have ever met! A good man, who doesn't look down on bad men. I don't believe you ever condemned a man or despised a man in your life, did you?"

"What makes you say that?" laughed Charles, taken aback by this outburst.

"Because if you ever had a chance to despise a man, it was when you were talking with me last month."

"Of course I don't despise you. In fact, I have such a wave of love for you in my heart right now this very instant that I would do anything in the world if I could help you."

Peters stared, open-mouthed.

"Well, I'll be damned. How did you know I needed help? If

any man on God's earth ever needed help, I am that man right now."

He sat down and gripped his hat in both hands.

"I am in a predicament and no one created the predicament but myself. I left the Wright Store with a lot of resentment in my heart, determined on revenge. Blocked from 'getting' Jonathan Wright, I was going to 'get' society. I played the game fast and loose. I didn't care where the chips fell. I was going to get rich and show up Jonathan Wright. The cards were all stacked. On every deal I held the aces and usually all the other face cards. I had already raked in one fortune and was starting to make another when you walked into my office that day."

He leaned forward, elbows on knees, and stared down at his hat between his knotted hands.

"If you had turned off a faucet, or turned off the light, or done something with your own two hands right there in the room that day, you couldn't have stopped what I was doing any more completely than you did. I won't go into detail. It's plenty sordid. Some people have got hurt, the innocent along with the guilty. I have kidded myself by saying that it would have happened anyway and if I hadn't got the apples someone else would."

He was breathing hard now, staring at the floor. Suddenly he tossed his hat onto a chair beside him and started clasping and unclasping his hands. He jerked up his head and glanced at Charles, a hunted look in his eyes.

"You said that day that there were three in that conversation. Do you think God and you can straighten me out?"

"God can. And I'll stand by you."

"Fact is, I'm in a hole. Last week my wife's dearest brother was held up at Sailorsville Junction and the savings of a lifetime taken. He has been digging and scraping all his life to give his two boys an education. His earning days are over now. This thing that happened to him is affecting his mind. Day before yesterday he was brought into our hospital here and my wife has been with him most of the time. When at the hospital she keeps calm for his sake, but when she's at home she goes into hysterics. It's hell and high water for me! Seeing her brother out of his mind, raving over his lost money, will drive her out of *her* mind if she keeps on. I never knew before how innocent people suffer through crimes committed by the guilty! And if she knew what you know—what you and I and God know— well, to put it in its mildest terms, all hell would break loose. Hearing her weep and keeping my mouth shut, I'm like a man in prison! If I open my mouth and confess everything to her— well—that's the hell of it. I'll do anything you tell me to!"

Bill's eyes stared pleadingly into his, hands clasped so tightly together they showed white around the knuckles. Charles Maxwell felt a great compassion for the poor soul before him.

"Remember, this secret is shared by three, not two," Charles began, "and the first step is to lay your repentance before the Father. Suppose you kneel down here—we'll both kneel—and ask God's forgiveness for our sins."

"Not *our* sins! *My* sins. But how can we ask that? I have piled up a mountain of karma that will take ninety-nine lifetimes to dig through."

"I see your much reading, your much studying, as you call it, has got you in another jail. There is one point where Christ goes so far beyond Buddha and Confucius and Zoroaster and all the other founders of religions that there is no comparison! He can wipe out your sin and even the remembrance of that sin if you are repentant enough and have faith enough in Him. Washed in the blood He shed on Calvary, cleansed by the Love He poured out for all sinners the world over, you can be a new man in one moment, provided—provided you have repentance, genuine, earnest and sincere repentance. If you have faith like a grain of mustard seed, Christ can cast a mountain of what you call karma into the uttermost parts of the sea."

"But I have never believed in this—this redemptive Love," Peters objected.

"Do you believe in it now?"

"Look here! It's either believe or curtains for me. I'll try to believe."

"All right—kneel down here and we will implore the good Father to help your unbelief."

Bill knelt heavily and whispered in a halting voice, "God, have mercy on my soul."

After praying together they resumed their seats. Tears had streaked Bill's face. Charles saw that the agony had not rolled away, but that the floodgates had opened, which he hoped would ultimately lead to full release.

"Besides repentance there is something else you must do, Bill. You must make every possible restitution of everything you've taken that isn't yours."

"How?"

"First of all, go to your brother-in-law and tell him that you will replace all he lost. If he remonstrates, tell him all police and enforcement officers in your position *should* feel morally responsible for the crooks who escape their net. Next, get busy to remove the hotbed of crime that you have established in this section of the state, and do it as quickly as possible. How best to do that, I don't know—it's up to you. Let us pray about that, too."

It was not till two hours later that Bill Peters parted from Charles.

"I feel a strange Otherness since we had those prayers," said Bill, a surprised look in his face. "Is that the way to put it? Is that feeling of Otherness, God's presence in our midst?"

"Yes," said Charles.

"It's like a sort of calm after a storm at sea. Will I keep it, do you think?"

"If you make restitution. If you are repentant. If you are brave. If you keep your mind on God. If you do all that, not only will you keep that Peace, but that Otherness will keep you."

CHAPTER 32

*"The harvest truly is great, but the laborers are few.
Pray ye therefore the Lord of the harvest, that he would
send forth laborers into his harvest."*

WHEN CHARLES parked his car at the beautiful Lakeside Camp Grounds on a warm May afternoon he found such a crowd of ministers, old and young, ahead of him trying to register and get assigned to their rooms and cottages that he decided to wait till the rush was over before asking about his own lodging. As he stood quietly at the edge of the throng of men in the lobby of the main building he was surprised to find that not a face was familiar. He heard the registrar say to one, "Yes, the registration has gone far beyond our expectations. The moment we opened the invitations to ministers outside our denomination and to men outside the state, we began to be swamped with applications. There will be close to three hundred and we will find our accommodations badly strained to take care of them."

The other remarked, "That is surprising, isn't it? And you say Bishop Patterson will be here only two days?"

"They aren't coming to hear Bishop Patterson. They are coming to hear young Maxwell. The theme for the week, you know, is 'What Would Jesus Do in an Age Like This?' He will address us every morning. The afternoons will be given over to discussion groups on this theme led by different leaders. After that come prayer groups which Mr. Maxwell insisted have the central place if we wanted to do justice to the theme. After supper we are to have a different speaker every evening, except the two evenings the Bishop is here."

The registrar had been busy filling out a card for the man he was talking with and now handed him his registration slip and started on another.

Charles slipped out of the hall and strolled down to the lake, where he found a secluded bench and sat down to get his thoughts in order. This was going to be a test of everything that had been wrought during the year. Where had these men come from—why had they come in such numbers? Was it not definite proof of the intense hunger of the church for Christ's answer to the needs of the day?

"Christ alone can give the answer, not I," he whispered. "I am but an instrument for Your use, O Master. Hold me in *Your* hands, speak *Your* words through my lips, let *Your* message reach these men, oh blessed Saviour."

As he recalled the words, "They are coming to hear young Maxwell" an overwhelming sense of inadequacy swept over him. Then he prayed, "Oh Lord, take Your biggest eraser and erase me completely out of the picture as I sit here by this lake. Don't let me put myself into the picture once, not once, but if I do, laugh me back into invisible nothingness so quickly that I will never do it again, never. Make me so invisible that no one can see me, so transparent that they can see only Christ shining through me."

For a few moments Charles sat motionless, unaware of the voices that came dimly from the throng in the distance, so deep was his meditation. Slowly the little sounds around him began to penetrate his consciousness: the whisper of the lake as it lapped the edge of the shore; a sudden flutter of wings in the green boughs above him; an awareness of the sun's warmth as it filtered through the leaves and touched his hands. The warmth and beauty of the summer day, the invigorating air, combined with the deep inner peace which had come to him after this quiet moment, brought about a delightful sense of well-being in body and mind. He leaned back on the rustic bench and stretched out his legs, luxuriating in this feeling, when suddenly a voice came from just behind.

"Oh, there you are!" Charles jumped up and turned to see Harold Parkman, an old seminary friend, walking towards him, smiling. "Someone said you were on the grounds. Come along— they told me to get you settled in your cabin before supper. Where have you been hiding yourself, old chap?"

The men clasped hands warmly as Charles exclaimed, "I'm so glad to see you, Parkman. You're the only one I've recognized so far!"

Parkman laid an arm across Charles' shoulder in friendly fashion as they started back, saying:

"Remember, you are new in this territory. It's a great conference we are anticipating under your leadership!"

"Under Christ's leadership, you mean. Well, lead the way!"

The next morning the little chapel was packed to the doors. Its capacity was three hundred, and extra chairs had to be placed in the aisles. Reverend Aldrich had arrived in time to conduct the service the night before, and his picture of what was happening in Raymond had brought the men out this morning with an openness of mind and an eagerness of spirit that filled Charles' heart with joy and gratitude.

"I shall want your prayers before I begin," he told them earnestly, "that Jesus and not I shall do the talking this morning. And I hope your prayers will keep going on every minute while I am speaking. If I bore you, or offend you, just lean forward and pray a little harder. You, as ministers, know as well as I do that your sermons depend only slightly upon yourselves. Your audiences either make or break you. Only when God and your audience and you all pull together do you have a good sermon."

As his eyes swept over the audience, a sea of responsive, friendly faces greeted him.

"When I began seriously to try to walk in Jesus' steps," he

226

began, "I found myself in a quandary. So many others had been attempting to follow in His steps that their crowding footprints almost obliterated the steps of the Master. If you have ever tried to track a deer in the snow when scores of hunters on horseback have already preceded you, you will know what I mean. The tracks of the particular creature which you wish to follow are very nearly obliterated. True you are able to follow the general direction. The more numerously the other tracks keep moving in the same direction, the more sure you are that you are on the right track. But if you want to walk right *in* Jesus' footsteps, the larger the crowd that preceded you, the more difficult it is to swing forward in exact rhythm with Jesus' stride.

"Well, when I started down the Christian trail I found that everyone in the churches for centuries and centuries were all going in the same direction. For instance, here is the violent revolutionary step of Martin Luther; here are the stamping, dogmatic footprints of Calvin; there go the swinging, enthusiastic steps of Wesley, and beside them the quiet, meditative steps of George Fox. If I follow the footprints of Charles Wesley I may become a mighty good Methodist; if I follow the prints of John Knox I may become a good Presbyterian; but if I find underneath all the footprints of the others the *exact* footprints of Christ Himself, and walk in rhythm with Him, then and then only am I *sure* to be a good *Christian*."

Charles saw from the thoughtful attention on the faces of his listeners that he had captured their interest, and continued forcefully:

"It is because we get so side-tracked by these footprints that have been stamped *upon* the Footprints of Jesus that the Christian world is so divided into rival factions, scattering our forces when we should be uniting our forces. Wars, intemperance, vice, graft, yes, crime and disease of every kind, might all have been brought under control if Christians everywhere had marched shoulder to shoulder in Jesus' steps down the years.

"As I searched for these half-forgotten footprints of the

227

Master, let me tell you what I found. I found Jesus one day asking His disciples who the people thought He was. They gave Him half-a-dozen answers. Then He asked them outright what *they* thought of Him. He didn't say, 'Think this over and sleep on it and come back and tell me later.' He said, 'I want the answer right now—the spontaneous, uninhibited, intuitive response that leaps to your lips the moment the question is given you!' Jesus knew that the greatest truths spring not from the mind, apart from God, but from the soul in tune with God. And sure enough, the answer came straight from Simon, son of Jonah, the most spontaneous disciple of them all: 'Thou art the Christ, the son of the living God.'

"Jesus had tried hard to make his disciples clear channels for the living truth to come through. And now at last in Simon he saw the inner spirit was in complete control, a perfect channel for God to speak through. And Jesus' immediate response was, 'Flesh and blood has not revealed this to you, Simon Barjonah, but the Father that is in heaven.' Upon clear channels like you, 'I shall build my church.' And he changed his name to 'Rock.'

"What was the function of a rock in Jesus' day? Not only did it make a firm foundation for a building, but it also made a perfect channel for living water to reach its destination without sinking into the sand and soil. The distinctive characteristic of the hills of northern Galilee at the source of the Jordan is that they consist of a rock formation that enables them to serve as a reservoir and permit the flow of the Jordan to continue all year; even during the dry season when other riverbeds are dry. Just as the Jordan is never empty because it comes from channels of rock, so would Christ's church never be empty if its message came from channels of God.

"And Peter, representing the churches, denied Jesus three times, just as the churches founded on that rock have denied Him three times."

A questioning look appeared on many faces in the group, but Charles took a deep breath and plunged ahead into the crux of his message.

"First, they have denied the healing ministry of Jesus. When the Master started down the hill to heal the epileptic boy Peter would have detained him, saying, 'Let us confine ourselves to the worship service only, let us erect three tabernacles and preach the gospel and leave the healing to the doctors and surgeons.' 'Get thee behind me, Satan,' was Jesus' reply.

"When I ventured into the field of spiritual healing and found a lot of criticism coming down upon my head from my church members I was tempted to deny part of Jesus' commission to his disciples 'Preach the gospel, heal the sick, cast out demons.' But one day I found in a little-used drawer in my study a secret journal of my grandfather's which I will read to you now:

" 'If I had it to do over again, I would give an important place in my church program for the teaching of health and healing. The Christian ministry need not be afraid to teach the healing power of God on the body through prayer. At what time in the history of the Christian life has bodily healing as a part of the church teaching been dismissed? It is still there, neglected and in some cases looked upon with fear and even disapproval. But it is a part of the Christian faith. I believe that the minister of today has as much right to pray for recovery of the sick in his parish as any minister in Paul's time or in the early centuries of the history of the church. Again, if I were back in my parish and could select the right men and women to assist me, I would maintain regularly a healing clinic of some sort and make prayer and faith regnant at the center of it.' *

"Then I turned to the commission Jesus gave to seventy young ministers he had trained. 'Preach the gospel, heal the sick, cast out demons,' and I saw that if I left out any part of this I would be denying Christ.

"The second denial of Christ by the churches was illustrated by Peter's cutting off the servant's ear, trusting to force instead of love. Whenever the church as a church puts its blessing upon a war, it is denying Christ. If the church truly realized the power of Prayer and Love as something infinitely more powerful than

* From the Journal of Charles M. Sheldon.

tanks and bombs war could be swept off the face of the earth. The greatest commentary upon the Christian church in all history is that it awaited one who was not a Christian to demonstrate the dynamic power residing in the teachings of Jesus when actually applied. Gandhi, with no other ammunition than the Sermon on the Mount, liberated his people from the greatest empire in the world.

"The third denial came when Peter counselled the 'comfortable' way instead of the sacrificial way. 'Big churches, wealthy congregations, big salaries,' are too often the way we measure the success of ministers today. 'Don't disturb the status quo; don't put yourself on the cross by talking of race prejudices and economic reforms.' When Peter begged Jesus not to go up to Jerusalem to suffer on the cross, Jesus turned to him and said, 'The Father is not now speaking through you, only the very human voice of Peter, who is made of flesh and blood. You speak not the things of God but of man.'

"The proud world that scoffs at religion, symbolized by the arrogant cock so sufficient unto himself, points the finger of scorn at the church and crows twice whenever it hears these three denials repeated, as they so often are.

"Jesus made no reservations, required nothing of his ministers except this one thing—this directly-channeled contact with the Father. He evidently wanted a church as free as air from bondage to anything but this direct, spontaneous contact with the Central Source. This was the church which He called, 'My Church.' Note that this is the only time he used that expression.

"There is no place in the Bible where Jesus ever spoke of the church as a building or an organization, but only as a channel for the voice of God. Indeed, in all the gospel He spoke the word church only twice, while He spoke the word kingdom continually. Paul uses the word church four times for every time he uses the word kingdom. Paul's footsteps are good, but I don't want them to obliterate the footsteps of Jesus.

"There are more and more persons coming to our churches in these critical days who are not looking for great sermons, not seeking wonderful music, or stately temples, or beautiful ritual. They are looking for a man who embodies in himself the second verse in the thirty-second chapter of Isaiah: 'And a man shall be as a hiding place from the wind, and a covert from the tempest; as rivers of water in a dry place, as the shadow of a great rock in a weary land.'

"My fellow ministers," Charles appealed to the close-packed faces before him as he stepped out on the edge of the platform. "With God's help we all might become that man Isaiah described! Bringing peace in the midst of storms and a spring of living water in a thirsty land! Without His help we can be only blind guides leading the blind. To become that man, we need above everything else more time for Quiet Spaces in our lives. My most urgent wish this morning is that we as ministers of the church of Christ will all save a period each day, perhaps many periods, when we can get very quiet, very close to Christ, very immersed in God, very filled with the Holy Spirit. Let us here highly resolve under God that we shall henceforth do everything we know how to do to help us to live, move and have our being in Christ. Amen."

CHAPTER 33

*"Ye are the salt of the earth; but if the salt have lost
his savour, wherewith shall it be salted?"*

Y OU CAN foretell the permanence of a species by the
strength of its heart," was the way Charles began his
address on the morning of the second day. "The dinosaur had a weak heart so it became extinct. The wild duck has a
strong heart so its kind will last forever.

"The heart of a church is prayer. Where prayer is beating
weakly against the stained-glass windows of a church, even
though that church were as colossal in its field as a dinosaur,
nevertheless its days are numbered. But if prayer is beating
with strength and power at the center of that church, even
though it has to hide in catacombs for protection, or flee from
persecution from one continent to another, that church will
live forever."

"Amen!" exclaimed an old man on the front row. Charles
smiled at him and went on.

"Some ministers seem to think that the old-fashioned prayer
meeting is as out of date as the one hoss shay. Suppose it is?
When the one hoss shay disappeared the need for transportation
didn't disappear. It merely changed its form. The old barn was
remodelled and changed into a garage and a Model T Ford was
substituted for the old sulky. As the years went by, still finer
models appeared, until the time is not far distant when the
airplane and automobile will blend into one vehicle through
development of the 'roadable airplane.' By adding wings to one's
car one will have an airplane; by taking wings off the plane one

will have a car suitable for shopping and travelling between airport and home. If the one hoss shay prayer meeting is out of date, let us add wings to our prayers and substitute the atomic energy of a dynamic faith and bring the very Kingdom of heaven into manifestation on earth!"

Smiling warmly at his audience, whose enthusiasm and attention seemed to have increased rather than diminished on this second day, Charles rested an elbow on the speaker's stand and continued:

"I believe the minister should study prayer as carefully as the heart specialist studies the human heart. And why not put the same zeal into improving the prayer life of our churches as automobile engineers put into improving the models of their cars? Steinmetz, the electrical wizard, said fifty years ago, after he had completed his 200th invention, 'We have been studying the laws of matter. Fifty years from now we are going to study the laws of spirit. We are going to take love into the laboratory and find more power in love than there is in electricity.' The fifty years are now up and the time has come for the clergymen to prove to the statesmen and scientists that prayer *is* the strongest force in the universe."

During the personal conversations with the men through the day that followed this morning address, Charles found that it was their united desire for him to "open up" and tell of his own personal experiences, and the experiences of his church members in the year that had elapsed since he put the challenge before them, "What would Jesus do?" "We are satisfied with your philosophy," they told him, "now we want to see how it works."

So the third morning he gave the hour over to telling personal experiences—Norman's in his newspaper, Wright's in his department store, and his own in the field of healing. As he piled illustration upon illustration, the lightness and responsiveness of his audience began to waver and a heaviness became apparent. Charles' speaking became more labored. When he had finished many questions were asked and answered, and then suddenly a square-jawed clergyman in the first row rose abruptly and demanded in a belligerent voice, "What should we think of a God Almighty who will answer some prayers merely because one person knows a special technique, and fails to answer others because the one who prays doesn't have the technique?"

"The hour is up for questions," said the chairman hastily. "We must go to our next gathering at once."

Charles Maxwell felt as though he had been slapped in the face. A great ache settled in his heart. Had he allowed his enthusiasm to out-run his reason and common sense? Had he let his ardor run too unrestrained in his desire to convince his fellow pastors that this dynamic power Jesus had proclaimed from one end of Galilee to the other was just as available for our use in this day as in the days of Caesar? Was his testimony of the invisible coming into visibility mistaken for coming into *conspicuosity?* Was he drawing attention to himself and not to Christ?

"I am sorry, friend," he said, "but I will have to answer that tomorrow. We have already gone over our time."

All day that loud voice kept ringing in his ears. When he retired that night he knelt by his cot in prayer for a full hour before he felt peaceful enough to sleep. In the morning he awoke with a new resolve, although not a joyous one.

When he faced the congregation of ministers that morning the atmosphere was entirely different from what it had been before. During the three opening days the ministers had listened not only with an open mind but also with an expectancy that was almost like a mesmeric spell. The sharp question cast forth at the close of the preceding lecture seemed to have shaken them all out of their dream of harmony into an atmosphere of controversy and revolt. The old watch-dog instinct so characteristic of a conscientious ministry had been evoked in all its force.

"This atmosphere," thought Charles unhappily, "feels as if they have arrived at the dead center that a great evangelist calls the 'paralysis of analysis.' God help me! I need your help, God!"

He would have given a great deal just then for a chance to

retreat—to flee headlong from that platform. The one thing he abhorred above everything else was to have pinned on him the reputation of egotism, of Pharisaic holier-than-thou-ness, of assumed superiority over that splended consecrated group of men, most of whom were much older than he.

As he arose an apology was already on his lips. He would tell them to forget and forgive everything he had said the day before, and today he would speak only of Jesus and His methods and give a solemn promise he would not have the effrontery again to witness to any experience of his own in following in Jesus' steps in prayer.

But before he began he paused instinctively at the pulpit and said quietly, "Let us step into the Silence for three minutes by the clock, and ask the Holy Spirit to listen through your ears and speak through my lips."

The silence that filled the room became a vacuum like unto the vacuum that fills the hollows in the hills into which the living water of the mountains flow. The power of it seemed almost to lift Charles Maxwell off his feet. When he finally ended it with a clear "Amen" there suddenly came a flow of words and a message that he never dreamed would be his.

His voice was firm and clear as he began, "My friends, I came here this morning intending to make an apology for offending you. The question that was flung at me at the close of the lecture yesterday left a sting that humbled me beyond words. I felt like a culprit before the bar of justice, and I came today prepared to beg your pardon for stepping outside the holy Scriptures to draw upon a few examples of answered prayer in modern times. But now, following this precious period of silence, that apology has been snatched away by some unseen hand—and a new message comes ringing through. It has come to me that if I apologize I should be demeaning not *my* voice but the voice of the Holy Ghost, and if there is an unforgivable sin I understand it is to retract or blaspheme the voice of the Holy Ghost.

"I was asked yesterday—and I know it was an honest and sincere question: 'What should we think of a God Almighty who answers some prayers merely because one person knows a special technique, and fails to answer others because the one who prays doesn't have the technique?'

"I am certain, friends, that you know very well that I never have implied that technique accomplished miracles of prayer— only the Spirit behind the technique. The only technique I have spoken of has been the technique of the Spirit, in the words of Paul: faith, hope and love; and of Christ: 'Whatsoever ye ask, *believing.*' Anyone who would substitute in his prayer distrust for faith, hate for love, and doubt for hope, would certainly have the wrong 'technique' and there is no way of denying it.

"But I stand here to remove once and for all any criticism, spoken or implied, against a God Almighty for answering prayers given with the technique prescribed by Jesus. Let us put the blame where the blame belongs—upon man, not upon God. Why blame God for saving the children of the rich when attacked by T.B. because they can have the best care; and for letting the children of the poor die like flies in the tenements? Of course the poor don't have the right technique, but let us put the blame not on God but on society where it belongs. And as the cries of the slum dwellers are unmet because of the blindness of society, so are the prayers of our church members unanswered because of the blindness of us spiritual leaders who are afraid to experiment and explore the mysteries of prayer for fear it *might* lead to failure. What fresh air is to the dwellers in apartment houses, prayer is to dwellers in churches. Just as greed has turned the heart of our beautiful cities into slums, so theological cynicism in regard to Jesus' teachings on the power of prayer has been turning our beautiful churches into slums of skepticism and doubt, monumental dinosaurs with the heart left out.

"I went yesterday from this platform rebuked and ashamed because I feared the condemnation of men more than I feared the shaming of my Lord. But, men, I have changed my mind since God got to me in this silence. I shall make no apologies for God. I shall reserve my apologies for ourselves."

He paused for breath. The silence, the absorbed attention, the

236

feeling that something great was happening in that room, was overpowering. From then on the words came effortlessly and fluently. From controversy and defense he stepped out into the vastness of the love and mercy of a personal Savior who had given His life that we might live—not only saving us from the evils of hell after this life is ended, but saving us from the hell of suffering in this world right now. When he had finished, a prayer sprang spontaneously to his lips for the beautiful Holy Spirit to bless all present.

The silence that followed this prayer was sweet and powerful. The complete transformation of the atmosphere of the room from controversy to concord, from supplication to serenity, from defeat to victory, had come so rapidly that it brought a deep peace to all present. When he retired to his seat on the platform, Dr. Aldrich did not rise to dismiss the men. He remained seated with his eyes closed. No one seemed anxious to leave. Finally Dr. Aldrich, with a radiant glow on his face, rose and said, "I don't think we should leave without singing a hymn like 'My Faith Looks Up to Thee.'"

It was on that note that the convention came to an end.

CHAPTER 34

"So shall the last be first and the first last."

S ANDY HAD just come out of the sanctuary when he heard a
loud knocking on the door to the pastor's study. He
looked down the hall where he could see the back of a
broad shouldered heavy set man.

"If ye want to see the pastor, ye'r wastin' your time," he
called. "He's oot."

The man turned. It was Bill Peters.

"In that case," Peters replied, "I'll go in and wait," and he
turned and opened the door. "I'm in no rush but I must see the
preacher."

Sandy shuffled toward him. "Ye will have to wait a verra
long time, friend. He's gone to a pastors' conference that will
keep him away for a whole week."

"Great scott!" Peters exclaimed. He sagged slightly. Then
looking straight at Sandy, he added, "Say, would you mind if I
stayed in his study for a few minutes? I want to get my bearings
before I go on. I might slip into his wave length."

"Sure, sure! Stay as long as you want to." Sandy was so
startled, he could say no more. As the door closed, he gasped
under his breath, "Bill Peters of a' men! Bill Peters! come to
visit the parson!"

Inside the study Bill Peters looked over the row of books.
Finding one that intrigued his curiosity, he opened LOVE CAN
OPEN PRISON DOORS and settled back in the big chair be-
hind the desk. A half hour later he was so absorbed in the reading

that he was hardly aware that the door had opened and a tall man had entered.

"Upon my word!" It was the voice of Andrew Marsh. "I come to see Charles Maxwell and who do I find in his chair but Bill Peters himself."

A smile slowly widened the cheeks of Bill Peters and his eyes twinkled. "A long way from the City Hall to the First Church, eh? But if you want to see the parson, you came the wrong day. He's at a pastors' conference—gone for a week."

"And you're taking his place? Well! well! The world *is* getting upside down." Andrew Marsh still stared. "I never dreamed I'd ever see you sitting in First Church. But if it's really you sitting there and not a mirage, you may be the man I'm looking for. Whatever brought you here, anyway?"

"Did you read the headlines this morning?"

"That terrible accident!" exclaimed Marsh. "Another case where alcohol and gasoline didn't mix. The governor was killed instantly, I understand. Will the lieutenant-governor pull through?"

"He passed away at 10 o'clock this morning."

"Good Lord! What will happen to the state?"

"That's what I came to see the reverend about," said Peters. "A special election is being called for August. Primaries will come off in three weeks. It's going to be a rush affair. That is what brought me here."

"Why here?"

"I want the pastor's advice on what man to back for the governor's race, to be frank about it. I've had a lot to do with the governor's campaign in the past and if I keep being lucky, I think I can put a governor in again. Only this time I want to find a man who will be worth electing. They're hard to find."

Andrew Marsh smiled, "Now I know you are the man I'm looking for and I think *I'm* the man *you're* looking for."

"Mr. Marsh," Bill Peters spoke slowly and carefully through firm jaws. "If a man of your standing and wide reputation in

239

the state would consent to run, I'm sure I could get you elected. It'd be a hot race, but you'd make it, I know."

There was something about the firmness in Peters' face that made Andrew Marsh draw back.

"See here, Bill Peters," he said, "On second thought, I'm afraid I can't do business with your crowd. I am in to clean up the state."

"Exactly what I'm in this for," ejaculated the other. "I got a reputation for cleaning up the city. I kept it clean, sure, but for the wrong reasons. I'll tell you all about that some day. But now I want to help clean up the state for the right reasons and I think you're the man who can do it. The gang that helped me clean up the city aren't going to be happy about this. But I can take care of them. I've been 'politicking' long enough for that anyway. But I need to have an organization if it's the right organization."

"Did I understand you right?" Andrew Marsh screwed up his eyebrows and squinted hard as he drew up a small chair and sat down within a foot of where Peters was sitting. "Did I hear you saying you were looking for a brand new crowd . . . was that it?"

"Didn't you ever hear of a car shifting gears when it comes to a long hill? Well we're coming to a long hill, a hill I never thought I'd come to. But thanks to young Maxwell I have. And it happens to be a hill that may lead this state right up to God, Himself, if we find the right man."

"Bill Peters!" Marsh didn't even try to conceal his amazement now. "When did you ever turn to God?"

"It's a little secret between Pastor Maxwell and me. If there ever was a straight-shooter he's the man. I've got a long way to go to make up for all the harm I've done and the sooner I get at it the happier I'll be. Since I'm out of the department store business this politics is all I know. So this is it."

The two men without a further word reached out at the same instant and took the other by the hand. Two strong hands in a powerful handclasp; two sets of eyes looking straight into the other's eyes.

"I believe you," said Marsh. He took a long breath and added, "And so you are on our team at last?"

"I'm on your team, all right! And if you don't get a move on pretty quick I'll be calling all the signals."

"Then what's keeping us. Let's go." And Marsh rose from his chair.

"Where shall we go?"

"Over to Old Man Babcock's," rejoined Marsh. "This is exactly what he has been waiting for. There's nothing can stop us now."

When Charles returned from the pastors' conference, he found First Church all agog over the proposed candidacy of one of its members to run for governor of the state. The primaries were to be held in June, the special election in August—"The 19th of August," said Richard Norman. "There is something significant in that. Remember, it is the anniversary of the day that you put that challenge up to us in First Church. What a fitting day for us to vote for a governor who will ask 'What would Jesus do?'"

"What are some things a governor should ask that question about?" asked Marsh one day of a dozen men Babcock had brought together in his home.

"What would Jesus do about the rural schools?" asked Mr. Paul. "That is a big need in this state."

"Will you help me find the right man to work that out?" asked Marsh. "It's too bad you are not in rural work."

"I was a superintendent in a little town for five years."

"Then that's your problem. Take it over and tell me what to do."

"Appoint a committee to work with me, then," said Paul.

"No!" exclaimed Marsh. "I am through with doing things through committees. I want to put it in one man's hands, one who is on fire about it—yes, one if possible whose heart is breaking over it. Get a few helpers, advisers, perhaps a special secretary, if you wish, but no committee. I have seen too many things 'committeed' to death."

"Halleluah!" smiled Charles. "Praise the Lord!"

"And then there is the State Hospitals," said Norman. "That is a black spot in our state. It's something I'm tremendously interested in."

"I intend to make that the major plank in my platform," said Marsh. "I am going to look into that matter and if you are the right man I'll make that your baby."

"I've got my best reporter making an investigation of that field right now. I'll gladly take that over," said Norman.

"The job is yours," said Marsh.

"And the crime wave," added Babcock.

"I'll put that in Peters' hands."

"It's put," said Peters.

"And the unemployment problem," said Norman.

"My secretary," said Marsh, "was in Minneapolis when the 'Organized Unemployed' solved their problem in 1933. If things get too bad I'll turn to him for the blue print."

"And the farm problem?" asked Peters.

"That's my baby," said Marsh. "I was raised on a farm. My heart bleeds for the way they have been exploited."

"That will be the open sesame that will get you into office, then!" exclaimed Peters. "As a corporation lawyer you will have one strike against you to start with out there. A strong plank for the farmers will drive in the home-run you want."

Out of these discussions was evolved a program that was constructive enough to satisfy the liberals and yet sound enough not to offend the more conservative. With this to hold to, Peters got him safely past the primaries. His only strong opponent withdrew when he saw Marsh was a candidate. The others were comparatively unknown politicians.

When Marsh's nomination was assured, Peters said, "Now

spend your time among the farmers. I'll take care of the cities. The farmers in this state hold the deciding vote."

All through the rest of June and July the campaign waged. Charles sat in every week with a prayer group that held up Marsh's constructive program for God's blessing. Beyond that he took no active part whatever in the campaign. But how he did devour the papers!

Deep down in his heart, he had to admit there was nothing he desired more than that Marsh should win the election. "Am I pressing down too hard on this?" he asked himself. "It's the old football spirit in me, I guess."

When late July arrived, it was with a sigh of relief that he packed his suitcase and departed for the state youth camp. "This will be a good interim," he thought, "to get away for a solid week from all newspaper reports and all telephone calls and all talk about politics. So Lord, here I come. You look after the election, and let me relax my soul with the young folks awhile."

CHAPTER 35

*"Blessed are ye when men shall revile you and perse-
cute you and shall say all manner of evil against you
falsely for my sake."*

HIGH SCHOOL and college students from all over the State
had been invited to the special Youth Camp which was
to be devoted entirely to the deepening of the spiritual
life. It was the first time the Young Men's and Young Women's
Christian Association had attempted anything on such a deep
scale.

"In previous years we have always given much time to organi-
zational phases of the work," was the remark of Ralph Smedley,
the Y.M.C.A. secretary who set it up. "I am sorry I can't be
there in person but I know that you have something vital for
the young people of the state, so we're turning over the entire
program to you."

Charles had asked Frances Page to lead the singing, and
Florence Bowen to lead the morning meditation hour, and a
number of "resource people" who were going to be present he
had assigned to lead afternoon discussion groups. He himself
assumed the responsibility of giving both the morning and evening addresses.

"I am so glad that Frances consented to come," Florence
confided in Charles. "Her mother had planned an auto trip
through the Black Hills with her but gladly let go when she
heard what was her chief reason for coming."

"And what was her chief reason?" asked Charles.

"To help bring about a change in Murray," Florence replied
gravely. "If she thought she could help win Murray Edwards

she would climb to the top of Pike's Peak on her hands and knees. She is convinced even more deeply than her father and I that the spiritual life of Lincoln College next year hangs almost entirely upon a change of attitude in him. He has been such a—a disrupting influence in the school—in many ways . . ." Florence broke off and sighed dejectedly.

"Is there any likelihood of his coming?"

"Oh, yes—if I paint up the outing features sufficiently—the swimming and boating and fishing." Florence looked thoughtful. "He loves those things, and I think—" she hesitated and a slight blush came to her cheeks—"I think he loves me."

"Do you love him?"

Florence's eyes dropped and the blush deepened.

"I am afraid I am falling for him, Mr. Maxwell—awfully hard."

"Well, if you love him, and if we all pray for him, and if Frances is here to help us, I think we can win him. I'm giving you the job of inducing him to come!"

Florence's face was radiant. "I shall surely try!"

There was a splendid spirit on the grounds right from the very start. The presence of Frances and the seeming joy with which she entered into everything was a constant source of happiness to Charles. The only thing that caused trepidation was the presence of Murray Edwards. But Florence Bowen insisted, and Frances Page supported her, that he was sincerely seeking, in spite of his argumentative ways, and they felt confident he would experience a real change before the camp was over.

"Even if there is a risk, it's worth taking," was the way Frances put it. "For Murray will have such tremendous influence at the college next year, as president of the student body, that if we don't get him we may lose the college."

"With your and Florence's help," he told her, "and with God behind us, we will win him yet!"

But as the days went by his hopes seemed doomed to disappointment. Evening after evening Murray not only absented himself but he enticed others to absent themselves as well.

"His spiritual endurance, he claims, isn't equal to such a marathon of religion," said Florence, with a little grimace, "But when he runs off to the movies in Greenville every third night, I wish he didn't take so many kids along with him. I wish he had never brought his car. Sometimes I wish I had never talked him into coming. But if we have just a little more patience and go with him the second mile we may have a chance yet."

"I wish I could share her faith," Frances confided worriedly to Charles, later.

The last afternoon of the conference was slated to be the climax and high point of the session, as Charles Maxwell had reminded them all along. He made a special plea for them to let nothing interfere with their presence at that meeting.

As the week drew to an end an idea came to him how best to use the night before the last day as a "build up" for the prayer laboratory that was to climax the camp experience. When the morning of that next to the last day came, he outlined with some enthusiasm the plan for the evening. To his amazement it fell upon indifferent ears and baffled faces.

After the meeting was over he inquired of Florence how she could account for the strange reception to his announcement and she explained hesitantly,

"We didn't foresee that you were going to make so much of this next-to-the-last evening, Mr. Maxwell, so Murray arranged a farewell dance at Logan's Beach Club, and told the boys they'd have to make a down payment. I am afraid they've gone so far they can't cancel it. I feel awfully sorry but I think now it's too late to do anything about it," she apologized. "There will still be a fair-sized meeting here that night," she added. "Only about a third of the crowd is going to the dance, you know."

"But that was the third I wanted to reach."

Deep down inside him, Charles felt his very blood boil. This was going the second mile a little too far! "Jesus never said we had to go the third and fourth mile!" he ejaculated under his breath. It appeared so obvious that there was a definite conspiracy to block his every move for bringing the spiritual experience he so craved for them. Charles even brought to the surface the lurking thought that this was the entire reason for Murray's having come to the conference—and that he had deliberately timed this dance so as to bring the biggest damage to the convention at its most climactic moment.

So heavily did this rest upon him that at supper time he made one of the great mistakes of his life. He let his anger show. Instead of drawing Murray and his ring leaders apart for a quiet conference on the matter, which at the time he felt would prove futile, he decided to do as Woodrow Wilson did when balked by Clemenceau and Lloyd George—he went over the leaders' heads to speak to the entire assembly.

He had hardly started to make his plea for the group to scuttle the dance and stick to him and his plans for the evening, when he suddenly realized that he was not doing as Jesus would have done. He had allowed anger and exasperation to show in his voice. He was evidently giving the impression that he personally resented being outsmarted by Murray Edwards. He realized painfully well that if he let this descend into a battle between two personalities he was no match for this brilliant youngster. When he sat down after a stumbling finish, he saw that his plea had fallen on deaf ears. Even those who were not going to the dance seemed ready to throw their sympathy with the rebels. He found he could not finish his meal because he felt so utterly frustrated. Immediately after supper he hurried to his cabin by the lake, resolved to make atonement for his mistake by spending the interval before the evening meeting began in prayer.

"Not my brother nor my sister, but it's me, O Lord, standing in the need of prayer." As he repeated this over and over again he could hear in imagination Frances leading the entire group in the refrain. No longer was his wrath boiling against Murray Edwards—all that was now quenched by his flood of shame and repentance. If any wrath remained it was all directed against his own bungling self.

247

"Not the preacher nor the deacon but it's me, O Lord."

He was kneeling at his cot, head buried in his hands, when a gentle knock came on the door. He didn't rise or even raise his head. If he remained silent, no one would know he was there. He wanted to be alone. He heard the screen door open and soft footsteps enter the room. Without looking up he knew it was Florence. He could hear the soft rustle of her skirts and knew she was kneeling by his side. He did not move or open his eyes but continued in prayer. He could hear the soft breathing of the one beside him. A great peace gradually descended upon him. He knew she was praying for that peace.

"When I can't plunge I can still pass," he thought gratefully. "Thank the Lord for the privilege of prayer! It's not the boys and it's not the girls, but it's me, O Lord, standing in the need of prayer."

An hour later when he finally opened his eyes and looked around his visitor had gone. He had been so deep in prayer he had not heard her go, but the peace he had felt seemed almost tangible in the air.

It was time for the Evensong. Across the lake Charles could see the boats loaded with a third of the campers, moving slowly toward Logan's Beach. There was an unhappy, wistful look on the faces of those remaining to sing by the lakeside. There was a sense of frustration and defeat everywhere. Try her best, Frances could secure only lukewarm participation in the Galilean Evensong. When Charles rose to give the message of the evening he found his enthusiastic plans to make this a real preparation and built-up for the closing climactic day fall flat. But toward the end something changed—first in him, then in the entire group.

"Friends," he found himself saying, "I feel that if there should be any condemnation it should fall on me. In some way, I don't quite know how, I forgot for a moment that this was Christ's job and not mine. Tonight at supper time I felt that this was the last straw—that I could stand it no longer. And thinking of myself, I forgot God. In wishing to save my own little plan I forgot that the only thing that mattered was God's plan. God can make His presence felt on a dance floor as well as in a meetinghouse. Let us send love and prayer for our absent friends."

On the first row a little serious-faced girl looked aghast.

"Remember," Charles continued, "Job said, 'Though I make my bed in hell, behold Thou art there.' I don't mean to be sacriligeous but you know what I mean. If we trust God, He can do anything.

"Friends, I have been in continual prayer from supper time until now. I realize that I have been carrying this conference too much on my own shoulders. I must put it entirely on God's shoulders and I want you to help me. Even while I have been talking here tonight, *God* has been talking to *me*. He tells me to ask seven of you to volunteer to come up on Vision Hill with me and spend the whole night in prayer."

The reproving look in the face of the little serious-faced girl changed to a radiant glow.

"Bless her heart," thought Charles, "I know she will be there."

"Those who come, bring wraps and blankets," he concluded. "There under the stars above the cross in the pines we will let God 'build up' the meeting for tomorrow afternoon and do what *He* wants us to do."

Thirty-three young people climbed the hill at the beginning of the vigil, but on the stroke of midnight Charles suggested that all who desired might go to their cabins and of those volunteering to stay on, six be elected to remain with him. Harlan Douglas was the first to volunteer, then Dorothy Calvert, the serious-faced little girl, and then Frances Page. Finally, Mary Lou Norman, daughter of the newspaper editor, put up her hand, followed by Gertrude Woods, a sweet-faced little Negro girl. And then there was a delay before anyone else offered. Finally Andrew Marsh, Jr., rubbing a pair of sleepy eyes, said, "I think I can stick it out."

As the rest rose to go, Charles reminded them to hold the situation in prayer while preparing for bed, and if anyone awoke during the night, to keep lifting it into the hands of God. After they left he remarked to Frances, "It was sweet of them to come, but I was surprised and a little disappointed that more didn't offer to remain. Oh well—it saved me the embarrassment of making a choice of whom should stay."

"I think," said Frances, thoughtfully, "that the cream of our crowd—yes, the majority of those who would have met this challenge most heroically—are among those who went to the dance."

CHAPTER 36

*"If two of you shall agree on earth as touching any-
thing that they shall ask, it shall be done for them of my
Father which is in heaven."*

AT MIDNIGHT eight boatloads of young people were shoving off from Logan's Beach. The air was full of the latest popular songs.

"Aren't we a gay and carefree bunch, though!" exclaimed Murray Edwards to Florence. "Eat, drink and be merry for tomorrow we die!"

"Don't talk that way!" she said. "You know I don't like it."

"See here, George," he called to a boat leader, disregarding Florence's remark, "it's our turn to use the canoe. You had your turn coming over. You can't have everything your way coming and going."

The boats were finally loaded, six in each of the seven boats, two in the canoe.

"This is nice," said Florence drowsily, as she settled herself on the floor of the canoe facing Murray. "A backrest, two cushions—why this is luxury-de-luxe! How did we rate all this?"

"And just we two alone," he added. "It's like heaven."

"Mention of heaven," said Florence, suddenly serious, "reminds me that I must make a confession to you, Murray. Tonight for me has been one long hell!"

"What do you mean?" exclaimed Murray, his eyebrows lifting in exaggerated surprise. "Now don't go religious on me! That's one thing I can't stand."

"I don't care what you can stand, you'll just have to stand

hearing my honest confession if it's the last thing you have to stand in all your life. I say I was unhappy tonight and I'm going to tell you why."

"Make it brief, then," Murray replied, with a wink. "The moon will be up in five minutes and confessionals and moonlight don't go together."

"Do you know what I admire in you, Murray?" Florence asked earnestly, leaning forward in the canoe.

"Sure!" He was now the debonair cavalier at his best. "I am so brilliant. Writer, orator—and, let's see, what was the other thing Professor Cochran said I was?"

"I don't care what Professor Cochran said you were—conceited, probably."

His response was a hearty laugh that rolled over the water.

"But this I do know, Murray, greater than your brilliance I admire your courage and your honesty."

"I'm glad to hear it wasn't my religion," he remarked wryly.

"I knew you weren't religious, Murray, but because I knew you were honest, I admired your coming to this conference, for I assumed you were making an honest quest to find something that you had been missing in life. But because religion was such a new atmosphere for you to breathe—"

"And how!" he ejaculated.

"I figured that it was perfectly normal for you to need some diversions. Yes, the only safe thing for you to do, really, because you were so new in a religious gathering of this kind, was to come up every-so-often for a breather."

"You're telling me!" he exclaimed, fervently.

"That is why I accepted your invitations to run off from the meetings so often—even though every time I went along it cut across all my deepest personal convictions to do it. But because I was so really deeply interested in you, Murray, I would do anything, anything to—to—oh! what word am I trying to say?"

"To save my soul, you silly little girl. You might just as well be honest and aboveboard about it! Florence Bowen, Salvation Army lassie, trying to save the soul of poor little sinner, Murray.

But alas! instead of picking a poor pagan from the burning, she found she had picked a peck of pickled trouble. Isn't that it?" There was a touch of grimness in his voice and he did not face Florence as he spoke.

"Murray," Florence was very serious now, "we have got to talk this out tonight, right now. We can't dodge it any longer. I have to confess that I have misjudged you. I still admit that you are the most brilliant and the most courageous—what shall I say—go-getter in the whole bunch of boys at this conference. But as to your honesty I am disillusioned. I don't think you came here with one bit of the sincere yearning to increase your religious life you professed when you offered to come. I think your one and only reason in coming was to discredit Mr. Maxwell and ruthlessly destroy in one week what it has taken him a whole year to build up."

"And what is so wrong in pricking a balloon?" he grinned. "When anything gets too inflated it is always good to let out a little air."

"It isn't air that Charles Maxwell has been filling us with. It is more like the blood that flows in our veins. Yes, the sacrificial blood that Jesus shed for us. When you pretended to be pricking a balloon in taking us off the conference grounds tonight, you were really driving a spear into the bleeding side of Christ."

"Now look here, don't go Pentecostal! In another minute you'll be in hysterics." Murray protested. "You talk like a border-line case already." His voice had lost its softening edge of humor.

"Murray, you are an artist in controversies of this kind. You draw your adversary on like the matador with his red robe draws the bull. And then when you get your victim so upset that he flies out of self-control for just one minute, you step in for the killing. I saw that happen this very night when you maneuvered Mr. Maxwell into a position where he looked like—like—"

"Thirty cents! Is that what you want to say?"

253

Florence's voice was accusing, but she was almost in tears. "No, even worse than that. You virtually destroyed the conference tonight."

"You mean *he* did!" Murray exclaimed scornfully.

"All right, Mr. Matador, there's no use trying to tell you anything." There were tears in her eyes as well as in her voice now. "And here I am letting myself be made a fool of by your clever baiting—trying to tell you things that I now see you never came out here to hear. I'd better finish this before I do go borderline by just simply saying that, in my opinion, you *are nothing but a clever hypocrite*. Take it or leave it, that is my final conclusion. You have wrapped me around your little finger by making me believe you were honestly seeking, when all the time you were making me part of the most diabolical scheme to destroy the finest man you or I have ever known, one who has the purest dream I have ever had the privilege of sharing."

"Well, what are you going to do about it?" he asked in a defiant tone.

"I will tell you what I am going to do about it, and what you are going to do about it until we reach the camp grounds. We are both going to remain perfectly silent. If you speak *one* more word I am going into hysterics! If you speak *two* I am going border-line and if you speak *three* I am going to jump right into the lake."

"O.K., if that's the way you want it." He cleared his throat. The moon was out now. The only sound was the drip, splash, drip, splash of the paddle in the still waters.

Half an hour later, as the canoe approached the landing pier, Florence broke the silence.

"Do you know, Murray, I feel as though someone has been praying for us all the time we have been coming."

Murray cleared his throat twice, coughed, and, after a little hesitation said, "If you won't go border-line and jump into the lake, Flo, I might say that perhaps I *have* been just a *little* bit of a cad."

"What!" She could hardly believe her ears.

"Don't let's talk any more, Flo. If you don't mind, I want to go straight to my cabin and let you go to yours. I want to sleep on this. If I don't, I'll go over the border-line myself."

It was exactly four o'clock in the morning, and the seven holding vigil on the hill behind the pines had just completed reciting the Lord's Prayer. They relapsed into silence again. Three were lying on their backs looking at the stars. One lad, lying on his side wrapped in a heavy blanket, was breathing so evenly that he may have fallen asleep. The other three, Frances, Charles and Harlan Douglas, were sitting side by side with their backs against three little birch trees, in silent prayer. Twenty feet below them, hidden behind a row of pines, stood the cross. The group had climbed above it where they could get a full view of the lake. Four hours ago they had seen the flashlights of the boats coming from Logan's Beach, and at Charles' request they had been "flashing prayers" and "swishing love" out to them as they came along.

"You never can tell what may happen," he said. "Prayers are never futile, and love is never wasted."

But now they were startled by footsteps on the dry leaves below the cross, heavy footsteps dragging over the stones along the path.

"Shall I call?" whispered Harlan to Charles, "and let them know where we are?"

"No," he cautioned, "it's only one and he may wish to be alone at the cross."

The group seated and lying under the pines was concealed from view from anyone below by the low bushes, but those in sitting position could see through the shrubbery the figure of a man in the moonlight getting down on his knees before the cross.

"I am not hysterical and I am not border-line," they could hear his voice saying, "but I am awfully close to something else that I never dreamed I would be."

255

Frances put her warm hand in the hand of Charles and whispered in his ear, "Can that be Murray?" In response he squeezed her hand for silence and nodded.

"Father," the voice went on, uncertainly, "this is a sort of prayer, as they call it, but in plain, ordinary, down-to-earth, every-day language, just man-to-God. Let's just say, if there is a God, and you are He, and a personal God like they say, and if religion is not largely bunk but largely true, and if—believe it or not—prayer is widely efficacious like they say—well, if all those things are true, I've been wrong in a lot of ways and I need prayer. Just between us, God, I wish You'd make the prayer for me, for any I might make would be much too weak."

The three figures lying beside Charles had silently risen to sitting posture, their faces in the moonlight all turned open-mouthed toward Charles. The sleeping boy was now wide awake, his arms folded beneath his head, every sinew tensed. Charles was relieved when he saw that all these varied movements had not reached the ear of the newcomer. Charles himself hardly dared to breathe.

Murray was speaking again: "I love this camp. It's physically a place of beauty. And I love these kids more than I ever thought I would. They are the best bunch I ever saw. You know I came here as an agnostic with a chip on my shoulder, and nobody knocked it off—until just now, tonight, You and Flo did something terrific.

"Forgive me, first of all, for being a cad and an egotist. I thought I could break this camp up. I thought pious Charley was one of those Pharisees with religion skin-deep. I found he is true-blue. Jehosophat, how deep it goes with that man! I don't know what he's got but it spreads like measles. Even while we danced tonight it kept spreading.

"But, Lord, I haven't even started on my sins of transgression and omission. I'm weak, selfish, cold, stubborn, hard-headed, quibblesome, vain, petty, narrow, dogmatic, pedantic, irreverent, over-gossipy, resentful, irritable, apologetic, self-excusing, rationalizing, superiority-complexed, impolite, rude, arrogant, impatient, impulsive, impetuous, undiplomatic, tactless, cross, churlish, sinful, unregenerate, unloving and unloved; well, maybe not all of those at once, all the time, but anyhow, some of them, most of the time, and that's aplenty! I don't know and can't imagine how one guy could accumulate and pick up all this rubbish.

"Personally, I don't have the slightest idea where You can find room for all these weaknesses and sins. But Preacher Charley told us to 'sweep all this trash out of our souls' and hand it up to You for Your incinerator. I surrender them to you—not just willingly or gladly but *gleefully*—that is, if You'll be kind and accommodating enough to take them. I'd like to have You take them all at once, but if Your incinerator can't work that fast, then I'd be glad to have You take them piecemeal, a little at a time.

"God, if we're still tuned in together on this receiver-transmitter, I want to add this to the script. This is the first time I ever really and truly tried to broadcast on this particular wavelength and so I know the program may sound pretty lousy coming in on Your antennae. I hope You can overlook the static and give this absolutely unrehearsed broadcast a better reception than it deserves.

"Lord, I hope it's just as good in Your sight to use this common, every-day talk, without the Quaker language, as it would be if I'd try to clutter up our talk with fancy 'Thees' and 'Thous' and 'Thines.' I have a sneaking feeling that maybe that won't make a particle of difference to You."

After a long silence, the voice came again, so low that Charles had to strain to hear,—in some subtle way a changed voice, full of a sincerity that belied the off-hand words.

"Since I'm still a doubter, God—if there is a God, a personal one—if prayer is efficacious and You're still tuned in—and if it is genuinely necessary for me not just to tolerate but to really believe this religious stuff, then help me to believe it, won't You?

"Thank You, God, for Your time and attention, and for

whatever You might be able to accomplish in my behalf I'll certainly be eternally grateful. Amen."

As Charles and his little brood watched, scarcely daring to breathe, the figure got to its feet and stood motionless for a long moment before the cross; then, incredibly, with a sweeping wave of the hand to the stars, and a murmured "s'long!" Murray Edwards turned and walked swiftly out of sight.

CHAPTER 37

"And the glory which thou gavest me I have given them; that they may be one even as we are one, I in them, and thou in me."

THIS HAS BEEN a Mount of Transfiguration!" exclaimed Frances when Murray's footsteps had faded away on the downward trail. All of the seven were wiping tears away.

"It was like—like seeing Niagara Falls and Grand Canyon all rolled up in one," said Mary Lou Norman. Her lips were trembling as she spoke.

"Do you remember what Jesus said to His disciples as they came down from the Mount of Transfiguration?" asked Charles Maxwell.

"Yes!" exclaimed Andrew Marsh, Jr., who had been asleep when the experience began. " 'Tell no man'!"

"That is what He is telling us now," cautioned Charles. "Let us obey that admonition of the Lord very faithfully. Let us give Murray the chance to tell of this experience first. If we wait, perhaps he will tell us what he wants to in his own way."

"It is four-thirty now," Andrew said. "Shall we continue our prayer vigil or can we go now?"

"I believe," said Charles, with an affectionate smile at his little group, "that God has answered our prayer and that His wish for us now is to go and rest, and be prepared for the grandest closing day any camp ever had. Let us join hands in a circle and have Harlan and Frances offer prayers of gratitude and thanksgiving before we go."

That morning at breakfast seven pairs of eyes were searching the dining hall for Murray Edwards. These seven were carrying a secret that was almost exploding to get out. Florence Bowen had her eyes alerted also, not to find him but to avoid him. But Murray Edwards was not at breakfast. He did not come to the morning meditation nor to Charles' nine o'clock address. Later in the morning Harlan Douglas returned from a survey of the boats.

"One is missing," he told Charles, excitedly. "He must have taken it while we were eating breakfast. Maybe he has gone over to the island."

"He may have taken it when he came down from the cross," said Charles. "Something wonderful may be happening if he is spending the morning alone."

"With God," added Harlan.

"With God," repeated Charles, as their eyes met in understanding.

The discussion groups followed their customary routine that afternoon but when all gathered together at the Council Ring at four-forty-five for the final prayer laboratory, Charles Maxwell suddenly became aware of a wave of suppressed excitement passing through the throng of young people gathering around him. Their eyes were all focussed upon the dock where Murray was fastening his boat. A silence fell as he strode toward the group.

Murray Edwards had always studiously avoided all prayer groups. He had been a faithful attendant only at the discussions, where his active voice and agnostic views had been a very disrupting influence. He had attended a few—only a few—of the Maxwell lectures. And now for the first time he was coming toward the group gathered for prayer.

One hundred boys and girls had seated themselves on the stone circle of the Council Ring. About fifty others were seated on the grass inside, their backs against the encircling wall. Charles stood in the open entrance way, his back to the lake. Two sitting on the Council Ring moved over and made a place for Murray at Charles' right hand when he arrived.

Looking down, Charles noticed that Murray held a Bible in his hand.

"Let us begin this last hour that we shall be meeting together," he said, quietly, "with a prayer for the Father to be in our midst."

After five long minutes of perfect silence, closing with the Lord's Prayer, Charles said, "Beginning at my left, each one of you give a verse from the Bible that means something special to you. Not just a nice set of words that you picked up yesterday, but a promise straight from the heart of God to the heart of you —a verse that has become alive to you since some of you took the pledge a year ago that you would ask yourself before every undertaking, 'What would Jesus do?' "

One by one the verses were given until the circle was well nigh completed. Last of all came the turn of Murray Edwards. To the surprise of all he slowly rose.

"I can't give a verse that I have lived by this past year because to be very frank I haven't lived by any. But would it be okay to give a passage I memorized just this morning?"

"Certainly," said Charles. "Go ahead."

Laying the Bible down on the ring Murray began, his voice a bit hesitant at first: his hands clasped tightly behind his back: " 'But where shall wisdom be found? and where is the place of understanding? Man knoweth not the price thereof; neither is it found in the land of the living. The depth saith, It is not in me: and the sea saith, It is not with me. It cannot be gotten for gold, neither shall silver be weighed for the price thereof. It cannot be valued with the gold of Ophir, with the precious onyx or the sapphire. The gold and the crystal cannot equal it; and the exchange of it shall not be for jewels of fine gold. No mention shall be made of coral or of pearls; for the price of wisdom is above rubies. The topaz of Ethiopia shall not equal it, neither shall it be valued with pure gold.' "

The golden words of the Old Book took on new freshness and meaning in the voice of this new disciple. All present thought that he had finished but instead of sitting down he suddenly lifted his eyes toward the sky and went right on, in ringing tones:

" 'Whence then cometh wisdom? and where is the place of understanding, seeing it is hid from the eyes of all living and kept close from the fowls of the air? Destruction and death say, We have heard the fame thereof with our ears. God understandeth the way thereof; and he knoweth the place thereof. For he looketh to the ends of the earth, and seeth under the whole heaven; to make the weight for the winds; and he weigheth the waters by measure. When he made a decree for the rain, and a way for the lightning of the thunder: then did he see it, and declare it; he prepared it, yea, and searched it out. And unto man he said, *Behold the fear of the Lord, that is wisdom; and to depart from evil is understanding.*' "

Murray paused and moved his gaze from the sky to the young people sitting before him. A new softness was in his voice that none of them had ever heard before.

"Last night under the stars I found wisdom—" his voice choked for a moment but he went on. "This morning on the island I found understanding. And here beside this beautiful lake, under this beautiful sky, surrounded by all you kids that I have learned to love as I never dreamed I could ever love anybody before, and in the presence of this God-like man whose shoestrings I'm not worthy to lace, I want to take publicly a pledge under God that for one whole year beginning today—and I hope extending through a lifetime—before everything I undertake I shall ask the question, 'What would Jesus do?' "

He sat down. No one stirred. In the deep silence that followed, Charles' eyes sought the face of Florence Bowen who was sitting directly opposite him, and saw tears streaming down her cheeks. Suddenly she slipped to her knees. Frances and Harlan, seated on either side of her, followed, and then one by one each of the one hundred and fifty young people joined them.

Charles choked a little as he saw Murray hesitate a moment and then drop to his knees. Then kneeling beside him, he put his arm around the lad who for one long year had relentlessly fought his every move to reach the young people. Suddenly Murray's arm shot around him and clasped him tightly.

And in that moment all *knew* that in their midst stood the blessed, forgiving Christ.

CHAPTER 38

"Peace I leave with you, my peace I give unto you; not as the world giveth give I unto you."

Arnold Eton told me before I left," Frances said to Florence as they were packing to leave camp that evening, "that if I came to this 'crackpot' camp he would break off our engagement. But I know that when I tell him of this wonderful miracle that has happened this afternoon, and of this triumphant climax following such seemingly hopeless odds, he will change his mind. What has happened here can happen there, if God so wills it," she finished, a tinge of wistfulness in her expression.

"Do you think anyone can change Arnold?" Florence's face reflected absolute skepticism.

"What do you mean?" Frances snapped the lock of her suitcase and stared at Florence. "It changed Murray. Don't you have any faith?"

"Frankly, no," grunted Florence as she bent over her packing. "Not about Arnold Eton."

Florence was right. Arnold had no intention of changing his mind. He was in deep dudgeon regarding Frances' open disregard of his expressed wish against her going to the camp. Her joy at its success incensed him still more. Every word she spoke added fuel to the red flame of anger burning within him. It ended with a white rage such as she had never witnessed in him before.

"This is it!" he flung at her finally, starting for the door—

"Never enter that church again until a new minister comes or I'm through!"

"Wait, Arnold! You'd better take this with you." And Frances held out her diamond ring in a trembling hand.

Eton gazed unbelievingly at Frances for a moment, reached out to take it, and then drew back. "Does this man mean that much to you," he stood unbelievingly, sorrow still written on his face.

"It isn't the man, Arnold, it is something bigger than that—something I begin to believe you will not understand."

He took the ring, "Some day you will come to your senses, young lady, until then, goodbye." And he walked out of her house and slowly closed the door behind him.

The next day Frances came down with a bad cold. The day after the doctor told her she was threatened with pneumonia and ordered her to bed.

Three days later Charles received a phone call from Rachel Page.

"I think you could help Frances," she said, pleadingly.

"I hadn't heard she was sick! I will be right over." Charles' voice was full of concern. Shortly after he arrived and was taken upstairs by Mrs. Page.

"I told her you were coming. Go right in."

"Oh, Mr. Maxwell," cried Frances eagerly, when he entered.

"Better make that Charles, Frances, after what we've been through together. But I'm sorry to find you in bed."

"Charles *is* a lot better, isn't it? Charles it will be," she said gaily. "But I am so glad you have come. I know you can help clear up something for me. There was such power of the Presence that last day of the Camp, that I thought everything was possible. It seemed such a natural thing the way young Murray got invaded by the Spirit, that I thought it could reach Arnold, too. All week I had been praying for Arnold. In that all-night of prayer I especially held him close to the Father for a miracle to happen. After that last climactic afternoon I could hardly wait to tell Arnold all about it. But—but, Charles—*it didn't happen.*" Her lip quivered and tears filled the lower corners of her eyes. "What did happen almost made me lose my faith in prayer. The absolute contrast between these two experiences was like a shock of lightening. Can you explain *why* one time it happened there, and why this other time that I wanted it to happen it didn't happen *here?* Was it because of something wrong in me?"

Charles drew a chair up beside her bed and laid his hand on hers.

"There may be a larger reason than any of us now know," he said thoughtfully. Then turning to her he added, "Do you really love him very much?"

"I know why you asked that," she sighed. "Most people don't like him. As a matter of fact, he doesn't like people. He is very choosy. It bores him terribly to meet most people. But when he *does* put his approval on anyone or smiles at one, he can be terribly charming. Maybe because it happens so rarely is the reason why those he favors with his attentions feel so—so honored."

"I see. One would naturally feel flattered, let us say, even to be noticed by him."

"If he notices them in a good way, yes," she replied, "but not if in the other way. Arnold has a terrible power of hating. I never saw anyone capable of such black hate. That is the only thing that ever came between us—that threatened our love time after time. When he hates he hates—and he hates with all his being. And when he turns this power against someone you love—"

She covered her face involuntarily with both her hands for a second. Then, replacing her hand in Charles', and gazing straight into his eyes she continued:

"But his greatest weakness may be his greatest hope. You brought that idea out in one of your sermons, Charles. Remember? You said that Paul, who was 'breathing threatening and slaughter against the disciples of the Lord,' once he turned his

266

enormous zeal-to-destroy into a magnificent zeal-to-save, became the chief architect of the Christian Church. And you explained how that happened because someone had prayed—Stephen's prayer, for instance, as he was dying."

"Then let us pray, Frances, to that end," he replied. "Let's do it right now—this very instant."

"Yes, yes!" she cried, "Right now!"

As he prayed he was aware that she was holding his hand in both of hers, clasped together like the Praying Hands of Dore, the picture which hung on the wall above her head.

When he opened his eyes he found her eyes glowing with a great peace, while she made no move to withdraw her hands.

"It just comes to me with tremendous power," she said, "that we can avail ourselves (as I heard you put it once), *avail* ourselves of Jesus' promise that where two *agree* touching anything on earth, in Jesus' name, that it shall be established. And we agree on that prayer, don't we, Charles, perfectly?"

"Yes, perfectly."

"A strange feeling came over me while you were praying just now, that someday Arnold is going to belong to you—heart and soul. That is what would make me happier than anything in all the world. But I don't see how this miracle can come to pass for forty or perhaps even for fifty years."

Charles gave a start. "Forty or fifty years!"

"Yes," she went on, "and what mystified me was that in spite of the long time to wait, when I seemed to hear those words a great peace came to me, the kind of peace that you say is a prophecy of a real answer."

Charles Maxwell smiled. "There is a great truth hidden in what you say. I have found that those who love us belong to us, and those who hate us also belong to us, for hate is only a mask of love. Only the indifferent ones, who blow neither hot nor cold, never really belong."

Frances turned to look at the picture of the praying hands above her head, and a far-away look came into her eyes.

"But just think," she mused, "for forty or fifty years he might still hate *you*. I couldn't wait that long. I couldn't live with him that long. Now I am glad we broke off the engagement. It doesn't really matter. The only thing that really matters is to let God and His will prevail."

Just then Mrs. Page came to the door.

"Pardon me, my dears," she said, "but Coach Wainright is here to see your father, and he brought little Meredith who wants to come up and see 'Aunt Frances.' Would she interrupt if she came in for just a minute?"

"Not at all," said Frances who had made no move to withdraw her hands from Charles. "There is nothing to interrupt. We are just talking."

As Mrs. Page departed Charles looked down at the two small, shapely hands clasping his large brown one, and the fleeting thought came, "This girl is as simple and unselfconscious as a little child; after God made her He must have broken the mould." In all his life, he told himself, he had never met anyone like her.

The next moment her hands were withdrawn, however, as she reached out to receive the little child who came rushing into the room like a bolt of lightening.

"Look who's here!" said Frances, merrily.

The curly locks swung around and the little freckled face looked up in Charles' face, two big brown eyes shining with joy.

"Oh, it's the preacher!" and both arms opened wide and shot around his neck as she buried a kiss on his cheek.

"Well, well," he said, "that is taking me by storm!"

Looking over the little shoulder while her bear-hug continued, he saw Frances' face watching the performance with a look of satisfaction. Charles seemed to detect a touch of wistfulness in her voice as she added with a smile,

"Little ones have some privileges that we grown-ups don't have."

"Goodbye Mr. Maxwell. Goodbye Miss Page," exclaimed Meredith, as she dashed out as quickly as she had come in.

Charles laid his hand on the bed but Frances made no move to take it now. The spontaneous, unselfconscious mood seemed to have left her, but her eyes were still on his face, but searching now, as though seeking something she had not yet caught.

"Supposing Arnold should come back to me now?" she said. "You wouldn't think I was wrong if I refused to take him back, would you? Do you think that is what Jesus would have me do?"

"That is your chief purpose in life now, is it? To do only what you think Jesus would do?"

"Oh, not my *chief* purpose in life now," she breathed, *"it's my ONLY purpose!"*

"Grand!" he exclaimed, startled by her intensity. "What a wonderful note to end on. It will help inspire me in preparing my sermon for next Sunday. Which reminds me, I must go now and get to work on it."

He paused when he reached the door and waved goodbye.

She did not wave back; instead, her eyes, dark and luminous, followed him to the door. Something very like a tear hung trembling in the corner of one eye.

CHAPTER 39

"Heaven and earth shall pass away, but my words shall not pass away."

WHEN CHARLES reached his study one afternoon, two days after his visit with Frances, he found a committee of three men of his congregation, who were also members of the Luncheon Club, waiting for him. The smiling faces that greeted him were those of Jonathan Wright, Egbert Page, and Richard Norman.

"We hear you had a wonderful time at the young people's camp," said Richard Norman, as he shook hands with Charles. "My daughter said it was a real Pentecost."

"Andrew Marsh says his son was thrilled over it," said Jonathan Wright warmly. "And it is partly because of that, and partly because of the general effect upon our whole city of your ministry at First Church in this past year, that we have come to see you. We have a very important proposition to make to you."

"Well, gentlemen, you quite take my breath away," laughed Charles. "I do hope it is not to electioneer for Andrew Marsh for governor."

"The time for electioneering is over," said Richard Norman. "The time to vote has come."

"Well, I cast my vote for Andrew this morning." Charles said.

"While the whole state is going to the polls today," said Egbert Page, "to put the government of the state upon the right man's shoulders, we have come to ask you to help put the government of this nation upon God's shoulders."

"Yes," exclaimed Norman, "we are planning to ask First Church for a three months' leave of absence for you this coming winter to send you on a journey to twenty-five selected cities of America to spread this gospel of walking in the steps of the Master."

"But, gentlemen, I am not an orator!" Charles protested, jumping to his feet in surprise.

"It isn't oratory that the world needs right now, it is contagion," insisted Norman.

"But I can't give great speeches." Charles spread his hands appealingly.

"It isn't speeches that people want today," replied President Page, with a warm smile, "it is manna."

"Well, what do you think I can do?" Charles sat down abruptly, still weak with surprise.

"We don't know whether *you* can do anything," said Richard Norman, in his deep voice, "and we don't care. But we all think that the good Lord can do something *through* you if enough of us pray behind you."

"This is what we had in mind," said Jonathan Wright, as he walked to Charles' desk and leaned over it. "We three men would like to underwrite this journey so there will be no concern about the money end whatever. We feel that the world is sick, and the only cure is a spiritual cure. We feel that there is only one way out and Jesus is that way."

"But next winter is still far off," said Charles, rising again. "This is only August. There will be plenty of time to talk this over later. When my congregation returns from their vacations and the church gets underway again this fall, you may change your minds. How do you know whether what I have done has any seeds of permanence?"

Jonathan Wright took him by both shoulders and gave him a friendly push back into his chair.

"Sit down, all of you gentlemen," he said, "while I tell this stubborn parson why we made a special point to come to see him today. Do you realize, Charles Sheldon Maxwell, that today is

271

the 19th of August, and that it was exactly a year ago today that you put that challenge up to the people of First Church? It would take a score of books to contain all the wonderful things that have transpired since then.

"And now, on this anniversary, we men—representing your congregation as well as the Luncheon Club—want to put the challenge back up to you. We want you to listen to God speaking through us just as obediently as a year ago you made us listen to God speaking through you."

"When you put it that way, I am on the spot," smiled Charles. "Let us pray about it right now, and then leave it in God's hands for a few weeks. If you feel as sure a month from now as you do today, if you find by then that the September winds have not chilled your August enthusiasm, then we can know that it is surely the Voice of God speaking through you, and I shall not leave a stone unturned until I have carried it out."

"Let us kneel," said Jonathan Wright, "and let each one of us pray."

Each prayed in turn, and when they rose Charles Maxwell said, in a voice shaken with emotion, "My friends, please don't go for a while yet. Please sit here with me a little longer. I felt the power of the Presence so strongly while each of you prayed that I want you to stay while that which is filling me to over-flowing may find utterance. That is, if God will give me the words to convey it to you."

While the others resumed their seats in silence, Charles, hands clasped behind his back, paced the length of the room. Suddenly he paused and faced them.

"It comes to me in a powerful way that this commission you dear men are laying upon me has come straight from God Himself. But I want to hold off my final reply until I have straightened out one limitation that seems to haunt me of late. One lack in me needs to be resolved and when that is done nothing can hold me back."

"You mean the message?" asked Wright, "I see no lack in your message."

272

Charles walked to his desk and rested back against it, in a half sitting posture. "I know the Father will furnish the message," he said, "and I know it will go far beyond anything I could plan or think. As we were kneeling just now, He spoke to me in no uncertain terms.

" 'A grain of wheat' I could hear Jesus say, 'unless it dies cannot produce a harvest. But if it fades away and gives up all of itself to the soil, it is multiplied a thousand-fold.' A piece of uranium has no power until it, too, is smashed and drops all its pride of personal identity. Then it, too, is multiplied in power a thousandfold. The same law that functions with metals and with grains functions also with humans. I, too, am perfectly worthless, absolutely helpless, unless I can make myself completely selfless, completely surrendered—in the words of Paul, be nothing but a slave of Christ,—unless I can meet that test I can't accept your request."

"We will certainly pray for that for you," said Norman.

"I believe there are enough praying people," continued Charles, "to save the world, if they can just become humble enough, and have love enough, and become united enough."

"That's the job we've cut out for you," said Egbert Page. "Go forth and preach that message and something will happen."

"We shall expect you," said Wright, "to gather up the praying people and make them as soft as putty in the hands of humility, and as powerful as the atomic bomb in the hands of faith."

"Sodom needed ten righteous men to save it from the fire from heaven," said Charles. "But there were only four that met the test. There are four of us. How many would we have to be multiplied into to save the world?"

"I think four million could do it," asserted Norman.

"Each one multiplied by a million!" said Charles. "That is certainly a big goal to aim at." He hesitated a second and then added with emphasis, "There must be a hundred men who are living the life of prayer more effectively than I am right now, and whose messages would carry far greater weight than any contribution that I could make."

"We won't debate that," said Egbert Page, "But if each of those hundred held back and said, 'Let George do it,' where would the world be? In fact that is exactly why it is where it is today—because the men of vision are saying exactly what you are saying right now."

"Yes," said Richard Norman, "We figured that the time had come for those who have caught the vision to say 'Here I am, Lord, send me.' "

"So you think," said Charles, "that if enough of us who believe profoundly that prayer and prayer alone can save the world, would go forth with our message, that we could roll the praying people of the nation, as it were, up into a great gigantic snow-ball of the Spirit, a great organic body of dedicated souls, united in prayer for the saving of the world and the glory of God?"

"You said it," said Jonathan Wright. "I don't think it—I know it."

"Yes," said Richard Norman, "That is it. Any further words would be out of place."

The three men picked up their hats and started silently for the door. Then as one man they paused and turned to Charles. It flashed upon them all that something still remained to be expressed—not *a word*, but *THE WORD*.

It came first to Egbert Page. He started it and all the rest followed:

"Our Father which art in Heaven, hallowed be Thy name. Thy Kingdom come. Thy will be done on earth as it is in Heaven. Give us this day our daily bread, and forgive us our debts as we forgive our debtors. And lead us not into temptation but deliver us from evil. For Thine is the Kingdom and the power and the glory forever and ever, Amen."

And as Charles watched these three splendid, consecrated men walk arm in arm down the street together he repeated, *"For Thine is the Kingdom and the power and the glory forever and ever, Amen."*

CHAPTER 40

"Mary hath chosen the better part."

RIGHT AFTER SUPPER the phone rang. Rachel Page's voice was like music on the wire.

"Can you spare an hour with me, dear Charles? My son Egbert told me of the wonderful dream of those three men— how they descended upon you this afternoon and how they hope you will accept the challenge."

"Yes, I capitulated to their combined frontal attack," laughed Charles. "Do you think I should?"

"I most certainly do!" There was joy in her voice. "If you have nothing planned for this evening, do come over. I am eager for us to step into the Silent Spaces together."

Out in the air he was strangely exhilarated. The moon was at its full. Something wonderful could happen. As he entered the Page home he felt as he had always felt in that house, as though he were entering a sanctuary. Rachel, looking younger than ever, her white hair more a crown and decoration than a sign of age, greeted him in the hall. She took him by the hand and led him into her private parlor which was lighted by two tall candles beside the picture of Jesus. The room was almost as bright as day from the bright moonlight falling through the large picture window. Before this window, where the flood of moonlight was brightest, was the large chair of his grandfather.

"You are to sit here tonight where you can look over the dear old college," she said, smiling up at him as she seated herself at the right of the window in a chair which also faced the campus.

He waited until she was seated before he spoke. Then he said quietly, "But do you think I deserve this chair? Remember, it is sacred to me."

"Sit down," she commanded, fondly. "This is a little ceremony that I have quite set my heart upon. It is not only what you deserve, but what your grandfather most devoutly would have wished were he here. I have been happy all day thinking what happiness this year must have brought to that sainted grandfather of yours in heaven."

Charles sank back in the soft contours of the great chair.

"We are not to talk for awhile," she said. "There is so much that cannot be put into words—let us not try. So many things have happened that we are to be thankful for, and I crave the privilege of doing it in your presence. Let us think back over all this year, and let us feel the presence of your grandfather and my husband joining us in this sacred hour of gratitude."

In response Charles merely turned his eyes upon her and nodded. How could she have divined so expertly what his whole being craved? The day had been so full that anything short of silence would have been an effort. But in this blessed silence in this dear, precious room there was at last all the space, yes, all the vast "elbow room" as he loved to phrase it, that the Father needed, to surround and envelop them in His priceless, unspeakable love.

In imagination he could see the young Rachel of fifty years ago singing in the Quadrangle; he could see his grandfather, young and vigorous, rise to address the group of unfortunate men on how to walk "in His steps." And now after all the years the lovely singer of the past was sitting beside him, and he, God be praised, was trying to walk in the footsteps of his grandfather. No, in the steps of the Master, whom his grandfather loved and adored.

The year that had just closed began to flow past him. The sweet face of Frances and her voice so reminiscent of the voice of her grandmother, seemed to appear in every scene. Such victories, such joys! How did he deserve them?

Almost an hour had elapsed when Charles was aware of Rachel Page's soft contralto voice. A strange experience, thought Charles; a voice and yet the silence is not broken by it. A voice, and the very stillness is enhanced and enriched by it. A voice like the voice of angels in heaven!

"Behold the days come, saith the Lord, that I will make a new covenant with you, and with your children; not according to the covenant that I made with your fathers."

The Bible lay open in her lap, but she seemed to be speaking from memory rather than reading from the printed page.

"This is the covenant that I will make with you, and with your children, in those days, saith the Lord: I will put my law in your mind, and in your heart will I write it; and I will be your God, and ye shall be my people. And ye shall teach no more every man his neighbor, and everyone his brother, saying Know ye the Lord: For ye shall all know me, from the greatest of you unto the least of you, saith the Lord."

That was the same scripture reading that Charles had used that Sunday a year ago. In the silence that followed he ceased thinking of the year that was past; his thoughts roamed to the year that was ahead. But try as he would, he could not visualize anything in it—his mind refused to accept anything short of God Himself. Finally another voice began to speak in the room, a voice that also did not break the silence but rather added to it. It was not a woman's voice this time but a man's. Charles was startled when he suddenly recognized it to be actually his own. The words that had been coming to him, he had intended to repeat only in the inner closet of his silent soul. But now the very room was echoing to them. It was as though the room had suddenly become his soul!

"He that dwelleth in the secret place of the Most High," his lips were saying, "shall abide under the shadow of the Almighty. I will say of the Lord, He is my refuge and my fortress; My God, in whom I trust." How he loved that ninety-first Psalm! How easily its stately promises rolled off his tongue! "Because thou hast made the Lord which is my refuge, even the most High, thy habitation; There shall no evil befall thee, neither shall any plague come nigh thy dwelling."

Toward the end the voice of Rachel Page joined his. "He shall call upon Me and I will answer him; I will be with him in trouble: I will deliver him and honor him. With long life will I satisfy him, and show him My salvation."

That seemed the perfect ending of a perfect evening. Rachel Page turned a radiant face upon Charles.

"When Egbert and Carolyn told me at dinner that their presence was required tonight at a college function, my heart said, 'Tonight Charles Maxwell is to have a tryst with Henry Maxwell and with Rollin and with me.' And when you said you could come, my heart leaped up like Wordsworth's leaped when he beheld a rainbow in the sky."

"My own heart leaped," said Charles, "when I saw the moonlight touching a fleeting cloud just now. It came like a token from God—like a rainbow of promise that the years that are ahead will be years of fulfillment even greater than those that are past."

"But before you go I do want us to have a prayer about Frances. I am really concerned about her. She has had a great shock."

"I know," said Charles.

"Anything that affects her love life affects her health seriously," Rachel continued. "To most people Frances appears to be a career girl. What few realize is that her own love life is by far the biggest part of her—, indeed almost all of her. That side of her nature has been going through such throes lately that— well, frankly, Charles, I am worried."

"Is there any possible chance of a reconciliation?" said Charles, with deep concern in his voice.

"What do you mean, reconciliation?" Rachel stared at Charles, a wistful incredulity in her eyes.

"Between Arnold and Frances, of course."

"Oh, Charles, her heart is no longer wrapped up in him. That ended long before the break up. She is in love with another man."

"No!" Charles was thunderstruck. "Another man!" he gasped. "You don't mean Henry, the choir leader?"

"Dear Charles, you *are* blind. She's eating her heart out right now because the man she is in love with is wedded—"

"Wedded!" Charles exclaimed, aghast.

"Yes, wedded so completely to an Idea that she wonders if she would be interfering in his life work even to show her love."

"You don't mean . . ." Charles whispered.

"Don't finish the sentence," smiled Rachel. "Grab your hat and drive down to the City Park as fast as you can. Frances is hardly over her fever and yet she has been down there all evening at the rally for Andrew Marsh making torches. She doesn't have any business to be there and you are the only one who could make her come back. And Charles, bring me the news of Andrew."

Half the city seemed to be gathered at the Park, milling about, shadowy figures silhouetted against the light that gleamed from the concave surface of the improvised bandstand shell. John Phillip Sousa's "Stars and Stripes Forever" was just starting.

Suddenly a feminine hand was laid on Charles' arm. In the half light he recognized the face of Florence.

"I guess I know whom you're looking for," she said.

"Yes, Frances. Her Grandmother thinks she should be home. Is she here?"

"I'm so glad you are getting her," said Florence. "She will wear herself out working over those terrible torches. She's only been out of bed two days."

A voice over a loud speaker was barking out, "Lynn County goes two to one for Marsh. Hackaberry's lead cut to 3,000."

At the far end of the Park, under the wisteria covered pergola, they found her. A group of high school boys and girls under her direction were rolling cloth around the tips of rods and dipping them in kerosene. Suddenly he saw the slender form of Frances, back turned, sleeves rolled up above her elbows, taking the rods, as the young folks handed them to her, and dipping them in kerosene.

Charles touched her shoulder. Just as she turned, the raucous loud speaker jarred the air, dwarfing the music, "Spencer County returns two to one for Marsh. Hackaberry's lead cut to 2,000."

Frances, arms hanging at her side, was staring up into the face of Charles. Her eyes remained fixed on his.

"Why are you here?" she said. "Oh, of course, you started this, Charles."

"Started what?" he asked.

"This victory for clean politics that this state is going to see."

"Marsh isn't elected yet." He tried to speak banteringly.

"But he will be. The western counties are all for him. They are just coming in now! He's going to win, I know!"

Again the loud speaker. "Webster County cuts Hackaberry's lead to 900." Before Charles could speak, again the voice jangled forth, "Polk County puts Marsh in the lead. Almost all the returns are in."

"Frances, your Grandmother thinks you should come home. I came to bring you in my car."

"In your car?" She drew a long breath, then took her eyes from his, Charles hoped, reluctantly. "I hate to leave before the procession starts, but I know I should be getting little Ned home. I brought him along to see the sights."

So Ned was going along. That was not in Charles' plan.

"Couldn't someone else bring him?" he asked. "I wanted to see you alone."

She stared at him. "Alone?" she seemed dazed. "I'm sorry, but I promised Ned's mother I'd get him safely back—not too late, and it's late already. But these torches. I can't leave a job half done."

"Let me help you," Charles threw his coat on a bench and picked up a rod. The milling people poured past them toward the bandstand. The voice shouting over the loud speaker and the blaring of the band that seemed to unloose all its noisiest instruments at once, made conversation between them impossible. The last torch was completed. Frances was plainly tired.

"Sit down and rest," Charles said.

She didn't hear him. He shouted it into her ear and then took her by the arm and led her to the bench. As he looked down at her sitting there like a fairy in the moonlight, he was about to give in to a sudden impulse to lean forward and kiss her when she suddenly exclaimed:

"Did you hear that, Charles?"

"Darn," he muttered under his breath. "It's just a siren."

"Many sirens!" she exclaimed, completely unconscious of what was going on in his mind. "Isn't it wonderful!"

Up the street rolled a whole cavalcade of cars. A spotlight from somewhere played upon them as they drew to a halt hardly a stone's throw from where Frances was sitting. Peters got out of the first car with several men and pushed through the milling throng, passing by the place where Charles stood. Suddenly Peters recognized him and leaving his contingent, rushed to Charles' side and seized him by the hand.

"We won!" he shouted. "We won!" Then lingering a moment longer, he said in a lower voice, "I want to thank you, Reverend. We not only won but we won in the right way."

Peters was starting to leave when a salvo of cheers greeted a man getting out of the second car. The spotlight upon him revealed the face and figure of Andrew Marsh.

"Come here, Andrew," Peters called as Marsh moved through the crowd towards the bandstand.

"Maxwell!" Marsh exclaimed, "And you, too, Peters. Here are the two men I owe most of all to. I've got something to ask you, Maxwell. Will you—" The shouts drowned out his words. People were pulling on him. The shouting was now a bedlam. The band could hardly be heard. Marsh put his mouth close to Charles' ear and shouted, "I have to go now. I'll call you later."

Charles watched him reach the bandstand. As he was lifted to the platform by a half dozen strong men, the cheers and the band together were deafening. "I don't know how long this cheering will last," said Charles as he sat down beside Frances, who he knew couldn't hear a word he was saying. All eyes were turned to the lighted bandstand. "No one would see me," he thought, "if I put my arm around her now." But just then little Ned, wearied by the excitement and noise, climbed into her lap.

"I have to be alone with her," the words shouted in his mind. "Good Lord, thanks for this victory, but do help us to get alone." The band was playing, "A Hot Time in the Old Town Tonight" but all Charles could hear was the beat—"Alone—alone—alone—alone."

Now all was quiet and Marsh was speaking. What a grand speaker he was! What a great governor he would make. And what a marvellous first lady Mercedes would be. But now the speech was ending—such a short speech but such a good one. He was quoting as his final words from the Springfield Speech of Abraham Lincoln, in paraphase, "Without the assistance of the Divine Being, I cannot succeed. With that assistance, I can not fail. Trusting in Him who can go with me and remain with you, and be everywhere for good, let me confidently hope that all will be well. To His care commending you, as I hope in your prayers you will commend me, I accept this great and new responsibility as a sacred trust from you, and bid you an affectionate farewell. We leave at once for Capitol City. May His blessing be with you."

The roar of applause filled the air like thunder. Charles led the way through the happy crowd to the car. Ned, holding a hand of each, stumbled along between them. They rode home with Ned and saw him safely in. His mother waved at the door and said, "Thanks, Frances." Half a block further Charles drew the car to a stop in front of the Page mansion overlooking the College Campus.

As they got out of the car Frances started to laugh. "All my fatigue has left me. Perhaps we should go back."

"Go back, nothing. I've something to tell you."

Just then, as they were passing the porch steps, an upstairs window opened and Rachel Page called down.

"Is that you, Frances?"

"Yes, grandmother, Charles has brought me home. It was a wonderful time at the Park. Andrew won! He was powerful. Wish you could have been there."

"I am so happy with Andrew's victory. He'll be a great governor. I must get to bed. But I left a pitcher of lemonade in my study, my darlings. Good-night."

"Oh, thank you, Grandma. You're a dear. Pleasant dreams."

Frances led the way. The candles were still burning. "Don't turn on the lights," said Charles. "The moonlight and the candles are enough."

"Lemonade," commented Frances, in a sing-song. "Made in the shade, But thank the Lord, not stirred by a spade."

Charles laughed. "And not, young lady, to be drunk by an old maid."

"That's what I'm doomed to be, Mr. Preacher."

"Not if I have anything to do about it," Charles said as he put down his glass. He started toward her when the telephone rang.

As Frances answered it, he smiled to himself. "I guess the Lord doesn't think I'm cut out to be a lover. Such interruptions! The Lord only knows how this will end!"

Frances was speaking over the phone. She shook with suppressed mirth over what she was hearing.

"See here, your honor," her voice rang with mischief. "Just because a man is governor doesn't mean that everyone else is his subject. I've got priority on this man and I'm not going to give him up for anybody. Anyhow, how did you know he was here?"

She laughed and wiggled with glee as a heavy voice vibrated into the receiver at the other end.

"We haven't had a chance to get one word in edgewise all evening, your majesty, and you are the chief cause—you with your big booming, noisy victory. Why couldn't you have stolen in to the governorship with gentle music. I thought you came in to stop rackets, not to start them."

Again the vibrant voice at the other end.

She glanced out the side of her eyes at Charles, mischief dancing in them. "All right, all right, Mr. Tyrant, I'll give him to you for just three minutes. Overtime on this long distance is a thousand dollars a minute. And say, your majesty, when the torch light procession starts, see that they come past our house."

"Here," she turned to Charles. "Take it. But remember what I said."

Charles didn't take it. Instead he put both arms around Frances and looked into her eyes. The mischief faded out and something deep and mysterious and overwhelming came in, as he drew her close to him. His breath and her breath suddenly become one and he planted his lips on hers, pressing deeply. Then seizing the phone from her hand, he said, "Governor Marsh, what are these orders you have been trying so hard to get through to me?"

"As my first official act as governor," came Marsh's booming, triumphant voice, "I want to appoint you as my spiritual advisor and ambassador. If I should ever appoint a Brain Trust, I shall empower you to appoint a Spiritual Trust to match it. For every man who thinks for me I want at least one to pray for me. Do you accept this appointment?"

"I do!" he started to raise his other hand as one going on oath, when he discovered it was still clasping Frances' and she was making no effort to escape. He smiled and hugged her, "I solemnly do!"

"This will not involve you, politically, Charles. You don't need to say a word in my behalf or talk politics to anyone. Just take Marsh's great need to God. And, Charles, one more answer I've got to get from you tonight. Will you take that commission to the twenty-five cities that those three men put upon you today. You know, roll up that snowball of prayer all over the United States?"

"You say you want that answer *tonight?*"

"Yes. Peters cleaned up the city. I am pledged to clean up the state. And it will inspire me no end if I know you are out there trying to clean up the nation."

Charles still hesitated.

Marsh's voice went on, "You said you had one limitation. Have you got that limitation cleared up?"

"I have been trying all evening to get that limitation cleared up. Only one thing has been blocking me."

"And what's that?"

"That's you, you big rootin', tootin', shootin' politician. With all your noise and all your interruptions you have pretty nearly wrecked the most important event in my life. But at last, not by you, but in spite of you, I think the problem is getting cleared up. I think I see a beautiful solution to my limitation. As a matter of fact I am looking right now into the eyes of the beautiful solution. Do you think I could take the solution with me?"

A low whistle at the other end of the line followed by a roar of laughter and applause so deafening he had to remove the receiver from his ear. The laughter reached Frances who smiled back at him, her eyes shining.

"See here," Charles had the phone to his lips again. "So you approve my taking my wife?" he questioned Frances with his eyes. She smiled and nodded her head. "Yes, Andrew, Frances has just promised she will marry me. We are wonderfully happy. And so while I accept your congratulations, Andrew, I want to congratulate you. We both do. It was a great victory. Frances joins me in sending our very best wishes to you and Mrs. Marsh, and Bill Peters, too. I know you are going to be a mighty instrument for God in the state. Goodnight, Andrew. It was a memorable night, indeed."

Meanwhile Frances had moved away and was standing in the window looking out at the moon-flooded campus. He walked over and took her in his arms. Her beautiful arms went around his neck and clasped him close.

"Darling," he said, "that wasn't the way I meant to ask you to marry me, but I want you so much. Will you? I love you."

"Oh, Charles, while you were phoning Andrew Marsh, I found myself saying, Can he really be proposing to me? Could he really? And my heart danced so I thought it would burst. I love your crazy way of doing things, Charles. Always, always do things that way, Charles. Always, always."

She nestled her head on his shoulder and gazed up into his face. His strong arms drew her slight figure close to him as his eyes, overflowing with a greater love than he had ever dreamed possible, returned her rapt gaze.

"This is heaven," he whispered. "Such as I had never dreamed possible before. With you at my side and God leading the way, nothing that He commands us to do will ever seem impossible—never!"